Fifty Years of Indian Independence and The Polity

FIFTY YEARS OF INDIAN INDEPENDENCE AND THE POLITY

Edited by

Dr. T. SURYANARAYANA SASTRY

A.P.H. PUBLISHING CORPORATION

5, ANSARI ROAD, DARYA GANJ

NEW DELHI - 110 002

Published by
S. B. Nangia
A.P.H. Publishing Corporation
5, Ansari Road, Darya Ganj
New Delhi-110 002
☎ 3274050
E-mail : aph@mantraonline.com

ISBN 81-7648-149-1

2000

Typeset at
NEW APCON
25/2, Panchsheel Shopping Centre
New Delhi 110 017
☎ 6490802
6494336

Printed in India at
Efficient Offset Printers
New Delhi-110 035

Foreword

The attainment of freedom on August 15, 1947, was itself a landmark achievement in the history of India. These fifty years of independence have witnessed tremendous changes with in India and the world in general. The present golden jubilee year of India's independence has great significance as this is a historic occasion reflecting laudable mile stones in the annals of free India. In these fifty years, the political framework of the Indian Union has absorbed the challenges of welding together different ethnicities, languages, cultures, and many socio-economic and political upheavals. This itself is a monumental achievement in the life of a nation—state, which India could ably demonstrate to the rest of the world defying the predictions of many that liberal democracy cannot survive too long here.

However, a nation cannot afford to be a static and it has to be dynamic and has to learn to realise itself structurally and functionally as it passes through the experience. Hence it is a significant occasion to make a proper assessment and an objective analysis to review its past and reform itself to meet the challenges of the 21st century.

During the last five decades, India can be proud to have safeguarded and enlarged the gains of freedom. We can also claim to have achieved significant progress in the diverse and interconnected spheres of democratic governance among the various institutions such as the Executive, Legislature and Judiciary. We can be legitimately proud that the Constitution could ably demonstrate that it is an ever-enduring document that we have adopted by ourselves. But at the same time, the assertion of caste, the resurgence of religious chauvinism, the erosion in the functioning of the political system and the escalating levels of political corruption, instability of governance at the Union are the few phenomenon that remind us to think twice, before we enter into the next millennium.

Considering all these, I am really happy that Dr. T.S.N. Sastry had succeeded in compiling all the scholarly contributions presented in a Nation Seminar on "Fifty Years of Indian Independence and the Working of Its Political System", Sponsored by UGC, ICSSR and Pondicherry University. The papers presented in this volume are highly commendable. There is no doubt, the present volume will certainly be received by the Politicians, Statesmen, Academicians and Scholars and all others interested in restructuring the Polity.

(Dr. A. GNANAM)
Chairman,
National Accreditation Council
Bangalore

Preface

In the 'Comity of Nations', on August 15, 1997 India had one more leap in its march ahead. It had completed Five Decades of its independent existence as a democratic polity. In these Fifty Years we have seen far reaching changes in the socio-economic, political, scientific, legal and intellectual life of this great nation. Notwithstanding the innumerable problems that afflict us, we are proud of our polity, which nurtured the roots of democracy without any wavering unlike many neo-democracies. There is no doubt, that this itself is a significant achievement in the life of a nation, specially if we compare our experience with that of other Nation-States that achieved their independence during this period and which have already fallen out of democratic governance.

However, there is a growing feeling among all the sections of the people of this country, that there is a need to have wide ranging debates and discussions and to review the overall functioning of our polity. It becomes all the more important especially as our accomplishments fall short of the noble values and ideals embodied in our Constitution and in the context of the fast deterioration of values in politics and business.

There is nothing wrong either with the Constitution of India or its Polity. It's the lack of will on the part of the political parties to adhere to the constitutional culture that is hampering us. The selfish motives of the political parties resulted in the involvement of money and muscle power in elections. It is also the cause for the escalating level of violence in various walks of public life, the widespread growth of unhealthy competition in all sections of the society. The recrudescence of social strife based on religion and caste factors, the imbalances in the functioning of our federal system, the erosion of values in the Administrative, Legislative, and Judicial Organs including the infighting between the three main Constitutional Functionaries in their quest for supremacy over the other, the negligence to strengthen the Democratic System from its Gross roots level and many more relevant factors taken together have made the people to doubt the tenacity of the Constitution and the very survival of our Country, as a functioning democracy. With the varied experience of living and working in the post-independent era, the present generation realised that there are many shortcomings and they except a thorough overhauling of the system. As an offshoot, a variety of opinions have been aired to reshape the Constitution and to re-organize the socio-economic, scientific and legal framework. The complexities of the problems confronting the nation internally have now been further exacerbated with the end of cold war and the reshaping of the Indian Economy. Apparently these efforts seem to have been largely engineered by the World Bank and the International Monetary Fund. All these changes have necessitated a fresh look at the changing India before we face the challenges of the next millennium.

In fact, no political system can succeed without having the backing of a sound socio-economic, educational, legal, scientific, and technological foundations. In order to strengthen the emerging economic imperative and the modalities, it is important to have a free and frank academic debate at the national level to update ourselves. Taking into consideration of these perceptions, the contributors of various articles wrote on various aspects on the functioning of the democratic polity in India during the last fifty years. The authors of these papers come from different disciplines and this strengthens our effort to provide a holistic approach to the subject of study.

I am thankful to Prof. A. Gnanam, Chairman of the National Accreditation Council for his ready acceptance to write the foreword. I am also highly grateful to the UGC, and ICCSR for their generous funding in conducting the National Seminar. I further express my sincere thanks to all the contributors for their active participation in this venture.

Last but not the least my sincere thanks to Managing Director and Staff of the APH Publishing Corporation, New Delhi for their keen interest in taking up this project and to publish it in a record time.

Dr. T. SURYANARAYANA SASTRY

Contents

Contributors

Dr. A. Laxminath, Prof. & Dean, Faculty of Law, Dr. B.R. Ambedkar College of Law, Andhra University Visakhapatnam.

Prof. T.S. Rama Rao, Senior Professor of Law (Retd.), P.G. Department of Law, University of Madras, Madras.

Mr. N. Ravi, Lecturer, Dr. B.R. Ambedkar Govt. Law College, Pondicherry

Dr. N.K. Jha, Reader & Head, Department of Political Science, Pondicherry University, Pondicherry.

Dr. M. Basheer Ahmed Khan, Professor of Management and Director, Centre for Tourism Studies, Pondhicherry University, Pondicherry.

Dr. D.S.N. Somayajulu, Professor of Law, Dr. B.R. Ambedkar College of Law, Andhra University, Visakhapatnam

Prof. R. Jaganmohan Rao, (Retd.) Dr. B.R. Ambedkar College of Law, Andhra University, Visakhapatnam.

T. Raghavendra Rao, Research Scholar, Dr. B.R. Ambedkar College of Law, Andhra University, Visakhapatnam.

Dr. S. Ambika Kumari, Lecturer, Dr. B.R. Ambedkar Govt. Law, College, Pondicherry.

Dr. Y. Satyanarayana, Reader, Dr. B.R. Ambedkar College of Law, Andhra University, Visakhapatnam.

Dr. A. David Ambrose, Senior Lecturer, Dr. B.R. Ambedkar Govt. Law College, Chennai.

Dr. K. Uma Shankar Patnaik, Reader, Dept. of Economics, Pondicherry University, Pondicherry.

Mr. S. Bhyravamurthy, Research Scholar, Dept. of Economics, Pondicherry University, Pondicherry.

Dr. Justice David Annousamy, Former Judge, Madras High Court, Pondicherry.

Dr. R. Venkata Rao, Professor of Law, Dr. B.R. Ambedkar College of Law, Andhra University, Visakhapatnam

Dr. T. Suryanarayana Sastry, Senior Lecturer, School of International Studies, Pondicherry University, Pondicherry.

Dr. K. Chandra Sekhara Rao, Reader & Head, Dept. of Commerce, Pondhicherry University, Pondicherry.

Dr. T. Subramaniyam Naidu, Co-ordinator and Head, Centre for Future Studies and Dept. of Anthropology, Pondicherry University, Pondicherry.

Dr. N.R. Madhava Menon, Member Law Commission of India and Vice-Chancellor, National University of Juridical Sciences, Calcutta.

Dr. V. Natrajan, Dy. Registrar (Retd.), Pondicherry University, Pondicherry.

Dr. Subhash C. Kashyap, Visiting Professor at the Centre for Policy Research, Former Secretary General of Lok Sabha and Director of the Institute of Constitutional and Institutional Studies, New Delhi.

Dr. B. Krishnamurty, Senior Lecturer, School of International Studies, Pondicherry University, Pondicherry.

CHAPTER I

Indian Constitutionalism and the Dynamics of Federal Polity

A . Lakshminath

The history of constitutionalism in India has been a story of the search for limitations on absolute power, a search for ways by which the powers of governments may be shared. While the search has yielded, significant results, the Indian polity is still looking for newer and better techniques by which political power may be allocated and exercised effectively by power holders.

The concepts of constitutionalism and constitutional democracy should now be treated as the final stage in the evolution of political systems, with the end of cold war and acceptance of constitutional democracy as a political system in a large part of the world. In such a case should we conceive constitutionalism as a full grown concept. Is constitutional democracy prey to internal contradictions, serious enough to undermine the political system in the long run? To put it in other words 'Do we face a crisis in constitutionalism?'

The contemporary complex pluralist and multi-cultural societies demonstrated a historical test for the fundamental tenets and inherent limits of modernity. More precisely the question is how far modern constitutionalism can be stretched beyond its roots to the normative order of Englightenment. This involves the problem of legitimacy of a given state and political order with its constitutionally laid down normative identity. Accordingly minorities, human-rights and social welfare principles receive a legitimising function which will have to be carried out by means of a constitution. This bears modern liberal, legal and political under-pinning. The relevance of the problem has much more to do with "stretching beyond" modernity and the post-modern constitutional paradigm.

The protective function of the sovereign is to establish peace inside the state and to guarantee security to its subjects (domestic peace) - Hobbes. On the other hand natural rights of life, liberty and estate (together making the right to property) mark out the limits to government which, in order to be legitimate, is not permitted to step out of its own by the citizens consented liberal purpose of being. (Human Rights Locke) (and Social Justice of Rousseau). The American and French revolutions from whom the concept of first constitutional acts emerged brought the inalienable natural rights and made them rights of freedom from public authority. The positivisation of universal natural rights into negative civil and political rights in the declaration of Independence and Bill of Rights, was the very means whereby the triumphant middle class, rising to power gave form to essential political limitations, of government. The indefeasible rights were intended to define legitimate sphere of power by providing qualifications upon powers actually granted by the people to the government (social contract), the former being and remaining the original sovereign. This is how the idea of popular sovereignty was related to natural rights and the consent of the governed.

With the first constitutions announcing the establishment of entirely new social contract basis of modern polity, the individual ceased to be a mere object of domination. Only a couple of years ago, the new constitution paradigm was emerging under the "leitmotif": *democracy as promotion of human rights within the welfare state setting*. Changes in international dogmas dealing with minority rights, however vague and insufficient they may still be, gave a pluralist discourse of constitution an additional tune, which is in favour of more comprehensive accommodation (also) of pre-political group diversities viz. ethnic, linguistic, religious. The emerging constitutional teleology also articulated as a quest for substantive values, gave rise to an alternative syntagm viz., security-diversity-solidarity. Thus there was a shift of emphasis from liberty, equality and fraternity to substantive principles of domestic peace and minimum of societal security, tolerance and promotion of diversity as well as social justice, supporting the legitimate political symbolism to human rights.

Viewed in this perspective the Indian Constitution drafted in the first half of this Century by the Drafting Committee headed by Dr. B.R. Ambedkar fulfils the aspirations of the Indian people and will be an exemplary model for the world constitutionalism of 21st Century, with an excellent alchemical amalgam of its preambular goals of Justice, Liberty and Equality, guaranteeing Fundamental Rights through Part III; Social and Economic Justice through Part IV and assuring, We, the people of India, positive content of 21st Century 'leitmotif' "security diversity and solidarity".

At a time, when the whole Indian sub-continent was in a state of, perhaps, contagious fermentation - when antiquity had lost all its relevance and all its effect on the minds of men, at the same time that novelty was attended with the suspicions that always will be attached to whatever is new the Constituent Assembly, the Drafting Committee and Dr. Ambedkar have been anxiously careful, in a rewarding business and an awe-inspiring venture which would give to us - 'WE THE PEOPLE OF INDIA' - the Constitution, so to conduct themselves that nothing in the progress of this great parliamentary process and constitutional exercise shall afford a pretext for its future disuse, misuse and abuse.

Law, as Prof. Cohen says, is not a closed independent system having nothing to do with economic, political, social or philosophical science. The Indian Constitution even architectured in such a way so as to reflect in it a harmonious blend of the ancient and the modern - by removing the undesirable elements of the old and filling gaps with the new. A constitution can perform many functions in a modern state. One of these tasks is to serve as a deposit for a cluster of a society's fundamental political values.

Constitution can reflect these values in substantive ways by guaranteeing Fundamental Rights and in procedural ways by providing remedies. It also reflects society's basic values in 'allocative ways'. It mirrors basic values about who shall govern and in what direction. In addition to structuring and allocating and limiting power, a constitution performs 'aspirational goals'. Through its institutional arrangements and commandments, the constitution reflects a particular vision of a good and achievable community life.

Our Constitution is the precursor of the new Indian renaissance. The basic objectives can be seen in the Preamble, which embodies in a solemn form all the ideals and aspirations for which the country had struggled during the British regime. These basic objectives are :

JUSTICE, social economic and political;

LIBERTY of thought, expression, belief, faith and worship;

EQUALITY of status and of opportunity; and to promote among them all;

FRATERNITY assuring the dignity of the individual and the Unity and Integrity of the Nation.

JUSTICE, LIBERTY, EQUALITY AND FRATERNITY

Structural equality demands equal opportunity for all sections of society and more so for the depressed ones. Structural inequalities tend to create an identity crisis among minorities and according to an analysis of the "official view" of national integration identity crisis is the main hurdle.

"Fraternity", the fourth objective in the Preamble was added because "the Drafting Committee felt that the need for fraternal concord and goodwill in India was never greater than now and that this particular aim of the Constitution should be emphasised by special reference in the Preamble.

Fraternity as an object is not reflected in any Article of the Constitution - no Constitution and no law can produce brotherly feeling or concord. There are provisions of the Constitution which are designed to promote fraternity, such as a common citizenship (Article 5) and the right of citizens of India to move freely throughout the territory of India, to reside and settle in any part of India, or to acquire, hold and dispose of property, to practice any profession or to carry on any occupation, trade or calling in any part of India [Article 19 (1) (d) to (g)]. There are, however, other provisions which militate against fraternity, such as the division of States on linguistic lines and the provisions relating to language. A fair and even-handed executive administration can do more to promote fraternity than any constitutional or legal provision. The fourth objective refers to a moral and political ideal, and it can throw no light on the interpretation of the Constitution, nor does any provision of the Constitution gave a clear content to fraternity. National Integration through Fraternity is the constitutional goal that can be achieved through individual pledge and commitment.

India, a polyglot society, is characterised by continental size, racial milieu, ethnic variety, cultural diversity, linguistic multiplicity, caste hierarchy, religious pluralism, rural-urban hiatus, disparities in the socio-cultural status of the people based on age and sex and historical factors such as feudalism and economic imbalances, offers a complex situation, for a meaningful and rewarding study. We, the people of India, gave unto ourselves a Constitution delineating not merely the instrumentalities for bringing about social change but also the goals of development and societal change - economic, social and cultural and also reducing the regional disparities.

In assuaging the rigour of rigidity and legalism the Draft Constitution follows the Australian plan on a far more extensive scale than has been done in Australia. Like the Australian Constitution, it has a long list of subjects for concurrent powers of legislation. Following the Australian Constitution there are as many as Six Articles in the Draft Constitution, where the provisions are of a temporary duration and which could be replaced by Parliament at any time by provisions suitable for the occasion. The biggest advance made by the Indian Constitution over the Australian Constitution is in the matter of exclusive powers of legislation vested in Parliament. While the exclusive authority of the Australian Parliament to legislate extends only to about three matters, the authority of the Indian Constitution will extend to 91 matters, while it stands at 97 entries. In this way the Indian Constitution has secured the greatest possible elasticity in its federalism which is supposed to be rigid by nature. What is to be noted is that it has added new ways of overcoming the rigidity and legalism inherent in federalism which are special to it and which are not to be found elsewhere.

Under Draft article 226 (Article 249 in the Constitution of India) Parliament can legislate when a subject becomes a matter of national concern as distinguished from purely Provincial concern, though the subject is in the state list. Article 227 (present Article 250) gives the similar power to Parliament in a national emergency. Under Article 229 (Article 252 of the Indian Constitution) Parliament can exercise the same power if Provinces consent to such exercise. Though the last provision also exists in the Australian Constitution the first two are a special feature of the Draft Constitution.

One can, therefore, safely say that the Indian Federation will not suffer from the faults of rigidity or legalism. Its distinguishing feature is that it is a flexible federation. The Draft Constitution has sought to forge means and methods whereby India will have a federation and at the same time will have uniformity in all the basic matters which are essential to maintain the unity of the country. The means adopted by the Draft Constitution are three :

1. A Single judiciary,
2. Uniformity in fundamental laws, civil and criminal, and
3. A common All India Civil Services to man important posts.

The fundamentals of a Constitution are recognised all over the world. Given these facts all Constitutions in their main provisions must look similar. He impressed upon the Constituent Assembly that the only new things in a Constitution framed so late in the day are the variations made to remove the faults and to accommodate it to the needs of the country.

Dr. Ambedkar agreed that administrative details should have no place in the Constitution. The Drafting Committee should see its way to avoid their inclusion in the Constitution. But this is to be said on the necessity which justifies their inclusion. Dr. Ambedkar quotes Grote, the Historian of Greece, who said that :

> "The diffusion of constitutional morality, not merely among the majority of any community but throughout the whole, is the indispensable condition of government at once free and peaceable; since even any powerful and obstinate minority may render the working of a free institution impracticable, without being strong enough to conquer ascendancy for themselves."

During the two world wars, even the 'classical' federations functioned as unitary governments. This was made possible by the widest interpretation put by the courts on the "Defence Power" vested in them by their Constitutions. The Indian Constitution makes express provisions in this regard in Articles 352, 353, 354, 358 and 359. This special feature was described by Dr. Ambedkar as follows:

> "All federal systems including the American are placed in a tight mould of federalism. No matter what the circumstances, it cannot change its form and shape. It can never be unitary. On the other hand the Indian Constitution can be both unitary as well as federal according to the requirements of time and circumstances. In normal times, it is framed to work as a federal system. But in times of war it is so designed as to make it work as though it was a unitary State....... Such a power of converting itself into a unitary State no federation possesses....."

Federalism is not a static paradigm. It is a changing notion. The classical concept of federation which envisaged two parallel governments of co-ordinate jurisdiction operating in isolation from each other in water-tight compartments, is nowhere a functional reality now. With the emergence of the Social Welfare State, the traditional theory of federalism completely lost its ground. After the First World War, it became very much a myth even in the older federational By the middle of the Twentieth Century, federalism had come to be understood as a dynamic process of co-operation and shared action between two or more levels of government, with increasing inter-dependence and Centrist trends. The framers of the Constitution took due note of these changing concepts and functional realities. Avoiding a dogmatic approach, they fashioned a *sui generis* system of two-tier polity in which the predominant strength of the Union is blended with the essence of co-operative federalism. Several features and provisions of the Constitution appear to have been deliberately designed to institutionalise the concept of co-operation.

The State of Jammu and Kashmir stands on a different footing in relation to the Union from other states. As Dr. Ambedkar said, it forms a part of the Union of India in an 'attenuated manner'. It's accession was not complete as that of other Indian States. Its final and complete accession was made dependent on a plebiscite which could not be held so far. Pending its final solution, the relations of Kashmir to the Union are regulated by Article 370 of the Constitution.

A special feature of the Indian Union is that the Union is indestructible but not so the States; their identity can be altered or even obliterated. This is a departure from the federal feature which obtains in a classical federation like USA. The Constituent Assembly rejected a motion in the concluding stages to designate India as a "Federation of States". Dr. Ambedkar, Chairman of the Drafting Committee, while introducing the Draft Constitution explained the position thus :

> ".......... that though India was to be a federation, the federation was not the result of the agreement by the States to join in a federation, and that the federation not being the result of an agreement, no State has the right to secede from it. The federation is a Union because it is indestructible. "Though the country and the people may be divided into different States for convenience of administration, the country is one integral whole, its people a single people living under a single imperium derived from a single source. The Americans had to wage a civil war to establish that the States have no right of secession and that their federation was indestructible. The Drafting Committee thought that it was better to make it clear at the outset rather than to leave it to speculation or to disputes."

Though there is no doubt that the constitution adopted by the people of India is a federal constitution, the word 'federation' has not been used anywhere in the Constitution. Article 1 declares India as 'a Union of States'. Dr. Ambedkar explained why the Drafting Committee used the word 'Union' instead of the word 'federation'. The word 'federation' is used whenever a number of hitherto independent states join together to form a new state for the achievement of some common purposes but desire to maintain their separate existence; it is, always, the result of a compact or agreement between independent units. The Indian Union is not the result of any such compact or agreement between pre-existing independent states. The states of the Union have no independent existence of their own; their boundaries can be altered by parliament even against their consent. Further, a federation need not be permanent; it can be disintegrated as happened in the case of USSR. The framers of our constitution wanted to make the union permanent and deny the right of secession to the units. Therefore, it can be said that it is a deliberate attempt on the part of our founding fathers, not to use the word 'federation' or 'federalism' anywhere in the constitution. Secondly, ours is a federal constitution in as much as it establishes a dual polity with the union at the centre and the states at the periphery, each endowed with sovereign powers to be exercised in the field assigned to them respectively. The states do not derive their authority and powers from the Union government. Both the union and the states derive their powers from the constitution. Neither of them is subordinate to the other nor agents of the other. They enjoy coordinate authority and are independent of each other. According to Prof. Wheare the existence of coordinate authorities, independent of each other is the gist of federal principle. Thirdly, as per Prof. Wheare's definition, federalism means the division of powers between the Union and the units. This is in principle embodies in our constitution. Dr. Ambedkar set forth the essence of 'federalism' in the following words :

> *"The chief mark of federalism lies in the partition of the legislative and executive authority between the centre and the units by the constitution. This is the principle embodied in our constitution. There can be no mistake about it. It is, therefore, wrong to say that the states have been placed under the Centre. The Centre cannot by its own will alter the boundary of this territory and the judiciary."*.

Fourthly, another requisite of federal constitution being it should be written, we have a written constitution. This written character confers upon it a great sanctity and makes it the supreme law of the land, which cannot be altered by the authority of executive, legislative and judicial organs of the national and state governments. This character signifies that since these organs derive their authority from the constitution they have to work within the constitution and cannot go beyond the limitations placed on them under the constitution. A federal constitution cannot but be a written constitution and a written constitution must necessarily be a rigid constitution. But our constitution can also be termed a rigid constitution in the technical sense as the process of amending it is different and difficult from the ordinary legislative procedure. But as the framing fathers realised that, too great a degree of rigidity makes the task of adapting and adjusting the constitution to changing requirements and to the changing times difficult, they introduced a certain degree of flexibility in it.

It is flexible enough to change and adjust in accordance with circumstances and can meet eventualities without being subjected to amendment in the formal manner. The fact that it is not so rigid as it should be for a federal constitution is evident from the fact that in the last 49 years the constitution has been amended about 80 times. According to Dr. Ambedkar, the distinguishing feature of our federation is that it is 'a flexible federation'. Lastly, the power to interpret and implement the provisions of the constitution, the power to declare any law, whether of the union or of a state to be void are unconstitutional, if it violates any provision of the constitution, and the power to keep each government within its defined sphere, is vested in the highest court of the land i.e., the Supreme Court.

Supporting the idea of federation with a strong centre, Dr. Ambedkar rightly observed "It is difficult to prevent the centre from becoming strong. Conditions in modern world are such that centralisation of powers is inevitable. One has, only, to consider the growth of the federal government in USA, which notwithstanding the very limited powers given to it by the constitution, has outgrown its former self and has overshadowed and eclipsed the state governments. This is due to the modern conditions. The same conditions are sure to operate in the Government of India and nothing that one can do will help to prevent it from being strong. On the other hand we must resist the tendency to make it stronger. It cannot chew more than it can digest.

Its strength must be commensurate with its weight. It would be a folly to make it so strong that it may fall by its own weight.

The unique feature of our constitution is that it is a federal state with a leaning towards central dominance in certain matters. The constitution envisaged the creation of a dual polity consisting of the Union Government and the States.

The dominant characteristics of India's political culture is unitary, high centralisation and authoritarian. Our political parties are unitary; they are not attuned to promote federal ethos or participative process; disposition to amend the constitution frequently itself reflects this ethos. Centralisation had been the characteristic of India polity - a tradition coming from the Moghul times through the British days. But the polity has no alibi now to justify the sustenance of distortions of history. A federal system can be sustained by a set of institutions operating in a complementary manner - but if the institutions are distorted or faulted by Individuals, it is the system that loses the credibility. The very concept of federalism implies mutuality and common purpose. Federal polity by the very definition is a relationship of mutuality between units. Such a structure can be operated only on a premise that conflicts will occur and that they can be resolved. Such a disposition alone can promote and sustain federalism in an organic, smooth and spontaneous manner. A balanced distribution of political power has to be supported by appropriate institutional framework and processes, contributing to what may be called an organic federalism, The ethos of an organic federalism could be brought about by a matching political culture, adjustment and distribution of the rules and operation of institutional mechanism. In this context the Supreme Court had to recognise itself as a federal court and make its creative contribution in promoting cooperative federalism.

Federalism whether centralised or decentralised, offers no panacea for the trials of regional conflicts or the dilemmas of social policy. In fact such structural prescriptions may serve to divert energies from the more difficult long term task of building a constitutional culture in which conflict can be channelled in productive directions. Whatever success the American system has enjoyed can be found in a constitutional culture incorporating a concept of federalism flexible enough to accommodate centralised power when required as in the Great Depression of the 1930s or the Civil Rights Struggle of the 1960s and yet devolve to the States the power to experiment and innovate when centralised programmes seem inadequate, inappropriate or counter-productive. Americans have gradually learned to apply that flexibility so as to moderate, but not eliminate, the periodic crises that have characterised the history of American federalism.

The constitutional structure of federalism in the U.S. differs markedly from that of India. The link between the centralising and decentralising trends was the development of the doctrine of administrative federalism using grants-in-aid and revenue sharing. Under this doctrine the federal government less constrained in its use of taxing power would make grants to the States for specific projects in return for state acceptance of federal standards in the administration and implementation of such projects.

India's success in maintaining democratic rule since independence (barring the brief interlude of the 1975-77 Emergency) in the world's largest-and most heterogeneous democracy runs counter to J.S. Mill's proposition that democracy is "next to impossible" in multi-ethnic and completely impossible in linguistically divided countries, has long been a puzzle besides two other puzzles. They are (i) its survival despite widespread poverty and illiteracy which casts grave doubts on the hypothesized link between the level of socio-economic development and stable democracy, further weakened by the fact that other third world democracies have by now established stable democratic rule (e.g. Barbados, Botswana, Costa Rica, Jamaica, Malta, Mauritius and Papua New Guinea). (ii) The second paradox is "the far more puzzling contradiction between India's high level of political violence and its success at sustaining a democratic political system (Lalloo Prasad Yadav's continuance as Bihar Chief Minister).

In contrast with Mill's thinking, power sharing theory holds that democracy is possible in deeply divided societies but only if their type of democracy is consociational, that is characterised by:

1. grand coalition governments that include representatives of all major linguistic and religious groups,
2. cultural autonomy for these groups,
3. proportionality in political representation and civil service appointments, and
4. a minority veto with regard to vital minority rights and autonomy.

Thus consociational theory maintains that power sharing is a necessary condition for democracy in deeply divided countries. Consociationalism, started as an incipient school (1974) became a theory "among the most influential contributions to comparative politics" which has now become a widely accepted paradigm for the analysis of contemporary democratic polities that can be regarded as the prototypes of power sharing such as the Netherlands, Belgium, Austria, Switzerland, Lebanon, Malaysia and Columbia. Moreover, consociational democracy has been proposed as a normative model for many ethnically divided countries, and it had a decisive influence in the shaping of South Africa's 1994 power-sharing constitution.

Newly Independent India embraced power sharing on the lines of consociational democracy during the first two decades and its success is, however, not a surprise as the conditions were favourable then. During the late sixties, as a result of greater mass mobilisation and activation and regionalism, power sharing became less strong and pervasive, evidenced by the centralisation of the congress party and the federal system, the decline of the Congress party's electoral strength, the attack on minority rights and the rise of the B.J.P.

With the United Front coming to power at the Centre as an alternative to Congress and the B.J.P., the States sharing power at the Centre, the power sharing is increasingly becoming stronger despite the increase in inter-group hostility and violence.

The values, aspirations and attitudes of citizens will provide soil conditions for federal or unitary ethos to set. Centralisation is the antithesis of citizen participation. Large majorities, centralised political parties without internal democracy, suppression-of dissent, provisions of anti-defection law agonising need for electoral reforms and absence of a process or mechanism for building national consensus through 'national debate' are some of the factors that are distancing the process and institutions of governance from the citizens.

Rajya Sabha as it seems today is more like a 'mini Lok Sabha'. It does not reflect federal equations as between the States. With the conferment of constitutional status on Panchayati Raj institutions through 73rd and 74th constitutional Amendments, it is necessary to have a second look at the composition of Rajya Sabha as a federal chamber. Federal ethos can be sustained and nourished by developing and strengthening conventions and not by constitutional amendments. Non-functioning or malfunctioning of constitutional provisions, as also extra-constitutional processes have had a greater but adverse impact on the federal ethos than the amendments of the constitution.

Federalism in India should not be reduced merely to its political and economic dimensions, but should be seen primarily in the backdrop of the socio-cultural perspectives of unity in diversity. Indian Constitution is a comprehensive, value-based document providing a vision of India encompassing political, economic, social and cultural facets of continuity and change.

While earlier forms of governments were characterised by grave defects that led to their eventual collapse. Constitutional consociational democracy is free from such internal contradictions.

During the last five decades India faced serious challenges to its constitutionalism and constitutional democracy. An evaluation of these challenges do not indicate a crisis of constitutionalism. The ideals of constitutionalism and constitutional democracy cannot be improved upon. The associates in the constitutional power-sharing should redefine their powers, limitations and functions to maintain high standards of constitutional morality and accordingly to save the Indian polity from constitutional: despotism, as is presently happening in some States like Bihar.

CHAPTER II

Quo Vadis Constitutional Values?

T.S. Rama Rao

The Indian Constitution is on the face of it a progressive document, embodying and giving effect to Western values like Parliamentary Democracy, Cabinet system of Government, adult franchise, justiciable fundamental rights, an independent judiciary to enforce these rights etc., and has borrowed extensively from British as well as American Constitutional systems. However, in its working, over the past fifty years, considerable deviations from these Western Models have come to light, due to the peculiar Indian political and social conditions.

The leaders of Indian National Congress, like Patel and Nehru, who played a crucial role in the shaping of the Indian Constitution were firm believers in Parliamentary Democracy, Adult Franchise etc., as they had fought for Indian independence and for achievement of these goals. The need for placation of the minorities had induced the Congress leaders in pre-independent India, to favour adoption of fundamental rights on the American pattern. However, these leaders were charismatic ones, due to their sacrifices in the fight for independence, and they soon exhibited a typically authoritarian attitude of impatience towards undue Constitutional constraints on executive and legislative power, especially by way of judicial review. Thus even in the Constituent Assembly, the due process clause was hastily dropped and during the deliberations on the eminent domain article (Art.31). Rajaji, then a Cabinet

Minister, told the Assembly that the result of judicial review of the "justness" of compensation would be that "Government functioning would be paralysed"[1]. Even on the issue of personal liberty, the leaders in the Constitutional Assembly decided at a very early stage to eliminate the due process clause and to sanction preventive detention in the very chapter on fundamental rights. The Judiciary however decided to interpret the Fundamental rights, liberally, expanding their ambit by way of interpretation, and this led to a series of Constitutional amendments seeking to nullify the effect of the Supreme Court Judgments.

In the immediate post-independence era, when stalwarts like Nehru, Patel and Rajaji exercised power, while these leaders sought to curb expansion of judicial review on the American pattern, they upheld the liberal traditions of Western democracy, in practice, with even preventive detention being confined to curb extreme cases of subversion by communal and anarchist forces; and corruption was also frowned at, as shown by the Mundhra Case etc. But there has been a steady deterioration of the political process since then. After the advent of Mrs. Indira Gandhi, as Prime Minister, the Indian political scene witnessed the emergence of personality cult, with political parties giving up the principle of inner party democracy and replacing the system of elected party committees with nominated committees at various levels and party legislators in States leaving the choice of Chief Ministers to the party head at the Centre. There was also systematic political castration of emerging tall poppies among party politicians who threatened developing independent political bases of their own. Thus, as I noted in an earlier article of mine, "Democratic formalism cloaking a voluntary submission to dictatorial leadership seems to be the unique Indian contribution to political science."[2] The further deterioration in the political process in recent years is evident from the numerous scams, ubiquitous corruption among political leaders, the increasing criminilisation of politics, growing nexus between the politician and criminals, with the bureaucracy also being increasingly involved in corruption, brazen attempts by politicians in power to ensure dynastic succession or succession by their spouses etc. One major cause for these political ills is the inability of the electorate to punish erring politicians, as for one thing, almost all political parties seem to be tarred with the same brush, leaving little choice for the people.

The Janata Dal was started on the initiative of Late Sri Jai Prakash Narain, to fight against corruption and its leaders are now accused by the CBI as involved in several scams. And while the earlier scams related to bribes being taken from middle men and industrialists for favours shown to them, the latest ones deal with the loot of the treasury itself by politicians and bureaucrats!

One contributing factor for this, is the hold of caste on the electorate. This is because when a politician is supported on caste-basis, not merely is a closed network of an alliance between the politician and his castemen set up, but the electorate is obliged to turn a blind eye to the corruption of the elected representatives, especially those in power.

This leads us to examine the role of casteism and communalism on the development of the political process. Adult franchise has led to the consolidation and augmentation of communal and caste loyalties and the 'emergence of these groups as political pressure groups as well as foci of political power. As the writer pointed out in an earlier article; "Casteism, if left unchecked, leads to the institution of the rule of groups for the rule of law. This may lead to some sort of stagment and low-temperature stability (with the different numerically strong caste and communal groups sharing political power), but....... the country would have to pay a high price for this stability in terms of loss of efficiency".[3]

As a result of these developments, the only aim of politicians seems to be to stay in power as long as possible and to keep in good humour the powerful caste and communal groups which vote them to power. This has its impact on the development of federalism also in the country. While regional parties have come to power in various states and in a coalition at the Centre also, and all-India parties like the Congress have suffered an eclipse, it is surprising that all parties want to retain Art. 356 of the Constitution authorising dismissal of State Governments. As Art. 356 comes in handy to threaten or dismiss a rival party in a power in a State, there is reluctance to delete this article, especially when the electorate does not choose to punish the party at the Centre for its violation of state autonomy. And when conflicts arise between two states as in the case of sharing of Cauvery waters, it is curious to find that all legislators in the two states unanimously vote in different ways in the two state

Legislatures, the same political parties adopting divergent attitudes in the two states. Besides the political consensus among all parties including regional parties seems not to be on devolution of more powers on the states, but only on acquiring power at the Centre. The electorate seems to have become a helpless captive in the hands of politicians, whose sole aim seems to be to acquire power and stay in power as long as possible.

While these developments represent a recession of the original constitutional values, we should take note of some positive developments also. First, is the very survival of political democracy, with regular elections being held, in this country, as compared to several Afro-Asian countries, where dictatorships have usurped power. The very diversity of India, with different castes and communities coexisting in the country, and competing for power, seems to prevent the possibility of a military take over or assumption of dictatorship by a particular political party, though the declaration of Emergency by Mrs. Indira Gandhi, should be treated as an exceptional factor, which came to an end due possibly to the loss of political legitimacy of this brief dictatorship. Secondly the very operation of democracy strengthens the hands of a free press the educated sections, the bar and the judiciary in keeping alive the liberal humanist values of fundamental rights. The Supreme Court and the different courts have played a notable role in bringing to trial the different political scamsters through the instrumentality of public interest litigation and in some cases through direct judicial initiatives. The very loss of legitimacy of the political class due to its corruption etc., has led to the courts taking the lead in initiating trials in the scam cases, and in evolving a steadily growing human rights jurisprudence as well as Environmental Law jurisprudence, where it has virtually assumed executive and legislative functions. Yet the threat of a frustrated political class adopting fascist methods on the basis of the Casteist support it enjoys, is a real one, as shown by the recent disclosure by the Chief Justice of India, of extraneous pressures to stop the reopening of the Hawala Cases, and the beating up of Advocate Vijayan in Madras, for daring to challenge the vires of the reservation policy, etc.. Hopefully, however, a free press and a judiciary committed to the protection of fundamental rights should mitigate the evil efforts of casteism and the canker of corruption, in the country, in the years to come.

REFERENCES

1. Granville Austin, The Indian Constitution-Cornerstone of A Nation P.88.

2. T.S. Rama Rao, "Supreme Court and the 'Higher' Logic of Fundamental rights" 1983 Journal of the Indian Law Institute, P. 186 at P. 188.

3. T.S. Rama Rao, "Law and Social Changes : A Historical perspective: Independence and After" 1974 Indian year Book of International Affair P. 460 at P. 481

CHAPTER III

Implementation of Human Rights and Fundamental Rights - Indian Perspective

N. Ravi

"The concept of Human Rights is the result of man's inhumanity to man. The story of Human Right is thus story of Human wrongs."

Human Rights and Fundamental Rights are based on mankinds increasing demand for a decent life and in which the inherent dignity of each human being will receive respect and protection. They are fundamental to our nature and are imprescriptible and inalienable. It is a 20th century name for what has been traditionally known as Natural. Rights or in a more exhilerating phrase, the Rights of Man. Much has been said about them and yet one still be left wondering what they are. In India for the teaming millions who, are oppressed, suppressed and depressed, who live in destitution, untold misery and suffering, it continues to remain an empty assertion, merely a teasing illusion and a promise of unreality.

The Universal Declaration of Human Rights recognised the inherent dignity and of the natural rights of all members of human family. It represents reaffirmance of faith in the dignity and worth of Human persons. It sets standards for achievement of Human Rights. But the Declaration was having the moral force of Law and not that of Law. It was more in nature of a moral commitment. Securing and enforcing Human Rights is more important to make it meaningful.

However the Declaration made tremendous impact throughout the world inspiring National Constitutions. Many a number of States drafted their Constitutions having these rights as part of their Constitutions and therefore enforceable by Municipal Courts.

The Declaration was followed by two important Covenants transforming the principle enunciated in the Declaration into provisions establishing legal obligations namely International Covenant on Civil and Political Rights and International Covenant on Social Cultural and Economic Rights. Member countries pledged themselves to achieve the promotion of Universal respect and observance of Human Rights and Fundamental Rights.

The Constitution of India embodies a number of Human Rights in its various forms, viz. Cultural Rights, Economic Rights, Social Rights, Political Rights and Civil Rights. Such of the justificable Human Rights namely Civil and Political Rights are enshrined in the Part III of the Constitution which is headed 'Fundamental Rights'. Part III also envisages the conditions under which these rights can be abridged. Our Constitution prevents the State from making any Law which takes away or abridge Fundamental Rights and renders such Laws void that contravene the mandate. Of these the Right that loms large over others is the Civil Right particularly the Right attached to the Person, i.e. Right to Life and Personal Liberty. It means the right that one's life shall not be taken away except under the authority of Law.

From the Right to Freedom of Life comes the Freedom of Person which means that one's body shall not be touched, violated arrested or imprisoned except under the authority of Law. The Right of Live and Freedom of Person are the foremost and primary rights, the realisation of which alone enables one to exercise a variety of other auxiliary rights. It is Right without which all other rights dwindle into insignificance.

In this paper it is intended to confine to the implementation of the Universal Human Right of Security of persons, i.e. the Right to Life and

Personal Liberty and the Right against arbitrary arrest under-our Constitution.

The charter of the Universal rights dwell on all aspects of the Right to Life and Personal Liberty. Much concern and stipulation for the protection of this right have been proclaimed under several Articles of the Declaration and Covenants.

Article 3 of the Declaration proclaims that every one has the right to liberty and security of persons and in safeguarding that right what is envisaged under Article 9 is of crucial importance. Providing for a Human Right against arbitrary arrest, Article 9 of the Declaration states

> "No one shall be subjected to arbitrary arrest, detention or Excile". Other aspects of personal liberty are covered under Articles 4, 5, 6, 11 and 12 of the Declaration."

The Covenant on Civil and Political Rights provides for these under Article 6, 9, 10, 14 and 15. Article 14 incorporating the same adds more rights viz. Right to be informed of the grounds of arrest, Right to be produced before a Magistrate within a reasonable time, entitlement to take proceedings before a court of Law to challenge the lawfulness of the arrest/detention, right to compensation for wrongful detention. etc.

Article 14(3) enumerates certain guarantees in the determination of Criminal charge.

The Articles of the Indian Constitution of India that correspond to the above are Articles 20, 21, and Article 22 that deal with the Right to Personal Liberty and Protection of Personal Liberty and Protection against arbitrary arrest and detention so that Human dignity is not violated and human being is treated as human being.

Our Constitution has not translated the entire set of Human Rights as envisaged in the Declaration and Covenants as Fundamental Rights enacting express provisions. Neither it permits the Apex Court to assume the role of Super legislature. A right which has not been enumerated and expressly declared to be fundamental right enforceable under Article 32 is not a Fundamental Right.

However in the wake of Human Rights realisation throughout the world, in India the Supreme Court has by its Judicial Activism transcended itself to meet the demand for Human Right protection in India. It has done a commendable role of expanding the Human right and it has found Article 21 as the most fruitful one. In the comprehension of the Supreme Court the Right to Life and Liberty as envisaged and protected under Article 21 of our Constitution includes:

- Right of Human Dignity
- Right to Privacy
- Right to speedy Trial
- Right to Bail
- Right to Free Legal Aid
- Right to Know
- Right to compensation for custodial death
- Right to Doctor's assistance
- Right of Prisoners to be treated with dignity and Humanity
- Right against unreasonable search and seizure.
- Right against . delayed execution
- Right against custodial death

Article 7 of the Covenant on Civil and Political Rights prescribes that no one shall be subjected to torture or to cruel and inhuman or degrading treatment or punishment. Like many other countries, India also has not included this immunity in its Constitution as a basic Constitutional Right. Even the Convention Against Torture and Inhuman or Degrading Treatment of Punishment adopted by the U.N. on December 10, 1984 was ratified very late and India has belatedly agreed to sign. It was the Judiciary that speed out this vital protection from Article 21 of the Constitution.

Article 20 corresponds to the protection enshrined in Article 15 of the Covenant but is wider in its scope as regards the doctrine it evolves. It lays down the principle that expost facto laws are bad as being unjust, Doctrine of Double Jeopardy and the Rule against Self Incrimination.

Corresponding to, the Articles 9 and 14 of the Convention, Article 22 of the Constitution of India expressly provides for certain protections viz. Right to be produced before a Magistrate, Right to be informed, Right to have Legal Aid/assistance Right not to be detained beyond 24 Hours etc. Obviously the entire set of rights set out in the said articles of the Convention are not enacted under Article 22 of the Constitution. Again it is left to the Judiciary to read all those rights to be inherent under Article 22.

IMPLEMENTATION OF HUMAN RIGHTS TO LIFE AND LIBERTY

There has been a remarkable progress in the field of enforcement of Human Rights. This is not merely because there is an inbuilt mechanism in the Constitution that ensures enforcement of Fundamental Right but also due to the fact that the Judiciary has made a striking advance in the field of Human Rights in our country.

The enforcement of Human Right is guaranteed by the Right to move the Supreme Court whenever there is an infringement. Article 32 provides a guaranteed remedy for the enforcement of Fundamental Rights. In fact Article 32 is itself a further right in this regard. It is the remedial Fundamental Rich, which gives teeth to all other Fundamental Rights. As Pathanjali Sasthri. J has put it, it is the protector and guarantor of Fundamental Rights. It can be brought into action by what may be compendiously called the Writ Jurisdiction of the Supreme Court and the High Courts.

Article 32 reads :

(a) The right to move the Supreme Court by appropriate proceedings for the enforcement of the rights conformed by this part is guaranteed.

(b) The Supreme Court shall have power to issue direction orders or writs, including writs in the nature of Habeas Corpus, Mandamus, Prohibition and Certiorori which may be appropriate for the enforcement of any of the rights conferred by the part.

The traditional rules of Locus Standi which was the ancient vintage was strictly applied whenever these remedial right were sought to be invoked. Only in the case of writ of Habeas Corpus which secures the instant release of person detained unlawfully that the petition could be filed by any other person on behalf of the person imprisoned or detained whose Fundamental Right is infringed. The Writ of Habeas Corpus is maintainable only when breach of Fundamental Right is alleged. Under Article 32 petition is not available against a private person who is allegedly to have unlawfully detained the petitioner. But under Article 226 petition of Habeas Corpus is maintainable in all cases of unlawful detention and against any detainee whether private of government. The purpose of this writ is to secure the release of a detainee from unlawful detention and not to punish the person who detained.

The remedial rights under Article 32 and Article 226 cannot be abdridged of abdicated by Statute of Limitation. In this regard the Supreme Court has expressed conflicting opinions. Finally in *R.S. Deodar v State* was not a rule of law but a rule of practice and the courts easily allow itself to be persuaded to relief on the ground of latches, delay or the like.

The requirement of Locus standi rule has been a serious stumbling block in the advancement of Human Rights. The restrictive rule of Locus Standi insisted that only the aggrieved could go to the court for relief and other members of the public had no access to the Court unless they suffered injury. Millions of our people find legal and Judicial process far removed from them for reasons of massive poverty, illiteracy, ignorance and helplessness. They have been constantly and continuously clamouring for Justice with a view to protect their Human Rights. Responding to demands, by the pioneering efforts of Justice V.R. Krishna Iyer and Justice Bhagvathi, the Supreme Court has liberalised the Locus Standi rule. While Justice Krishna Iyer, for the first time, advanced a liberal interpretation of Locust Standi in Dhabolkar case, Justice Bagwati gave a decent burial to the Locus Standi rule in the famous Judges Transfer case. Broadening the Doctrine of Locus Standi the Supreme Court made it possible for the poor to bring their problems before the Court through any person or Organisation.

The court speaking through Justice Bagwati held that any member of the public or social action group acting bonafide can maintain an application in the High Court under Article 226 and in the Supreme Court under Article 32 seeking judicial redress for the legal injury caused to such person or class of persons who, due to socially or economically disadvantageous position, cannot approach the courts for judicial redress. In such a case the Court will not insist on a regular Writ petition to be filed by the public spirited individual or social action group espousing their cause. Deciding the Asian Workers Case the Supreme Court stated that, "a new dimension has been given to the doctrine of Locus Standi which has revolutionised the whole concept of access to Justice in a way not known before it.

These developments have led to the introduction of new dimension in the Legal and Judicial process and opened up a new vista of entirely a different kind of litigation 'Public interest Litigation' or 'Social Action Litigation', as professor Upendra Baxi prefers to call it, - for enforcing the basic human rights of the deprived sections of the community and ensuring their basic human dignity.

The epistolary jurisdiction of the High Court and the Supreme Court has substantially contributed to the development of public interest litigation and the province of Public Interest Litigation is expanding wider and wider. Now the Supreme Court is able to widen the horizones and intervene whenever Human Rights violation and Injustice is caused and secures the rights of the helpless and the hapless who have no means to approach or do not know whom to approach. It is evident from number of cases where the court has taken appropriate action viz. Bahalpur under-trial blinding case, protection of payment and Slum Dwellers, case of Women in police custody, Flesh Trade, Children in Juvenile Holmes, Freeing of Bonded Labour etc. and the list continues.

JUDICIAL ACTIVISM IN HUMAN RIGHTS ENFORCEMENT AND SOME ILLUSTRATIVE CASES

By the significant contribution of the Judiciary striking advances have been made in the field of Human Rights in our country.

- For the first time, in *Hussainaara Khatoon's* case the Supreme Court liberally construed Article 21 so as to cover the positive concept of Liberty. The Court invested the Fundamental Right under Article 21 with a positive content requiring affirmative action on the part of the State. Till then it had interpreted Fundamental Right as merely imposing restriction on the authority of the State.

- The guarantee of Right to Life under Article 21 is not confined to mere physical or animal existence but also included within its scope ambit the right to live with Human Dignity. Expanding the reach and ambit of right to life enshrined in Article 21, the Supreme Court laid down in *Francis Muller's* case that the State cannot deprive a person of the right to live with basic human dignity and since no procedure which deprives a man of basic human dignity can ever be reasonable fair and just, the State is prohibited from acting in a manner which would trench upon the basic human dignity of a individual.

- A procedure prescribed by law for depriving a person of his life or personal liberty should be a reasonable fair and just and if a law depriving this rights prescribes a procedure which is unreasonable, unfair and unjust, the law should be void. Thus the Supreme Court held in *Menka Gandhi Case.*

- Taking a deviation from the system of monetary Bail the Supreme Court in *Hussainara Khatoon* case pointed out that a new insight should inform our approach in the matter of pre-Trial release and laid down a new and liberal norm consistent with the Human Rights on which accused person should be released on Bail. The court held that the accused may safely be released on personal bond without insisting on a monetary bond and sureties if the court is satisfied that the accused has his roots in the society. Thus the Supreme Court has helped to advance Human Right envisaged under Article 9 Cl. 3 of International Covenant on Civil and Political Rights.

- Again the Apex Court, in *Hussainara Khatoon* case gave due recognition and significance to the Right to Legal Aid in a Criminal Trial and Right to Speedy Trial as basic Human Rights. "Legal Aid to an indigent caused in a criminal trial is implicit in the guarantee of Fundamental Rights enshrined in Article 21, because a procedure which does not provide for a Legal representation to a person when he is in jeopardy of his life and liberty, cannot be regarded as reasonable, fair and just."

- The State is under a constitutional mandate to provide free legal aid to the accussed who cannot afford legal service". *Khatri v State of Bihar*. In categorical terms the Supreme Court, in *Sheela Barse* case, held that the constitutional obligation to provide Free Legal Aid emanates from Articles 14, 21 and 39-A. "The right of a poor person to have legal aid exists even if it is not demanded by him. Failure to provide legal aid to an accused vitiates the trial" *Shuk Dass* vs *Arunachal Pradesh*.

  "Right to a reasonably and expeditious trial is an integral and essential part of the Fundamental Right embodied in Article 21 and that the State is under a Constitutional mandate to do whatever is necessary to ensure expeditious investigation and speedy Trial" *Khussainara Khatoon* case. Reinstating the same and emphasising that right to speedy trial flowing from Article 21 encompasses all the stages namely the stage of Investigation, Trial, Retrial, Appeal and Revision, in - *A.R. Antulay* v *R.S. Naik*, the Supreme Court laid a set of guidelines concerning the right to speedy Trial. In *Raghubir Singh* v *State of Bihar* the Supreme Court observed that the right to speedy Trial is one of the dimensions of Fundamental Right to Liberty and Life.

- Arrest and detention in police custody of a person can affect seriously the reputation, self-esteem and human dignity of that person. To uphold the constitutional guarantee of Human Rights under Article 21, the Supreme Court, in *Joginder Kumar* v *State of U.P.*, evolved standards and safeguards against arbitrary arrests by the police. The court explained the powers of the police to arrest an accused and laid down that no arrest can be made just because it is lawful for the police to do so. The police officer must be able to justify the arrest apart from the power to do so. It also made a direction that Director General of Police of all States in India shall issue directions that a police officer making an arrest should also record reasons for making the arrest.

- Though India is a party to the Covenant, the Constitution does not contain a specific analogous provisions for right to compensation for wrongful arrest detention and torture. Article 9(5) of the Covenant on Civil and Political Rights reads. "Any one who has been victim of unlawful arrest or detention shall have an enforceable right to compensation." Again it was the Supreme Court that considered the right to compensation for wrongful arrest and detention as an aspect of personal liberty. (*Rudul Shah* v *State of Bihar*).
- In *Nilabhati* vs *State of Orissa*, a case for compensation in custodial death, Justice Verma, quoting the text of Art. 9 (5) of the Covenant on Civil and Political Rights said that an enforceable right to compensation is not alien to the concept of enforcement of guaranteed rights.
- Right to Privacy is part of the fundamental right guaranteed by Article 21. It is part of individual's personal liberty. It is available to any person whether he or she be a person of easy virtue or a virtuous person" so held the Supreme Court in *State of Maharashtra* v *Madhukar*.
- Again in *Menaka Gandhi* case the Constitutional Bench of the Supreme Court, placing reliance not merely on Indian Constitutional provision but also on the provisions of the Declaration of Universal Human Rights, held that no person can be deprived of his right to go abroad unless there is a law made by the State prescribing the procedure which is not arbitrary, unfair and unreasonable.

SOME IMPEDIMENTS - WHERE IT GOES WRONG AND WHAT IS TO BE DONE?

The declarations made and the resolutions passed about Human Rights, in reality in number of cases, remain idle ideals, empty assertions and pious declarations. New tools and innovative strategies are to be fashioned for the purpose of actualising the human rights and making them meaningful for the large mass of people who are denied their basic human rights. Most of the human rights are made a part of the fabric of social welfare legislations in our country. But these laws remain to be symbolic laws. They should be de-symbolised and be made available for the exploited mass to use them to secure their rights.

A firm impediment in the advancement of Human Rights is the formalities and procedural technicalities under the law. The systematic constraints and traditions frustrated the humanistic expectation from the Judiciary. The enormous delay and expenses of the legal system barred many from getting access to justice. Access to justice should be broadened. The court has to put into action procedural justice as given by Article 39(A) of the Constitution.

The advent of the Public Interest Litigation and Legal Aid Movement has cracked the serious stumbling block in the advancement of Human Rights, the Locus Standi Rule. Notably, since then the Human Rights Fundamental Rights are being translated into living realities and thus the Human Rights Movement accelerated. But still there is a grave contradiction between the victims of the privation and the class who use the laws as intimidatory instrument. The unfortunate lot often get entangled in the web of law which is tuned against them as instrument of repression. And the deprivations and exploitations continue unabated. As commented by Justice V.R. Krishna Iyer, "What we need is a new Justice Jurisprudence charged with the egalitarian ideology of socialist development and dignity of personhood, tuned to the living realities of our people."

It is true that the Constitution of most of the Countries embody a number of Human Rights and it is equally true that governments of all countries are united in violating them in a greater or lesser degree. It is a parodox of history that those who fought against dictators and tyrants for liberty and championed human rights, themselves commit many crimes against human rights.

The State forces meant for maintaining law and order are self impediments and high violators of human rights. As pointed out by Justice V.R. Krishna Iyer 'the police and para-military forces have become weapons in the hands of the state and were pitted against those who speak up for their rights, the poor and the downtrodden'. And instances are on the increase where the police also eliminate unwanted people through what is described as "encounters".

Permissive approach towards the use of third degree methods has lead to violation of Fundamental Rights of Citizens. Having acceded to the 'Convention against Torture' the government should take early and firm decision to ban and eliminate use of third degree method and torture in investigation.

The scene of Human Right violation behind the bars or the tall dark boundary of Law, as Justice Iyer puts it, is still more gruesome. Men and women who are behind the bars and in political lock up lose their dignity because police operate under their own rules without any respect to the provisions of Constitution. What is needed to be done is to go for a total revamping of the police organisation to infuse confidence in the minds of the public. Steps should be taken to impart knowledge and awareness in the minds of the police people of the Human Rights and its importance. Different approaches to the methodology of teaching Human rights to the police can be adopted.

The Legislature should be more sensitive about the protection of Human Rights of Citizens and the Judiciary should be more vigilant to ensure than Human Rights are not violated at the hands of the machinery enforcing Law and Order. Justice V.R. Krishna Iyer observes: "The fundamental task of the day is the dynamic legislative action and purposeful judicial reforms and sensitive administration, streamline so as to transform our conditions of social life."

The State bears an obligatory duty to ensure and protect in its territorial jurisdiction, the civil and political rights of all its people. To achieve this and for the implementation of Human Rights enough development in the political, social, economic and cultural spheres should be made as these have a close relationship with the Rights. It is also the duty of the State to set up adequate machinery to discharge its legal and constitutional obligations regarding protection of Human Rights.

The role of the Legislature, Judiciary and the Administration is just one part in the scheme of implementation of Human Rights. What should go along with this is the social awakening and public participation. A majority of the masses who are oppressed, exploited and deprived are not aware of their Human Rights and that they are violated. Ignorance and illiteracy of the masses, poverty, backwardness, caste feelings and religious superstitious feelings offer fertile ground for exploitation. And then there are victims of evil social practices that have the backing of tradition and religion. There should be an awakening and the masses should relieve themselves from the shackles of exploitation and relieve themselves from being mute victims and witnesses of Human Right violations.

Education and enlightenment with the aid of Government, Mass Media and Social Organisations can check this exploitation. Human Rights Organisations should play a more constructive role than a partisan role in bringing to light the cases of Human Rights violations by the police and others. Participatory organisations of the poor at the grass root level should be created, developed and should be taught how to fight for their rights through legal process. The existing scattered social organisations groups should be organised on regional basis and should be provided legal support to promote their effectiveness. What is necessary to enable the weakest and poor to get the benefit of implementation schemes is the operation through sincere and dedicated non-political social action group. Human Rights Movement should be action oriented and should be taken up at the grass root level by social activists dedicated to the noble cause.

CHAPTER IV

The Fifty Years of Human Rights Jurisprudence in India

Dr. Nalini Kant Jha

Once we review the history of past fifty years of independent India, one of the remarkable achievements of this period that immediately comes to our mind is the evolution of the human rights jurisprudence. The Indian Supreme Court has played an unique role in this regard, perhaps incomparable to any other court in the world. Undoubtedly, the Indian Supreme Court is one of the most powerful courts in the world. It is at once a federal court, a court of appeal, a guardian of the Constitution and a court of record in the sense that the law declared by it is binding on all other courts within the territory of India. Its jurisdiction extends to around 900 million people and it has the power of judicial review not only over executive action but also legislation and extends even to reviewing the validity of Constitutional amendments - a power incomprehensible in most parts of the world.

II

The power of judicial review is conferred on the Supreme Court by Article 32 of the Constitution and this power is granted in the widest terms. The power of the Supreme Court is thus not limited to the issuance of the traditional writs of mandamus, certiorari or prohibition, but is of the widest amplitude. Indeed, the Indian Supreme Court possesses larger powers than the American Supreme Court in several respects.

In *Gopalan V. State of Madras* (1950) and *Jaynarayan V. State of West Bengal* (1970), the Indian Supreme Court had, however, propounded the view that by adopting the expression "procedure established by law", Article 21 of the Indian Constitution had embodied the English concept of personal liberty in preference to that of American principle of "Due Process of Law" (5th and 14th Amendments of the US Constitution) which protects Americans not only against arbitrary executive actions but also against any legislation the court may regard as undue, unreasonable or unfair. In other words, the Indian apex court held the view that unlike the American Constitution, the founding fathers of our Constitution preferred the supremacy of the legislators to that of the judiciary. As such, they believed that like the British Constitution, personal liberty in India was "a liberty confined and controlled by law", even though the minority of judges in the Gopalan's case held that such an interpretation of Art. 21 could only throw "the most important fundamental right to life and personal liberty" "at the mercy of legislative majorities".

The majority opinion of the Supreme Court had reasons to make a restricted interpretation of the right to personal liberty granted by Article 21 of the Constitution. It may be recalled here that the Drafting Committee of the Constitution Assembly, headed by Dr. B.R. Ambedkar, had rejected the "due process" clause proposed by B.N. Rau. This was done after a detailed scrutiny of the Constitutional Advisor's draft of the Constitution and other matters, notes, reports and memoranda placed before it. Undoubtedly, the founding fathers of the Constitution could not anticipate the irresponsible and highly selfish behaviour of present legislators. Unlike American counterparts, they, therefore, placed certain trust in.them.

III

Once, however, our elected representatives began to increasingly display their scant regard for democratic ethos and popular welfare, the Supreme Court had to come forward to safeguard a common individual's rights. After a long struggle, which may be said to have started tangibly since 1971, the minority view in Gopalan's case could, therefore, come to triumph in the 7-Judge landmark decision in the *Meneka V. Union of India* case (1978). In that case, the Supereme Court held that the procedure contemplated by Article 21 was not any procedure, but had to be just, reasonable and fair. For the first time, it took the view that Article 21 afforded protection not only against executive action but also against legislation. The court thus introduced in the Constitution the procedural due process of the American Constitution.

From *Gopalan* to *Meneka,* thus, the judicial exploration completed its trek from the North to the South Pole. The decision in Meneka's case has been followed by the Supreme Court in subsequent cases such as *Sunil V. Delhi Administration* (1978), *Hassainara* V. *State of Bihar* (1979), *State of Maharastra* V. *Champaklal* (1981); and *Shri Singh* V. *State of Punjab* (1983), etc. The Supreme Court developed through these cases three notable basic commitments to human rights in the last few years. First is the commitment to participative justice, the second is the commitment against arbitrariness and third is the commitment to just standard of procedure.

The Supreme Court affirmed its commitment to just standards of procedure in preventing administrative regression. Relying on the requirements of a reasonable, fair and just procedure, the court made legal aid to a poor accused in a criminal case a constitutional right by treating it as an integral part of a reasonable, fair and just procedure. It also held speedy justice in a criminal case to be part of a reasonable, fair and just procedure.

In the process, the Supreme Court repudiated its traditional view that fundamental rights merely impose negative restrictions on the state. Since the landmark judgement of the *Meneka Ganhdi case,* the court started reading fundamental rights as imposing affirmative obligations on the state. It marked the beginning of a new era of judicial activism. It further expanded the scope and ambit of Article 21 by placing an expansive interpretation on the right to life enshrined in that Article in the Francis Coral Mullin case. In this case the court held that the word "life" did not mean a mere physical or animal existence but included the use of every limb and faculty through which life was enjoyed and also a safe and healthy environment was included in the right to life. The right to travel abroad was also recognized as an integral part of the right to life and personal liberty.

In addition, the court extended the reach of fundamental rights by holding that not only the state but also any instrumentality or agency of the state such as public sector corporation would be subject to the discipline of fundamental human rights set out in the Constitution. At the same time, the court held that the state action must not only be non-arbitrary, but also be in the public interest.

As the above mentioned rights which the Supreme Court spelt out from the language of Article 21 by a process of judicial activism and creative interpretation would have no meaning for the large masses unless they have access to justice, the court proceeded to develop the law in regard to access to justice. In order to enable the weaker section to rights, the Supreme Court changed the traditional rule of locus standi that permitted only the victims to approach the court against violation of their rights. As the poor and illiterate victims were unable to approach the court, the apex court enlarged the doctrine of locus standi by providing that where a legal injury is caused or a legal wrong done to a person or class of persons - who, by reason of poverty or disability or social socio-economic disadvantaged position, can not approach a court of law for justice - any member of the public or social action group acting bonafide can bring an action seeking judicial redress for such a person or a class of persons. This can be done even by addressing a letter to the court. Thus came into being the public interest litigation in the Supreme Court and the High Courts and a new jurisdiction evolved, namely, epistolary jurisdiction.

IV

The use of public interest litigation has evoked widespread applause as well as considerable controversy. While the human right activists have hailed it as a revolutionary step towards advancement of individual dignity in India, the politicians and bureaucrats have attacked this on the ground that the strategy of public interest litigation is being misused and that the courts are lending themselves to such misuse. It is also alleged that the court is trespassing in to the field entrusted by the Constitution to the executive and legislature.

No one can, of course, dismiss the above mentioned apprehensions lightly. As the framers of the American constitution had discovered long back that an individual's liberty can be secured best only through checks and balances among various organs of the government. Judges are also human beings. In the event of concentration of powers in their hands due to the failure of the executive and legislatures, they too can become arrogant. This is already, happening in lower courts. Even a well educated person is not allowed to speak in his defence by some judges only in order to please their legal fraternity. This only erodes peoples faith in the judiciary. While this malady is not as widespread in High Courts and the Supreme Court as in the lower courts, certain blacksheeps have penetrated the higher judiciary too.

Supreme Court has, however, played a major role in championing the cause of liberty in India. The lower judiciary needs to emulate their apex body. Judicial activism, therefore, needs to be examined in the proper perspective. While hailing the virtues of judicial activism, proper methods have to be devised for checking judicial excesses. One must also not forget that security forces had to fight the merchants of death and terrorism for the protection of innocent civilians. A tendency has developed to condemn only the security forces without uttering a single word against the foreign inspired agents of death and destruction. This tendency has to be condemned by all right thinking persons. Judiciary, too, should not succumb to populist temptations while dealing with such enemies of innocent civilians.

V

Judicial activism or excesses should not, however, lead to hysterical response. At the same time judicial accountability must be ensured. The language used in the judiciary reflecting feudal tendency needs to be corrected. Even the most junior lawyer, for example, is addressed as the learned counsel, a victim seeking justice in the court is not addressed properly even if he may be an established scholar. Judicial functionaries, therefore, needs proper training for adjusting themselves to the democratic ethos.

In fact, adjudication is a delicate process where diverse factors and considerations have to be weighed, adjusted, and harmonised and that requires not only wisdom and courage but also faith in constitutional values. This can come only through proper selection of judges and training. Otherwise, we will continue to see the elevation of such persons to the august offices in the temple of Justice, some of whom believe that justice means only shutting the mouth of victims. One can only hope that the executive, the legislature and the Judiciary will show their commitments to our constitutional ethos and human dignity.

CHAPTER V

Managing Sustainable Democracy for a United India - A Review of the Election System and its Needed Reform

*Dr. M. Basheer Ahmed Khan**

- *Since the writing of the paper, countrywide elections for the 18th Loksabha were held vindicating the doubt expressed.*

INTRODUCTION

In about half a century, 'Mera Bharat Mahan' held a dozen country wide elections and established globally that it is one of the 'greatest' democracies of the world! Considering the lower socioeconomic position of the nation in comparison to the western developed world, its greatness and importance only enhance having continued the electoral ritual with a religious tenacity. Prediction is not possible if we will have the same 12th Lok Sabha on the morn of January 1, 2000 when we would be literally entering the 21st century considering the political dynamics of the country and the inherent inconsistency of the generation. Nevertheless, we can be proud of the fact that we have come of age as a democratic polity at the time when we are celebrating the Golden Jubilee Year of our Independence and our life as a Sovereign Democratic Republic.

It is not at all a mean achievement for India to reach its current position in the world considering the multifarious challenges faced by the country during the past five decades. It can always be pleaded that we could have achieved better it we had performed better. Of all said words of pen and tongue, the saddest are 'we could have been'! While invoking the electoral process is a robust faith in the democratic power, the need for invoking it often also proclaims aloud that "something is rotten in the state of Denmark". The development of a mature, empowered polity is not only an end in itself for a democracy, but also a means to achieve the end of a higher quality of life in all its realms in a democracy. While the electoral process is set in motion to gain political power, the nations economic power is eroded due to its high socio-economic costs for a comparatively low priority reason, which is avoidable. The fact that we have had only 12 Lok Sabha elections, which is marginally more than an ideal number is not an alarming one, but certainly sends warning signals that if the nation wants to sustain its democracy for a United India, the electoral process and its representative credentials have to be reviewed and if necessary reformed and restructured. The founding fathers of Indian Constitution have been careful in laying the precincts of the system and if the leadership of the polity and society is to maintain the same standards of the political behaviour at the time of the framing of the constitution, nothing would have gone wrong with the country and the nation. As some argue, (TSN Sastry, 1997) "there is nothing wrong either with the constitution of India or its polity. It's the lack of will on the part of the political parties, to adhere to the constitutional culture that is hampering us. The selfish motives of the political parties resulted in the involvement of money and muscle power in elections. According to Subhash C. Kashyap (1997) "the new breed of the so called representatives of the people have lost their representative credentials and respect and trust of the people. Therefore, we need new mechanisms and devices for ensuring and enforcing responsibility of Ministers and Members of Parliament to the people at large. The hard operative reality of our polity today is that it is no more representative or parliamentary or even democracy."

In the past five decades, what has happened in the country that make people lament against the electoral system, that make people different about their democracy, that make the people guilt conscious, that make people apologetic, that make people feel that all is not well with their existing system and urgent measures are needed to reformulate the electoral process? It is argued (D. Sundar Ram,1998) that "the framers" of the constitution have given a foolproof electoral mechanism to ensure free and fair elections. However, four factors have shaken the foundation - increase in the use of money power, reliance on muscle power at the time of elections, kindling the caste and communal prejudices of the voters and the misuse of official machinery...... Today what is needed is sweeping electoral reforms and accountability of the representatives to the citizens of India." If these and similar factors are responsible for eroding the values and diluting the quality of elections, perhaps what would be needed would be to manipulate these factors in the best interest of maintaining the old system in its true spirit. However, before proceeding to analyse these factors, it may also be of interest to review the concepts underlying the election system.

ELECTIONS IN DEMOCRACY

The following couplet of Pope is oft remembered while talking about polity and governance: "O'er forms of government let fools contest, What'er is best administered is best." "The same couplet can also be remembered when debating the forms of elections or their reforms. Many a times, the problem of elections in India arise out of their mal-administration than that of the system itself as the complaints about our elections are not same everywhere in the country! So the elections as a mechanism to provide democracy are certainly playing an important role notwithstanding their time specific, situation-specific and region specific limitations. After all, as Richard Robinson (1949) said "democracy is usually an attempt to find, in the sphere of government, the ideal state of things or the best constitutional means of approaching the ideal, it being already agreed that this ideal includes or involves a large participation of the common people in the forming of public policy." Looking democracy from this angle, the elections do help to a significant extent in the participation of the common people, especially those who are politically active in the forming of public policy. However, when it comes to the point of identifying democracy by definition, with everything that is good, i.e. with the good laws, policies etc. which we want (Mayo, H.B.; 1967) the problem starts. Our inadequacies, situational improbabilities, inequities etc. will be quickly assigned to the democratic governance, rather than admitting them as our failures of performance.

The elections are also supposed to play different roles in the democratic system of governance. According to Mayo, (1967) elections manifest the following:

1. the Individual voter takes his share in political power by voting for the representative of his choice.

2. voters as a group bring the decision makers under popular control. This control is ever present in the minds of representatives because any of their behaviour in office may affect their chances at the next elections.
3. the election result is also an authorization of representatives to make decisions to govern within the broad drift of a policy platform. Thus the election results invest representatives and decisions with legitimacy. This point answers the criticisms of some (Subhash C. Kashyap, 1997), against the coalition governments of '13 or 14 small parties stay together to share the fruits of power'.

However, realistically speaking, the voter does not always consider that his vote is a share in political power. In India with the extent of illiteracy, social alienation, rural and tribal life, votes are cast for reasons other than the expression as a share in political power. Infact, if the voter is treated as a sharer of political power, his job should not be made complicated with long and confusing lists of electoral candidates. But this is not avoided either in India or even in U.S.A. As Mayo says (1967) 'perhaps nowhere else in the world is the ballot - and much of the other political and governmental machinery - so bewildering and cumbersome as in the United States, a country which is a model to the world in its efficient technology and corporate organization. Let us be frank about it; much of the United States electoral machinery is a national disgrace, and the fact that it can be seriously defended compounds the disgrace and shows how far Americans are willing to tolerate abuses in what should be the simplest feature of democracy."

If the electoral machinery is so bad as to be a disgrace for the Americans, the Indian situation is indeed tolerable. Collectively, the voters bring the political stewardship under the control of the people during elections. In India, over and again the various governments have been punished for their misdeed by the voters by using their ultimate weapon - the ballots. Political parties have undoubtedly been made to behave through the anger of the electorate. To that extent, in the Indian elections, the anti-incumbency factor has decided the fate of the political parties in many states as well as at the centre.

Elections are the production centres for the legitimate governments. Irrespective of the motives with which an individual voter casts his or her vote, the ultimate aim is to help the system produce a government which is legitimate. With the presence of multiple parties and groups, the prediction of the result may be difficult, except for psephological calculations carried out through opinion polls or exit polls. Even in a two party system, it would be difficult for the individual voter to decide who would be the government-to-be or opposition-to-be. However, once elected, the groups and parties are able to formulate within an acceptable paradigm and establish a government within the limits of the constitutional provisions. Thus they get the legitimacy to govern the country. In India, we have the anti-defection law, which also helps to keep the loyalty of the individual to the group to which he belongs which is also a conceptually sound practice for the democratic dynamics.

In the context of elections in democracy, a few other issues should be kept in mind to have a pragmatic view. It is often asserted that voters decide policies directly by their votes. Infact, this does not happen always because political platforms contain many issues, some vague and some specific with a deliberate mixing so that the parties can win the elections. The BJP in India had the Ayodhya issue, income tax issue, Swadeshi issue, reforms issue etc. in its manifesto. After the formation of the coalition and the National Agenda, the issues had to be re-prioritised.

The elections also do not reflect the exact wishes of the people or do not manifest the 'popular will'. The parties that come to power may or may not actually implement their manifestos or campaign promises. The legislators are forced to decide on matters where they know the popular will or the wishes of the electorate are different. The governmental decisions will not only reflect the majority views, but also views held by others. The majorities are many a times considered to be fickle and the governments would be considered to be foolish which would try to implement every transient public mood because of its sense of electoral obligation.

The majority syndrom of a democracy is temporary. It keeps shifting. Besides, a government is not passive. It can influence the public through its actions and convert the electoral mood through campaigns in its favour before the next elections.

It is also debated as to why should there be a popular control at all. The basic principle in democracy is that the people are sovereign and the authority to govern the people must flow from the people as against in monarchy or in any other form of government. However, this authority does not mean that all decision-making should be scrutinised or controlled by the people. Hence, the concept of popular control is and should be as practised limited to the universal franchise rather than a narrow franchise.

Similarly, it is also essential to look at the issue of representation. Elections justify the representation of persons and not interests. When we make a segregation like this between 'persons' and 'interests', it would be easy to understand the current practices among the legislators. It is often held that representatives are 'microcosms' of the electorate. This also does not hold good. It is not that people want to be represented by others of the same profession, job or caste or creed etc. Political workers have to raise above their limited groups to which they belong to represent larger groups of people in democracy. The political parties are informal systems of representation to supplement the formal structure of government.

The tenure of legislators, size of the legislature, compensation for legislators are also issues that crowd the discussion about election in democracy. The simple fact here is democracy being a system of governance of people by themselves for themselves, the society at large should be least troubled by the burden of democracy.

A REVIEW OF THE INDIAN ELECTION SYSTEM

Indian Constitution has carefully examined the issue of elections in India and a separate chapter is provided on the elections. "In this respect, it has made departure from the usual practice of constitutions to leave elections as comparatively unimportant subject to be dealt with by the legislature" (Pylee, M.V.; 1984). The political right of the Indian citizen has been safeguarded by the constitution and a constitutional authority was created in the form of Chief Election Commissioner with permanence to hold general elections after a five year term and by-elections at any time. The Chief Election Commissioner was entrusted with such matters as election of the President of India, election of Vice President of India, Parliament and its two chambers, qualification of members of Parliament, composition of State Legislatures, duration of Parliament and the State Legislature, elections to Parliament and the State Legislatures, reservation of seats in the House of People and the State Assemblies for the Scheduled Castes and tribes and the determination of population for the purposes of election. Articles 327 and 328 give powers to the Parliament and State Legislature respectively to legislate on all matters relating to elections. The two important legalisation that arose from these are the Representation of People Act, 1950 and the Representation of People Act, 1951. Statutory rules under these Acts were made called as the Representation of People (Preparation of Electoral Rolls) Rules, 1950 and the Representation of the People (Conduct of Elections and Election Petitions) Rules, 1951. There have been amendments to the Acts from time to time. Under the laws enacted, the Indian nation had its first general elections in 1951-52. Since then, there should have been ten general elections and the tenth parliament should have been formed. However, due to mid-term elections and the general elections advanced in 1971 by one year, currently the 12th parliament is formed. Looking at the issue this way, India has not committed much wrong especially compared to some other countries of the world. Our election history is without much blemishes. This does not mean that all is well with us and in perfecting our system and in maintaining the spirit of the constitution, we have a long way to tread, which of course is full of challenges. But the warning signals should not be ignored if the country is committed to sustaining its democratic traditions and boast the luxury of enjoying democratic living in a united India in the future. In the break up of the East European nations, India has a lesson to learn. Similarly, in the formation of CIS (Commonwealth of Independent States) also, India has a lesson to learn.

SOME FACTS OF THE ELECTORAL SCENE IN INDIA

We are fresh from the current parliament election scene of 1998. Out of a population of approximately 95 crores, as on January 1, 1998, 60 crores and 53 lakhs are eligible voters. Article 326 of the Constitution ensures adult suffrage and the current voting age is 18 years. Out of the eligible voters, only a small percentage has been exercising their frachise. The voter turn out for 1998 elections has been 55%. In 1996, it was 58%. A quick look at the percentage of voting in the past will give us the following figures : 1962 - 55%, 1967 - 61.3%, 1971 - 55.3%, 1977 - 60.5%, 1984 - 64%, 1989 - 62% and in 1991 - 61%. These percentages mean that a substantial number of the population (perhaps as high as 1/3rd) remains outside the election process. Among those who participate in the election, the votes are divided among the many contestants and those who win the elections win as a result of the approbation of a small number. The elected candidate thus sometimes represent with as low a percentage as 15% or at best with 25%. This sort of a situation raises the eye brows of many who, hence prefer to call the elections a mockery of democracy!

To add to this situation, the frequent complaints of criminalisation of election, corruption, whipping up sectarian, caste, creed feelings during election campaigns, literal purchase of votes or vote banks, deliberate lowering of the status of the democratic institutions, all have left distressing trends in the polity of the country. The result of all these has led to emergence of sub-national feelings, partisan politics, small group interactions and the feeling of self righteousness of individuals. It is in the midst of the confusing scene that prevails in the electoral system, management efforts are to be made to correct the trends for the sustainability of the democracy for the continued unity and integrity of the Indian state.

It could be realised that in the recent past an apathy towards our political system has emerged among the common people. While they are politically conscious, a sense of helplessness has engulfed them as they find it impossible to change the undesirable trends in the polity and society. The liberalised economy has marginalised the Indian common man and the over play of money power has become visible and goes undeterred. A sizeable section of voters prefer to abstain from the electoral process due to inertia and apathy.

There are at least some groups who boycott the elections at the call of some political activists or on their own convictions. There are people in some regions who are scared to come out and exercise their franchise. Political leadership has lost its credentials and political activists and party position holders and people who occupied high public positions continue to be in public life shamelessly inspite of their being charge sheeted by courts for various acts of omissions and commissions. In the land of 'Sitaji' who has been subjected to the test of fire ('agni pariksha'), there are people who shun elections due to the presence of these culprits in public life. As a result, people are now promoting persons with clear criminal records and convicts as their representatives in the parliament and legislative assemblies. Former dacoits, smugglers, forest brigands etc. are accepted for public life with a vengeance!

With illiteracy at such high levels, prevailing poverty, rural population, tribal people and people in all regions who do not know the value of their votes, political manipulators are able to convert them as their votes by offering the right incentives.

But notwithstanding all these negative features, the elections are also able to return the right candidates as well as carry out the game as required by the constitution. At all times in the history of the country, many reverred leaders could find a place in the legislative bodies and some who secured public approbation continue to get elected from more than one constituency. Where the leaders or the parties could either reach out to the heart of the people or to their minds, people have responded well in continuing to support.

The electoral scene in India is thus a mixed one with many negative and positive features. While matters have not yet reached a breaking point, it would only be wise to review the situation from time to time and take appropriate needed steps to correct the situation and march towards perfection. It is here that management of the democracy plays an important role.

MANAGEMENT OF THE ELECTORAL SYSTEM THROUGH NEEDED REFORMS

Dr. B.R. Ambedkar, the Chairman of the Drafting Committee of the Constituent Assembly remarked about the constitution: "I feel that it is workable, it is flexible and it is strong enough to hold the country together both in peace-time and in war-time. Indeed, if I may say so, if things go wrong under the new Constitution, the reason will not be that we had a bad constitution. What we will have to say is that Man was vile." Groups of vile and honourable persons always existed all through history in every country and culture. The situation is not different to India any way. However, it has been of late realised that there exists the generation "Is" in terms of human behaviour i.e. people have become Individualistic, Iconoclastic and Inconsistent. These behaviours will certainly affect the smooth functioning of any democracy. Looking Indian situation from this angle, even Indian people are subject to such behavioural commonality thereby affecting the democracy and the constitution. Criticising the quality of behaviour of our legislators from what happens in the Indian legislative assemblies like UP Assembly or even Indian Parliament, we tend to feel that all is lost, little realising that worse things happen in other centres of culture like Japanese parliament or Italian Parliament to name a few. Undoubtedly within the precincts of our reverred constitution, we can still think of many actions that can help correct the electoral scene and reinject the spirit of credibility to the system.

Perhaps a total revamp of the system will be well neigh impossible given the sociopolitical conditions nor that be required. A management strategy would be to look at the administrative and judicial aspects of the reform system. We may perhaps ask questions like why corrupt practices become necessary, why large money is required for the elections, why muscle power comes to play its role in selected areas, why caste and sectarian feelings have to be whipped up etc. The answers to the question will give us clear line of action to improve the system.

It may not be out of place to recall that Mr. T.N. Seshan as the Chief Election Commissioner has earned the respect and approbation of the people for efficient and near clean conduct of the elections. This means that 'where there is a will, there is a way.' Recently several articles have appeared (Subhash C. Kashyap, 1997; N. Shyamasundaram, 1998; RV. Shenoy, 1998; P.L. Prasada Rao, 1998; D. Sundar Ram, 1998 etc.) which touch upon one or the other issue relating to the political system and elections. The prominent aspects referred in these views are:

1. A viable time period for elections
2. Performance based voting decision
3. Smaller states
4. Empowering and revamping civil services
5. Judicial activism and quick delivery of justice
6. Deterrent punishment to all including elected representatives
7. Better anti-defection laws
8. Proportional voting system
9. Need to enhance the minimum votes for winning
10. Declaration of wealth and Assets of people in public life
11. Mechanism to avoid litigation and speed up settlement of cases
12. Educating the voters about democratic rights
13. Increasing the representation of groups and classes in the legislative bodies
14. Debarring people with criminal records in the participation of elections
15. Setting an ethical dimension and laying down modes of behaviour of the elected representatives
16. Absentee representation to be avoided and one candidate to file nomination from one constituency alone
17. One person to hold only one office at a time
18. Inner party democracy to be made strict
19. Rotation of public office and avoidance of monopoly of office
20. State going to polls to be under President's rule and prohibition of use of official machinery by contesting or canvassing persons who are in power
21. Elected representative to be available in the constituency all through election time and a few years well ahead of the

election time. Then after, the elected legislator to be basically stationed at his constituency.

22. Election to be organised in such a way to bring down the expenses which can be met by any ordinary citizen
23. Common campaign system for all aspiring candidates
24. Non-serious candidates to be prohibited through Organisation of limited parties based on clear ideological polarisation
25. Direct elections to be confined to panchayats and local bodies and Legislature and parliament to be elected through indirect election.
26. Ceiling on the number of ministers and rotation of minister from among the party workers
27. Elected representative to be paid salary and all perks to be withdrawn
28. Only one term to be enjoyed by party men in public office
29. Gun trotting security of political activists to be prohibited and all government special security to be withdrawn to any selected persons
30. Decentralisation of political decision making and power of the parliament and legislature to be limited to the essential.

It is indeed necessary to consider all the above point of view for evolving a system to better manage our election process for the sustainability of our democracy. The above issues will nonetheless reduce the privileges of some people who gained positions of benefit to them through the political dynamics that followed independence. But a time has now come when people started looking at these privileges of some in the name of democracy without any benefit to the nation at large and at the cost of the honest tax payer.

CONCLUSION

This country belongs to all the 950 million and odd people who live here. The so called managers of the destiny of the people will have to now change from 'self seekers' to 'public servants', the stage from where they came during the pre and post-independent India. The various groups of people in the country have awakened and political assertion has taken place. The coalition governments, however much any one tries to wish away, has come to stay. It only conveys the message that people now mean business and the days of hoodwinking are slowly but surely passing away. The constitution framers had imagined this possibility and framed a constitution that can hold the country together. But we must learn to live together under the constitution by giving the legitimate right of every citizen to him-perhaps by giving 'the devil his due'. One can only conclude by recalling what Aristotle had said:

"To live by the rule of the constitution ought not to be regarded as slavery, but rather as salvation." Let us attain this salvation.

REFERENCES

1. Sastry, TSN: Fifty - Years of Indian independence and the working of its political system, School of International Studies, Pondicherry University, Pondicherry, August 1997.
2. Subash C. Kashyap: Working of the Constitution - Model for Reformed Polity, National Seminar, Pondicherry University, August 1997. P. 2.
3. Sundar Ram, D.: Electoral Reforms a must to Preserve Democracy The Hindu, Madras, Feb. 24, 1998.
4. Richard Robinson: Definition, Oxford. 1949 P. 166
5. Mayo, H.B.: Introduction to Democratic Theory, Sterling Publishers, Delhi, 1967 P. 55.
6. Mayo, H.B.: ibid
7. Subash C Kashyap: ibid
8. Mayo, H.B.: ibid
9. Pylee, M.V.: Constitutional Government in India, S. Chand and Company, Ltd., New Delhi, 1984.
10. Subhash C. Kashyap ibid
11. RV. Shenoy: "Goals achievable in the next fifty years." The Hindu, January 6, 1998.

12. L. Prasad Rao: Educating the Voter, The Hindu, Feb. 24, 1998
13. D. Sundar Ram: ibid
14. N. Shyamasundaram: Performance the basis of Voter Decision The Hindu, April 21, 1998.

CHAPTER VI

Socially and Educationally Backward Classes

D.S.N. Somayajulu

The expression Backward Classes is nowhere defined in the Constitution nor any exclusive method or agency for their determination has been provided.[1] The question who are scheduled castes was roughly settled before independence and gave no scope for judicial determination. Compensatory discrimination in favour of the scheduled castes and scheduled tribes has never been a source of intense social conflicts, court cases or political stalemate.[2] Inspite of the ameliorative measures envisaged under the Constitution for uplifting them they have to travel a long way for catching up and become part of the mainstream of the national life.[3]

The term backward classes had no definite meaning at all India level. It's meaning varied from province to province depending upon local contexts.[4] To appreciate the true meaning of the term "Backward Classes", it is necessary to look into the debates of the Constituent Assembely. Some members felt the expression backward classes used in Article 16(4) (then draft article 10) was vague, and some understood it as synonyms for scheduled castes.[5] While some others considered it as something more.[6] Representatives from southern states like Mysore and Bombay assured the other members of the Constituent Assembly that "Backward Classes" was a distinct term having a technical meaning. In Mysore state Backward Classes included all but

Brahmins.[7] In Madras it meant a stratum of untouchable Hindu Castes.[8] In Bombay it included not only scheduled castes and tribes but also all others who are economically educationally socially backwards.[9] Chandrika Ram from Bihar, explained that backward classes were a section of society between the highest castes and the schedueled castes, i.e.[10]

> "the third section occupying the middle position... and consisting of a large portion of our people is what may be termed as the backward class... doubt they are not treated as untouchables".

K.M. Munshi opined that the term includes scheduled castes. When doubts were raised he explained the necessity of finding a generic term. According to him.[11]

> "it signifies people... touchable or untouchable, belonging to this community or that, who are so backward that special protection is required in the services".

Dr. Ambedkar explained the exact import, and significance and the necessity for using the word "Backward Classes" in Article 16(4). Further, he declared that there were three points of view namely.[12]

(i) that there shall be equality of opportunity for all citizens.

(ii) there should not be reservation of any sort for any class or community at all, that all citizens, if they are qualified, should be placed on the same footing of equality so far as the public services are concerned.

(iii) Theoretically equality of opportunity for all citizens though a good principle, there must at the same time be a provision made for entry of certain communities which have so far been outside the administration.

He clarified that Article 16(4) was intended to serve as a happy formula to reconcile the competing claims of equalities[13] and that wholesale reservation of services would be incompatible with the principle of equality of apportunity.[14] Defending the Article (draft) he explained that:[15]

"We have left it to be determined by each local government. A backward class community is a community which is backward in the opinion of the government".

T.T. Krishnamahari was prophetic when he said that, Article 16(4) would be a "Paradise for lawyers."[16] Further, allaying the fears of some members, that the article was loosely worded and that the word backward is susceptible of different meanings, he said that[17].

"there is no need for such a fear, because I have no doubt it is going to be ultimately interpreted by the Supreme Court on some basic caste, community religion, literacy, or economic status".

Keeping in mind the various views expressed by the members in the Constituent Assembly, the drafting committee had to work out a formula for reconciling these view, namely,[18]

(i) That there shall be equality of opportunity.

(ii) that there shall be reservation in favour of communities which have not so far had a proper "look in" so to say into the administration.

Article 16(4) is a result of such a compromise. The debates of the Constituent Assembly give an impression that backward classes under Article 16(4) are not merely economic groups but historical and social categories whose backwardness is associated with discriminatory social structure of the Indian society.

Reservation by definition entails some element of preference for the disadvantaged who may otherwise lose in an open competition with those who are lucky to have good education training and upbringing.[20] Reservation in favour of the scheduled castes and scheduled tribes are by and large acquired. Harijans and adivasis alone are for centuries victims of active social discrimination through segregation in the former and isolation in the later respectively. They alone have suffered the kind of psychological and moral injury that now call for special treatment to got over their earlier disadvantaged position.[21]

But the extension of reservation in favour of "other backward classes" is seriously objected, on the ground that they are not victims of historical injustices like the scheduled castes or at any rate did not suffer them in a gross form. Castes or communities called as "other backward classes" have never suffered collectively or individually that kind of injury either recently or in the distant past. Viewed in that sense reservations or advantages in favour of "other backward classes" or religious minorities are basically directed towards a balance of power. Reservations made in favour of scheduled castes and scheduled tribes are in tune with the spirit of the constitution, while in favour of other backward classes will sooner or later become what Gajendragadkar former Chief Justice of India called it as "fraud of the constitution."[22]

The intention of the constitution in providing the reservations was to make available special opportunities for the most disadvantaged sections of the society. Preferential policies in operation results in creation of special opportunities for some over and above the equal opportunities available in principle to all. Preferential opportunities may lead to tension between "special opportunities to some" and "equal opportunities for all" and it obviously can not be ignored. If preferential policies are used judiciously, and with restraint, tension can be kept under control and prevent subversion of institutional system.[23]

The principle of redress is broad one and it can be carried on by different kinds of affirmative action. Job reservation or quotas in public employment touches only a fringe of the problem. It is by no means the best one for reducing the social and economical disparities between castes and communities. They have serious institutional costs that far out weigh the benefits they bring to the some individual members of the backward classes.[24]

The basis of reservations rests upon a combination of number of concepts. The most important being the welfare concept i.e., the upliftment of socially and economically weaker sections of the people[25]. The other factor is in relation to scheduled castes and scheduled tribes where to a considerable extent though not solely, the concept of reparation or compensation for least injuries and deprivations suffered by them find place. The other factor is distributive justice.[26]

CRITERIA FOR DETERMINING BACKWARDNESS

The Supreme Court in *M.R. Balaji v. State of Mysore*[27] held that "the backwardness" under Article 15(4), must be social and educaitonal. It is not either social or educational, but is both "social and educational", caste may be considered as a relevant criteria for determining back-wardness. The special provisions are contemplated for classes of citizens, and not for individual citizens as such, and hence though the caste of the group is considered, its importance should not be exaggerated. If the classification of backward classes of citizens was based solely on the case of citizens, it may not always be logical, and it may perhaps perpetuate the castes themselves. Social backwardness in the ultimate analysis is the result of poverty to a large extent, the occupation of a citizen may also contribute to make classes of citizens socially backward. The place of habitation also plays a part in determining the backwardness of the community of persons.

The question of constitutional validity of the reservations to backward classes and quantum of reservations was raised in *M.R. Balaji v. State of Mysore.*[29] Here the Mysore Government by order provided that 68 per cent of the seats in the professional colleges were reserved and 32 per cent of the seats were open to competition on merit basis. Of the 68 percent reserved, 28 per cent were reserved for the backward classes, and 22 per cent for the more backward classes, 15 per cent to the Scheduled Castes and 3 per cent to Scheduled Tribes. The Supreme Court held,[30] that the classification into backward and more backward was not justified, since it was not the scope of Article 15(4). The State is allowed to make special provisions for the advancement of backward classes in the interests of society and to promote advancement of weaker sections of the people in the society. Article 15(4) is a provisions in the nature of an exception excluding the rest of the society who are not backward. It would be unreasonable to assume that by introducing Article 15(4) the Constitution intended to provide that where the advancement of backward classes, or the Scheduled Castes or Scheduled Tribes are concerned, the fundamental rights of the citizens of the society were completely ignored.[31] As a result of Government order 90 per cent of the population was treated as backward, and the classification divides the population into two classes backward and more backward.[32]

The reservations made for the backward classes of citizens should not exceed 50 per cent in any event because, if it exceeds it ceases to be reservation at all.[33] The state has to determine the extent of reservation by taking into account the prevailing circumstances in each case. The State has to determine the issue objectively in a national manner taking into account the needs of the community, and the formula so evolved, should be a reasonable balance between several relevant considerations. In the interest of higher education and in the interest of boys of backward classes themselves, it is undesirable that the boys in the higher education should consist of boys of backward classes admitted under the reserved quota and not boys on merit basis, if it were so permitted the national effort becomes wasteful.

The Kerala High Court in *R. Jacob Mathew v. State of Kerala*[34] hold that the classification of socially backward classes based predominantly on the test of caste, community or religion was inconsistent with the requirement of Article 15 (4). In this case the basis to include Ezvahas and Muslims as a whole as backward classes was pre-dominantity based on the test of caste, community or religion without making any attempt to investigate their economic condition.[35]

The classification and reservation of seats for backward classes must be based on an objective approach, having regard to the materials that have been collected by the Government after making proper investigation of the data relevant for such purposes. The State Government cannot be subjectively satisfied in determining the backwardness of a class. It is the duty of the court to see whether the Government has applied the proper test in determining the backwardness of a particular group.[36] Though a class is treated as a backward class under Article 15(4), it does not take away the right of any of the member of the group from competing on the general merit basis, and securing as many seats as possible. The few seats that are obtained by them in competition on a general merit basis seats secured in accordance with the guarantee given to them under Article 29(2) and not as members of the backward class.[37] Similar view was taken by the Andhra Pradesh High Court[38] and also by the Supreme Court in relation to reservation of posts in services.[39]

CASTE AS A FACTOR FOR DETERMINING BACKWARDNESS

The Supreme Court in *M.R. Balaji v. State of Mysore*[40] hold that caste can be considered as one of the matters for determining backwardness. But it cannot be the sole question for the determination of social backwardness; if it were to be the sole question it comes under discrimination based on caste.[41] Article 15(4) permits reservation on the ground of social and educational backwardness for classes, and not for castes.[42] But in *P. Rajendran v. State of Madras*[43], the Supreme Court justified reservation of seats made castewise. The Supreme Court observed that in this case at any rate caste is synonymous with class. The Advocate-General made this contention and it was not opposed by the other side. On admission of the parties, caste was treated as a class, but it is difficult to accept the correctness of the proposition in regard to all castes. However, in *R. Chitralekha v. State of Mysore*[44], the order of the Government making a classification of socially and educationally backward classes based on economic condition only was held to be justified, the Government did not take into consideration the question of caste. The Government observed that caste is only a relevant and not a compelling circumstance for ascertaining the social backwardness of a group of citizens. The Mysore Government laid down the following conditions for being regarded as belonging to socially and educationally backward class:[45]

(1) the annual income of the family of the students should not be more than Rs. 1200;

(2) the parent or guardian of the student should be pursuing one of the occupations mentioned in the order. Such occupation is one involving manual labour.

The classification thus made is not open to objection because it determines social, and educational backwardness not based on caste. It was held[46] that if the parent was a purohit, it was not an occupation based on manual labour making the boy eligible to be regarded as socially and educationally backward. When the applicant's mother had no occupation, the Mysore High Court did not admit the claim of the child to be treated as one belonging to backward classes.[47] In *Miss Laila Chacko V. State of Kerala,*[48] the High

Court hold that, while accepting means-cum-caste/community test for classification of backward classes several factors have to be taken into consideration. It was not on the basis of income alone that the question whether the class is backward can be determined. Merely because the income of the petitioner's father is less than Rs. 6000 that would not entitle the petitioner to claim that he belongs to the backward class; classification on the basis of the test of income was rejected.

The question of reservation under Article 15(4) was again considered in *K.S. Jayasree v. State of Kerala*[49], where the Supreme Court was called upon to determine the constitutional protection which could be extended to a person who belonged to a backward community, but the family income exceeded the prescribed limit of Rs. 10,000 per annumm. The court said that in ascertaining the social backwardness of the class of citizens it may not be irrelevant to consider the caste of the group of citizens.[50] Caste cannot, however, be made the sole or dominant test, as social backwardness is in the ultimate analysis the result of poverty to a large extent, though social backwardness which results from poverty is likely to be aggravated by considerations of the caste.[51] This shows the relevance of both caste and poverty in determining the backwardness of citizens, but neither caste alone nor poverty alone can be the determining test of social backwardness. It was therefore, held that the impugned order prescribing the income limit was valid as the classification was based not on income but on social and educational backwardness.[52] It was recognized that only those among the members of the mentioned castes whose economic means was below the prescribed limit were socially and educationally backward and educational backwardness was reflected to a certain extent by the economic consideration of the group.[53]

The Supreme Court observed in *S.R. Balaji v. State of Mysore*,[54] that reservation of seats for backward classes cannot really be for their upliftment. The backwardness in the ultimate analysis is due to economic backwardness. The considerations for determining the question of social and educational backwardness are :

(1) Traditional apathy for education on account of social and environmental conditions or occupational handicaps;

(2) Poverty and lack of educational institutions in rural areas;

(3) Living in inaccessible areas;

(4) Lack of adequate educational aids, such as free studentships, scholarships and monetary grants;

(5) Lack of residential hostel facilities;

(6) Unemployment among the educated, which acts as a damper on the desire of the members to educate their children; and

(7) Defective educational system which does not train students for appropriate occupations and professions.

The Director of Social Welfare, Andhra Pradesh made similar suggestions in O. Sagar v. State of A.P.[55] The consideration for backwardness are[56] :

1. Poverty
2. Low standard of education
3. Low standard of living
4. Place of habitation
5. Inferiority of occupation
6. Caste.

Therefore, the courts have suggested that the economic position of the backward classes should be improved.[57] It may be done by creating employment opportunities for the members of the class, the court also suggested that if necessary, polytechnics may be started wherein the boys from the backward classes may obtain training leading to employment. If necessary, the court suggested, cash grants may be made to the deserving persons.[58].

JOB RESERVATION

Job reservations being intended for the benefit of the backward classes, the question then, who are the other backward classes came up for consideration again in Indra Sawhney v. Union of India.[59] All the judges excepting Thommen J., held that the expression 'backward classes' in Article 16(4) is wider than the expression socially and educationally backward classes under Article 15(4).[60]

This is a striking departure from the Balaji Chitralekha ruling that the expression 'backward classes' in Article 16(4) is same as the expression 'Socially and Educationally backward classes' under Article 15(4). However, Kuldip Singh J., made a succinct distinction between the two provisions as[61]

> "The expression 'backward' in the context of Article 16(4) is entirely different than the expression socially and educationally backward classes in Article 15(4). Under Article 16(4) the backward class has to be culled out from amongst the classes who are not adequately represented in the State services. Any species to backwardness is relevant in the context Article 16(4). By contrast any special provision to be made under Article 15(4). e.g. grants out of the public exchequer can only be made for 'socially and educationally backward classes'".

Following Balaji and Chitralekha, Thommen J. held, that backwardness of the other backward classes should be comparable to that of the scheduled castes and scheduled tribes.[62] Rejecting this view, the other judges hold that if the backwardness of the other backward classes was to be similar to that of the scheduled caste or scheduled tribes then the other backward classes would have been included by the Presidential order in the list of scheduled castes or scheduled tribes, as they no longer belong to other backward classes.[63]

Interestingly, Thommen, Kuldip Singh, Sahai J. were of the views, that "class" under Article 16(4) cannot be read as 'caste While the other judges holds that 'class' for the purpose of Article 16(4) is used in the sense of a 'social class' denoting a number of persons having certain common traits which distinguish them from the other and not in the sense it is understood In Marxist Jargon.[65] In other words class is often a caste, the connection between the two is too close, This strengthens the observation that caste has all the attributes of a class, a caste is also a class of citizens and is nothing but a social class, a socially and occupationally homogenous class and so on.[66]

Jeevan Reddy J. (on his behalf and on behalf of Kania C.J, Venkatachaliha and Ahmadi JJ) clarified that classification is not on the basis of caste, but on the ground that caste is found to be a backward class not adequately represented in the services of the State.[67] According to Sawant J. a caste in order to constitute a backward class, the caste must be socially backward and its educational backwardness and economic backwardness must be on account of its social backwardness.[68] While Ratnavel Pandian J. was of the view, that a caste perse generally cannot be within the meaning of a backward class of citizens under Article 16(4), if it does not satisfy the primary test of social as well as economic and educational backwardness.[69]

From this it is clear, that all the judges recognised the relevance of caste for identifying social backwardness. The Central idea and overall objective should be to consider all available groups, sections and classes in society. Since caste represents an existing identifiable social group/class comprising an over whelming majority of the country's population one may began with it and go to other groups, sections and classes. Article 16(4) speaks about backward classes.[70] Reservation is not made for castes. It is only when a caste satisfies the criteria of backwardness it falls under 'backward classes' for the purpose of Article 16(4). Further, the backward class must be one which is not adequately represented in State services.[71]

Ratnavel Pandian J. (concurring) held, caste is a primary criterion or a dominant factor though not a sole criterion for identification of backward classes under Article 16(4).[72] Thommen J. emphasizing the relevance of caste factor in identification of backward classes aptly said that[73]

> "the constitution is neither caste blind nor caste prejudiced nor caste overcharged, but fully alive to caste as one of the relevant criteria to be reckoned in the process of identification of backward class of citizens."

The constitution seeks to identify backward class and not backward caste. In this process, it may so happen in many cases either partly or in some cases predominantly or even solely backward classes are identified with particular castes.[74] The caste must apply objective criteria for identifying a caste as socially and educationally backward class. A caste is backward for the purpose of Article 15 or 16 if it is subject to prior discrimination and its illeffects are continuing and are comparable to those of scheduled castes and or scheduled tribes.[75] In the scheduled castes or scheduled tribes the proof the past discrimination is presumed while in the case of other backward classes the burden is on the state to show that the other backward classes are victims of past discrimination and that has reduced them to a state of helplessness and poverty.[76]

Sawant J. making a departure from the dicta in *Trilokinath case* added that the expression backward class becomes synonymous when the members of an entire caste are backward and on that account are treated as a backward class.[77] However, Kuldip Singh J (dissenting) hold that caste cannot be adopted as collectives for the purpose of identifying backward classes.[78]

RESERVATIONS IN PROMOTION

The question of permissibility of preferences or reservation came up before the Supreme Court in *Indra Swahney's Case.*[79] As reservations are intended to benefit the other backward classes they should be a one time affairs and confined only to initial appointments and not to promotions. In Rangachari's case,[80] the majority held that Article 16(4) contemplates or permits reservation in promotions as well. Overruling this view, in Indira Sawhney's case[81] Jeevan Reddy J. considered that reservations in promotions would be a serious and unacceptable in road into the rule of equality of opportunity. To say that such a handicap should be provided at every stage of promotion throughout their career would negative the principle of equality of opportunity. Further, this would result in creating a permanent separate category apart from the mainstream resulting.[82]

> "a vertical division of the administrative apparatus. The members of the reserved categories need not have to compete with others but only among themselves. There will be no will to work, compete and excel among them. Whether they work or not, they tend to think, their promotions is assured. This in turn is bound to generate a feeling of despondence and "heart burning" among open competition

members .... Putting the members of backward classes on a fast track would necessarily result in 'leap frogging' ...."

Reservations at promotional level if permitted will have serious consequences and 'leap-frogging' has a deleterious effect on the efficiency of administration.

Sahai, Thommen, Kuldip Singh and Sawant JJ. concurred with Jeevan Reddy J. that reservation in promotions was impermissible Sahai J. held that[83]

"...once in order to treat some persons equally we must treat them differently has been done and advantaged and disadvantaged are made equal and are brought in one class or group then any further benefit extended for promotion on the inequality existing prior to be brought in the group would be treating equals unequally it would not be eradicating effects of past discrimination but perpetuating it".

Thommen J. was of the view that[84]

"once appointed in a service, any further discrimination in matters relating to conditions of services such as salary, increments, promotions retirement benefits etc., is constitutionally impermissible, it being the very negation of equality, fairness and justice.

Kuldip Singh J opined that[85]

"Article 16(4) does not permit reservations either to the selection posts on in any other manner in the process of promotions".

Sawant J considered that,[86]

"The reservations in promotions are inconsistent with the efficiency of administration and are impermissible under the constitution".

All the judges were unanimous in holding that reservation in promotions is violative of Article 16(4). They realised that promotions out of turns, or 'leap frogging' will have a telling effect on the efficiency of administration. However, and considering the gravity of the effect in overruling the majority view Rangachari case, which was the law till today, Jeevan Reddy J. with whom Ratnavel Pandian J. concurred declared, that this decision will apply only prospectively and shall not effect promotions already made, whether temporary, officiating or regular/permanent basis. They directed the appropriate government or authority falling under the scope of Article 12, that such reservations shall continue for a period of five years from the date of this decision. Meanwhile the appropriate governments are asked to bring about the necessary modifications in the relevant rules to achieve the object of Article 16(4).

Modern state being a welfare one, the state considers equality as not merely an abstract ideal but a politically aggressive idea. Inequality perse as a thought is utterally repugnant to modern sensibility.

To do away with inequalities existing in the Indian society due to Caste system, Dr. Ambedkar strongly articulated the cause of backward classes in the constituent Assembly. This has led to the inclusion of the provisions of compensatory discrimination in the Constitution.

Neither the Constitution nor the debates of the Constituent Assembly provide any tests or criteria for determining backwardness or the extent to which preferential treatment be allowed be work. Ultimately it fell on the Supreme Court to evolve a formula which would not only achieve the object of advancement of these classes without perpetuating class distinction and also to see that in the garb of eradicating inequality, inequality is not perpetuated in the country.

The classification of backward classes in the States depended upon the local conditions and the varying degree of caste feelings. There is no uniformity either in methodology adopted or in quantum of reservation allowed in the States.

If benefits are conferred on caste basis then more and more castes - clamour to be called as backward classes. If more and more castes are netted than backwardness is reduced to a mockery. This is nothing but a movement towards 'backwardisation' or 'Sanskritisation in the reverse'. This will in long run may lead to division and animosity and have a telling effect on national integration. National integration through fraternity is the constitutional goal that can be achieved through individual pledge and committee. The ambiguities inherent in court's jurisprudence manifest the judicial anxiety to adjust the competing inequalities. It remains to be seen whether future courts will adopt a more rational approach, which permits such remedies only where specific individuals can identify instances of intentional discrimination aimed at them personally rather than generally at the caste group of which they are members.

REFERENCES

1. Marc Galanter "Competing Equalities" - Law and Backward Classes in India, P 154 (1984).
2. Dr. Parmanand Singh "Reservations, Reality and the Constitution: Current Crisis in India", Vol. XI C.U.L.R. 284 (1987).
3. Parmanand Singh "Some Reflections on Indian Experience with Policy of Reservations". Vol. 25 J.L.I.P. 47, at 48 (1983) : See also Supra Note 2, at P 285.
4. Ibid, P 159.
5. Vol. VII C.A.D. - Pandit Hirdayanath Kunzuru - U.P. P 680 : Sri Ari Bahadur Gurunt (West Bengal) P 685 : Sri R.M. Nalvade (Bombay) P 686, Dr. Dharam Prakash (U.P.) suggested the use of the term scheduled castes or depressed classes in place of backward classes, as the former term had a definite meaning, P 687.
6. Ibid - H.J. Khandekar (C.P. Berar) preferred the use of the term scheduled castes lest the people of other castes would also claim to be backward. P 692 : Sardar Hukum Singh (E.P.) expressed a doubt whether the term covers the scheduled castes and religious minorities. P 694.
7. Ibid - Sri Chennaiah, pp. 689-90.
8. Ibid - P 692.
9. Vol. VII C.A.D. - Dr. K.M. Munshi, P 697.
10. Vol. VII C.A.D. P 687.

11. Ibid, P 687.
12. Ibid, P 701.
13. Ibid, P 701-02
14. Ibid.
15. Ibid.
16. Ibid, P 699.
17. Ibid.
18. Ibid.
19. Rajeev Dhavan "Reservations Equality or Deceit?
20. B.R. Bhagat "Reservations - A National Perspective" The Hindu Open Page 17, Col. 3, Tuesday, October 30 1990.
21. Andre Beteille "Caste and Politics Subversion of Public Institutions". P 8, Col. 1, The Times of India (New Delhi), Tuesday, September 11, 1990.
22. M.R. Balaji V. State of Mysore A.I.R. 1963 S.C. 649.
23. Andre Beteille "The Problem" 268 Seminar 10 (1981).
24. Ibid.
25. Supre Note 48, P 37.
26. Marc Galantar "Caste Disabilities and the Indian Federalism". Vol. 3, J.I.L.I. 205, at P 207.
27. AIR 1963 SC 649 at 658 and 659.
28. Ibid.
29. Ibid, at 662
30. Ibid.
31. Ibid.
32. Ibid at 659.
33. AIR 1964 Ker 39.
34. Ibid.
35. Ibid.
36. Ibid.

37. AIR 1963 SC 649.

38. State of Madras V. Champakam Darairaja, AIR 1951 SC 226.

39. Mr. R. Balaji V. State of Mysore, AIr 1963 SC 649.

40. AIR 1968 SC 1012.

41. AIR 1964 SC 1823.

42. Ibid.

43. N.S. Sudha V. Selection Committee for Admission to Medical *Colleges, Bangalore*, AIR 1967 Mys 221.

44. Zakir Ahmed V. Chairman, Medical College, Bangalore, (1967) 1 Mys LJ 82.

45. AIR 1967 Ker 124, 128.

46. AIR 1976 SC 2381.

47. Ibid.

48. Ibid.

49. Ibid.

50. Ibid.

51. AIR 1963 SC 649.

52. AIR 1968 AP 165.

53. Ibid.

54. M.R. Balaji V. State of Mysore, AIR 1963 SC 649.

55. Ibid.

56. J.T. 1992 (6) 273, AIR 1993 SC 477.

57. *Ibid*. Ratnaval Pandian J. P 322, Kuldip Singh J.P. 401 Sawant J. P 441, Sahai J. P 519, Jeevan Reddy J. P 625 (on behalf of himself and on behalf of Kania C.J., Venkatachaliha, J. and Ahmadi JJ.)

58. Ibid., P 104.

59. Ibid., P 377-78.

60. E. Radhakrishnan "Judicial Pragmatism, Political Opportunism". The Hindu Magazine Section - 2, P. I, Col. 6 Sunday, March 12, 1993.

61. See Supra Note 43, PP 369, 399, 504.

62. Ibid P. 619.

63. Ibid.

64. Ibid P 623.

65. Ibid. P. 460.

66. Ibid., P 323.

67. Ibid.

68. Ibid.

69. Ibid., P 314.

70. Ibid., P 371.

71. Ibid.

72. Ibid.

73. Ibid., P 373.

74. Ibid., P 448.

75. Ibid. P 399.

76. Supra Note 59.

77. A.I.R. 1962 SC 36.

78. Supra Note 59.

79. Ibid., P 537.

80. Ibid., P 382.

81. Ibid., P 413.

82. Ibid., P 482.

83. Ibid., PP 354, 650.

CHAPTER VII

Uniform Civil Code : A Myth or Reality

R. Jagan Mohana Rao and T. Raghavendra Rao

There has been great controversy in the country about the desirability to introduce changes in the personal laws to suit uniform civil code through out the territory of India as provided in Article 44 of the Indian Constitution.

India is a secular nation and as such has to serve to all her citizens irrespective of caste or religion on an equal basis and ensuing them all universally accepted human rights. This applies as well to the domain of conjugal relations, inheritance etc, as to any other social or Political domain. This was the vision of the founding fathers of the Indian constitution and was embodied in its directive principles. The constitution on the one hand has guaranteed freedoms, to profess, practise and to propogate religion in the form of fundamental rights (Part III)[1], on the other hand in Part IV (Directive Principles of State Policy) has laid down the responsibility on the State "to secure for the citizens a uniform civil code through out the Territory of India"[2]. In order to avoid any controversy about the various provisions in the constitution, Article 13 of the constitution has clarified the position which provides "the state shall not make any law which takes away or abridges the right confessed by this part and any law made in contravention be void."[3]

The need for the Uniform Civil Code was felt as soon as the constitution came into force. Even after 47 years this directive could not be implemented for reasons better known to all the concerned with this directive.[4] It is true that in bringing a common code for all religions is not an easy task for the legislature. Indian secularism, has therefore to develop the philosophy of co-existence. To achieve the philosophy of coexistence the support of a high degree of tolerance by all concerned to the principles of equality and nondiscrimination are necessary.[5] The claim of separate laws of different Religions and the aspiration of a common code have co-existed in our country for a long time. It is naive to blame the British for the existence of separate personnel laws in India or to attribute it to the British Policy of divide and rule. It is equally naive to believe that the inclusion of the objective of a Uniform Civil Code in our constitution in the chapter containing Part IV (Directive Principles of State Policy) was an earth shaking revolutionary step. The separate personnel laws were not invented by the British, nor was the idea of a Uniform Civil Code a sudden discovery of the founding fathers of the constitution.[6] It is interesting to recall that fundamental rights subcommittee of the Constituent Assembly had dealt with both the Justifiable and non-justifiable Fundamental Rights (i.e. the Rights and Directive Principles of the State Policy.) Shri M.R. Masani had suggested that a provision for a common civil code applicable to all citizens should be included in the body of Justifiable Fundamental Rights to be incorporated in the constitution.[7] It was decided in the sub-committee by a narrow margin (5 to 4) that the proposed provision was out of the scope of fundamental rights. The distinguished minority consisted of Dr. B.R. Ambedkar, Shri M.R. Masani, Raja Kumari Amrit Kaur and Mrs. Hamsa Mehta. Two days later, it was decided by a majority to insert a clause regarding a unified civil code for the country in the directive principles of state policy. The debate in the Constituent Assembly on what was at that time Article 35 and which became Article 44 of the constitution is instructive. Three most important speeches in the constituent Assembly on the question of a uniform civil code were those made by Shri K.M. Munishi, Shri Alladi Krishna Swamy Ayyar and Dr. B.R. Ambedkar.[8] The debate was concluded by Dr. B.R. Ambedkar. He declined to accept the amendments which had moved to that Article. He felt that the objections to the ideas of a unified code were too late in the day. He said Muslim Personal Law it-self was not immutable and uniform in India, and gave certain examples of Muslim Communities following the Hindu Law in the matter of succession and in other matters until the Shariat Act 1937 was passed.

In the context of fighting the poison of communalism, the relevance of a uniform civil code cannot be disputed. In fact it will provide a juristic solution to the communal problem by stracking at its root cause. Since our constitution envisages one society with singular citizenship, it is highly desirable that one single set of civil laws should govern all its citizens. The need and justification to have a uniform civil code as mandated by Article 44 of the constitution cannot be over emphasised.

Mainly the objections to the enactment of a uniform civil code have all along been raised by the largest minority community in the country, the Muslim community. Not merely the formulation of a uniform family code is objected to but the orthodox Muslim public opinion, the Moulavis and Ulemass as well as some intellectuals have vociferously opposed any change or reform in their personal law.[9] Apart from the Vocifero from opposition of our Muslim brothern, religious fundamentalism and fenatism of some political parties are also a hindrance for healthy and conductive environment for achieving the goal of uniform civil code. In view of these fissiparious tendencies on the part of some sections of the society, Muslim minority in particular, it looks as though the goal of uniform civil code remains a mere wishful thinking.

Despite the progressive judicial pronouncements[10] and juristic opinions in favour of carrying out the directive under Art. 44 of the constitution, parliament has done nothing to achieve this noble ideal. However the recent direction from the Supreme Court to the Union Government to take necessary steps to see, that uniform civil code is formulated and successfully implemented in accordance with Article 44 of the Indian Constitution. But the former Prime Minister Shri P.V. Narasimha Rao, made it clear that the time has not come to implement Article 44 of the Constitution and formulate uniform civil code for reasons best known to the Government. The authors is of the opinion that it is only because of political reasons the party in power is reluctant to formulate uniform civil code. Further, the negative attitude of Muslim brothern adds fuel to the fire. It may be mentioned here that almost all fenatic Muslim countries have successfully, reformed their laws to keep pace with the changing times and countries like Turkey and Sudan have family codes governing their people. Pakistan has issued number of Family Law Ordinances reforming Islamic Law to Modernize their legal systems. So also Egypt has introduced number of drastic reforms in their laws.

CONCLUSION

In the light of above discussion the authors would suggest:

1. the concept of religion should be defined confining it to the individual's faith and beliefs and his personal relations with his Creator.
2. Article 29 needs some modifications by way of amendment.
3. An atmosphere of mutual confidence should be created among all sections of the people.
4. Some amendements immediately however in the Shariat Act of 1937 will have to be made. Before doing so, in the present political climate, certain well thought-out strategy will have to be pursued if we wish to avoid stirring the hornet's nest.
5. It is necessary that the Government must shed its apathy and complacency in the matter and without waiting for the demand for reforms being backed up by majority members of the any minority community, the Government must take the initiative in pushing through the needed reforms with the support of the existing progressive elements available in the concerned community irrespective of their strength.

In the final analysis, we have to conclude that it is a herculean task to bring about a Uniform Civil Code in the present circumstances surcharged with the intransedent attitude of our Muslim brethren and the indifference of the Union Government which has been sleeping over this matter for the past 5 decades. For this reason the authors are contained to conclued that the formulation of uniform civil code only a myth but it can never be a reality.

REFERENCES

1. Articles 25, 26 of the Indian Constitution.
2. Article 44 of the Indian Constitution.
3. Article 13 of the Indian Constitution.
4. CULR (1988) P.339.
5. Ibid.
6. Dr. L.M. Singhvi 'Towards a Uniform Civil Code' Religion and Society, Vol. XXVI No.4, Dec. 1979 P.8.
7. Minutes of Proceedings of the Fundamental Rights Sub Committee of March 28, 1947.
8. Constituent Assembly Debates Vol. VII P. 541.
9. AIR 1987 (Journal) P.20.
10. AIR 1977 SC 1344, AIR 1985 SC 945.

CHAPTER VIII

Need for a Common Civil Code

S. Ambika Kumari

Article 44 of the Indian Constitution provides that the State shall endeavour to secure for the citizens a uniform civil code throughout the territory of India. Since our constitution envisages one society with singular citizenship, it is highly desirable that one single set of civil laws should govern all its citizens. The Directive Principles of State Policy set out in Part IV of our constitution are paramount to the governance of the country and mandate the State to implement them without playing political hide-and-seek with them. Two objections were put forward in the constituent Assembly against the making of a uniform civil code applying throughout India, firstly, it would infringe the fundamental right to freedom of religion mentioned in Article 25 and secondly it would be a tyranny to the minority.[1]

India is a country of diversities; Hindus, Muslims and Christians follow their own personal laws in family matters which to a great extent differ from one another. The diversities in these spheres of the personal laws governing these religions are so great. Some of the rules in these spheres are so unfair, inequitable and humiliating. Such type of laws instead of serving the purpose of unity and integrity of the country encouraged separatists tendencies which are detrimental to any growing democracy. Keeping the interest of the nation, the Constitution makers incorporated Article 44 in the Constitution which provide for the establishment of uniform Civil Code. The Constitution makers were very well aware of the fact that it is highly difficult to enact a uniform Civil Code. So they directed the 'state' to 'endeavour to secure' it. They wanted both the legislature and the executive to lead the nation jointly to the era of a uniform Civil Code. In otherwords it can be stated that they wanted the code to be enacted and enforced at the end of an evolutionary process during which the People would be prepared to accept and actually practice the same in their day to day domestic life.

The words 'endeavour' and 'secure' are of most significance. These two words indicate that State can apply the liberal approach as well as can adopt intermediatory arrangement for securing a uniform civil code for the citizens of India. The word 'States' used in Article 44 is of wide amplitude and has a close reference to Article 12 of the Constitution of India. Article 12 defines state as 'Government and Parliament of India and the Government and the legislature of each of the States and all local or other authorities within the territory of India or under the Control of the Government of India. Thus it is evident that all authorities functioning within the Territory of India are under obligation to make efforts towards one Civil Code. Part IV of the Constitution puts positive duty on the state to make such laws and policies which may help towards achieving the objectives laid down in this part. The relevant provision which authorises the parliament as well the State Legislature towards the uniform Civil Code provides as follows.[2]

"Marriage and Divorce; infants and minors, adoption; Wills; intestacy; and succession; joint family and partition; all matters in respect of which in judicial proceedings were immediately before the commencement of this constitution subject to their personal law".

The very purpose of our democratic system is to remove all kinds of barriers i.e. religion, caste, creed and to provide with a law which may help to maintain rule of law in the Indian Society. It can be stated that the common Civil Code will provide Social justice to the weaker sections of the society. The idea of social Justice as envisaged in the preamble can be achieved only when we have a single law for all citizens. Article 44 had placed a greater responsibility on the Executive than on the legislature. It is the responsibility of the Government to prepare the People gradually to accept a uniform Civil Code, without much compulsion. It is pertinent to state that Government has not done anything towards the uniform Civil code eventhough almost 50 years have elapsed after the enforcement of the Constitution. Whether the Government has taken any step to educate the People on the Social ideal dealt with in Article 44 of the Constitution? It is submitted that so far Government could not take any step to draft or enforce a uniform Civil Code.

The vehement opposition of a uniform Civil Code came from the Muslims. It is because of the Government's failure to make them understand the real issues in their true perspective. Undue weightage is being given in this respect to the views held by conservative sections of the citizens. The result is that this can have only political motivations. It is however unfortunate that a few orthodoxical thinkers have opposed the introduction of uniform Civil Code in India. They were, of the view that state had no jurisdiction to reform Muslim Personal Law even as a measure of social welfare because it had devine origin and therefore immutable and inseparable part to Islamic religion.[3] Their attitude towards the adoption of uniform civil code was even more stiffer than that of the British Government. They propagated the view that personal law is a comprehensive code of life. It has its origin in divine revelation and is therefore immutable. A few Advocates of Muslim. Personal Law argue that the Muslim Law relating to marriage, divorce and inheritance has been handed down by the prophet and must therefore be unquestionably obeyed.[4] They have gone to the extent of arguing that if anything is done affecting personal laws, it will tantamount to interference with their freedom of religion and hence transgress Article 25 of the Constitution[5]. Justice Tulzapurkar in an Article entitled 'uniform Civil Code'[6] quoted Chief Justice Gajendragadkar that 'in the event, the non-implementation of the provisions contained in Article 44 amounts to a grave failure of the Indian democracy and the sooner we take suitable action in that behalf, the better'.

Political leaders, time and again have declared in and outside the parliament that the Government will not touch the

Muslim Personal law unless a substantial number of Muslims themselves demand reforms. The politicians are always under a strong belief that by talking of uniform Civil Code they will loose-their vote among the minority community. In fact they are adopting a neutral stand so that they are not taking any attempt to promote the spirit of uniformity of legislations. However, one should appreciate the Indian Parliament for enacting the Muslim Women (Protection of Rights on Divorce) Act, 1986. This legislation has settled the controversy that arose in *Shah Bano case.*[7]

India is a democratic country having a written Constitution. If there is a written constitution the judiciary has more special role to play. The Judiciary is competent to declare any law or administrative action as unconstitutional if it is inconsistent with the Constitution. The State is under Constitutional obligation to make efforts towards the establishment of one Civil Code for all persons. If these provisions come in direct conflict with related provisions in Part III, then it is the duty of the judiciary to control. The Courts in India have sought to establish a secular polity founded on social justice ineffective of the tenets of religion. Judiciary has carried out the spirit of Article 44 and decided the controversy arising, out of the personal laws. In *Shah Banos' case* the issue regarding the application of Section 125 of Criminal Procedure Code in case of divorced Muslim Woman was raised. In this case the Appellant drove the Respondent out of the matrimonial home. The Respondent filed a Petition under Sec. 125 of the Cr.P.C., before the Judicial magistrate. Thereafter, the Appellant divorced the Respondent by an irrevocable talaq. The Appellants' main contention was that the Respondent ceased to be his wife and so he was not under any obligation to pay maintenance. The trial Court decreed the Suit in favour of the Respondent and directed the Appellant to pay an amount of Rs. 25/- per month to the Respondent. The High Court enhanced the maintenance allowance from Rs. 25 to Rs. 179.20 per month. Against this Order the Appellant filed an Appeal before the Supreme Court. The Appellants' contention was that under Muslim Personal Law he is not under obligation to provide maintenance after divorce. 'After divorce the wife is entitled to maintenance during the period of iddat. If an Order is made for the maintenance of a wife under Cr.P.C. and the wife is divorced afterwards, then the Order ceases to operate on the expiration of the period of iddat'.[8] The main issue before the Supreme Court was whether the Muslim Personal Law impose any obligation on the husband to provide for the maintenance of his divorced wife. The Supreme Court held that Sec. 125, Cr.P.C. deals with cases in which, a person who is possessed of sufficient means neglects or refuses to maintain, among others, his wife who is unable to maintain herself. Since, the Muslim Personal Law limits the husband's liability to provide for maintenance of the divorced wife to the period of iddat; it does not contemplate or countenance the situation evisaged in Section 125 of Cr.P.C. It can not be said that the Muslim husband is not under an obligation to provide maintenance, beyond the period of iddat to his divorced wife who is unable to maintain herself. The true position is that if the divorced wife is able to maintain herself, the husband's liability to provide maintenance for her ceases with the expiration of the period of iddat. But if she is unable to maintain herself she is entitled to take recourse to Section 125 of the Cr.P.C. Therefore there is no conflict between Section 125 and Muslim personal law on the question of maintenance of a divorced wife who is unable to maintain herself.[9] Thus overriding operation was given to the general law of the land by ignoring the texts of the personal law. Thus it can be stated as a welcome step of judicial activism to archieve and encourage the goal of common civil code as intended by the Constitution makers.

The issue which was decided by the Supreme Court in Shah Bano case was again raised before the Court in *Begam Subanu and Saira Banu* V. *A.M. Abdul Gafoor.*[10] The Apex Court reiterated that irrespective of the husband's right under his personal law to take more than one wife, his first wife would be entitled to claim maintenance and separate residence if he takes a second wife. Thus the Supreme Court reaffirmed the decision of Shah Bano Begum and laid down solid foundation for the Uniform Civil code in spite of Muslim Women (Protection of Rights on Divorce) Act, 1986.

A deep investigation of the judicial trend discloses that it has always made earnest efforts to ensure the implication of the mandate contained in Article 44 of the Constitution. The judiciary has gone to the extent of holding that the institution of polygamy is not based on necessity. If there is no son out of the first marriage then instead of taking recourse to the second marriage the proper course is adoption of a son. The court bravely stated that religious practices are always subject to the State Regulation. This can be governed through appropriate legislations irrespective of their religious emotions. In *Ms. Jordan Diengdeh* V. *S.S. Chopra*[11], the Supreme, Court after analysing the various laws, viz. Indian Divorce Act, 1869, Hindu Marriage Act, 1955, Parsi Marriage and Divorce Act, 1935, Special Marriage Act, 1954 and provisions therein regarding the dissolution of marriage emphasized the need for one common code relating to judicial separation, divorce and nullity of marriage. "The time has now come for a complete reform of the law of marriage and make a uniform law applicable to all; people irrespective of religion or Caste. It is necessary to introduce irretrievable breakdown of marriage and mutual consent as grounds of divorce in all cases".[12] Again in *Mary Roy* V. *State of Kerala*[13] the Supreme Court clarified that after the Part-B States Laws Act, 1951, the members of the Indian Christian Community will be governed in case of intestate succession by the Indian Succession Act, 1925 and not by the Travancore Christian Succession Act, 1092. Thus, the Supreme Court endeavoured to give less importance to laws based on particular religion and made applicable to the law which also applied to other communities in case of intestate succession to the property. This decision also is again a welcome decision of the Court.

The judicial response to encourage the Constitutional Philosophy of Uniform Civil Code is praiseworthy. But unfortunately the legislature has not done anything to promote the philosophy of Article 44. "Legislator's, especially those who must some time face the polls, move slowly and by indirection into areas where the community's conduct tells them that they must venture but the community's mores warns them that they must not".[14]

The Forty nine years old legislature could so far enact very few legislations under the heading of common civil code. They include the Special Marriage Act, 1954. The Hindu Code of 1955-56[15], and the Dowry Prohibition Act, 1961. The Special Marriage Act is a secular Code of Marriage, divorce and inheritance. The law of inheritance applicable to the property of a couple governed by the Special Marriage Act, 1954 is contained in the Indian Succession Act, 1925. The Special Marriage Act enable any two

Indians irrespective of their religion to marry and to give up their personal law without abandoning their religion and to adopt a common and secular law of marriage and inheritance. The Hindu Code deals with Uniform Laws of Marriage, Divorce, Minority, guardianship, adoption maintenance and succession to Jains, Sikhs, Buddhists and Hindus. The only Uniform law compulsorily applicable to all citizens of India is the Dowry Prohibition Act, 1961. But it remains a dead letter ever since its enactment. Dowry transactions are not only freely taking place among the Hindus, but have become popular even among the Muslims. The evil of dowry is assuming new dimensions and finding new adherents day by day. Thus the unifying or partly unifying legislations has miserably failed to achieve the desired objectives.[16] The legislature has kept its eyes shut to the said state of the personal laws of all the minorities.

To promote the spirit of Uniform Civil code, the state has to raise the social, educational and economic standard of the ignorant people. This will help them to know about their rights and obligations. The State should create an atmosphere of confidence and prepare them to accept the reforms in the light of the changing values of the society. The media can be of great help in this regard. It is the moral duty of the academicians to promote the feelings of secularism and explain the contents of uniform civil code to the community at large. A committee of eminent jurists belonging to different religions may be constituted to help the parliament to implement the uniform civil code. To conclude it is submitted that the objective of uniform civil code can be achieved only if the three organs of the state untiedly take the initiative.

REFERENCES

1. "V.N. Shukla, Constitution of India 9th edn., p. 307.
2. Constitution of India, Schedule VII, List III Entry 5.
3. Constituent Assembly Debate (1948) Vol. III pp. 541, 721.
4. H.A. Gani, Reform of Muslim Personal Law (1988) p. 58.
5. Kiran Deshta, Uniform Civil Code in Retrospect and Prospect (1995) p. 120.

6. J.I.L.I. 1987, page 17 at 22.
7. *Mohammed Ahmad Khan* V. *Shah Bano Begum* A.I.R. 1985 SC 945.
8. Mulla, Mohammadan Law (18th Edn.) pp. 301-02.
9. Ibid at 950. Chief Justice Chandrachud.
10. AIR 1987 SC 1103.
11. AIR 1985 SC 935.
12. Justice Chinnappa Reddy, Ibid.
13. AIR 1986 SC 1011.
14. Julius Stone, Social Dimensions of Law and Justice (1966) at p. 314.
15. Hindu Code includes, The Hindu Marriage Act, 1955, The Hindu Succession Act, 1956, The Hindu Minority and Guardianship Act, 1956 and the Hindu Adoption and Maintenance Act, 1956.
16. Tahir Mahmood, An Indian Civil Code and Islamic Law (1976) at p. 10.

CHAPTER IX

Governor's Discretionary Powers under the Constitution — A Study on the Post Sarkaria Scenario

Y. Satyanarayana

The role of Governor has emerged as one of the key issues in Union-State relations. The Indian political scene was dominated by a single party for a number of years after independence. Problems which arose in the working of Union-State relations were mostly matters for adjustment in the intra-party forum and the Governor had very little opportunity for exercising his discretionary powers. The institution of Governor remained largely latent. Imposition of President's rule in Kerala in 1959, brought into some prominence the role of the Governor, but thereafter it did not attract much attention for some years. A major change occurred after the fourth General Elections in 1967. In a number of states the party in power was different from that in the Union. The subsequent decades witnessed the Fragmentation of political parties and emergence of new regional parties. Frequent, sometimes unpredictable realignment of political parties and groups took place for the purpose of forming governments in the states. These developments gave rise to incurable instability in the governments of several states. As a consequence, the Governors were called upon to exercise their discretionary powers indiscretely and more frequently. This has had a direct impact on Union-State relations.

The role of the Governor has come in for attack on the ground that some Governors have failed to display the qualities of impartiality and sagacity expected of them. It has been alleged that their actions lacked necessary objectivity either in the manner of exercise of discretion or in their role as a vital link between the Union and the States. It has often been alleged that the Union Government utilises the Governors for its own political ends.

In this background it becomes pertinent to discuss the scope of discretionary powers of the Governor under the Constitution of India.

Whatever might have been the views of the framers of the Constitution, it would appeal from a plain reading of Article 163 that clauses (1) and (2) of the Article confer on the Governor, the general power to exercise discretion in respect of any of the functions entrusted to him by the Constitution. The expression 'by or under the Constitution' in clause (1) can be taken as covering all situations in which the power to exercise discretion is either expressly mentioned or necessarily implied in the relevant Articles. Further, a decision of the Governor to act in his discretion in a particular situation is protected from being questioned by any Court or other authority by clause (2). In practice, situations have arisen and will arise in which a Governor may necessarily have to exercise his discretion even though they may be no express provision to that effect in the relevant Articles. Thus, there may be no Council of Ministers duly responsible to the Legislative Assembly to advise him, or the advice given by the Council of Ministers cannot be reconciled with the course of action which, in the opinion of the Governor, should be adopted in view of his responsibility either to the Centre under the Constitution or to the Constitution itself which in accordance with his oath of office he is required to preserve, protect and defend.

The following are some examples:

(a) Appointment of a Chief Minister [Article 164 (l)] when no single party has a clear majority;

(b) dissolution of the Legislative Assembly [174 (2)(b)] when no stable Ministry can be formed.

(c) reserving a state bill for the consideration of the President (Article 200); and

(d) A Governor may require that any matter decided by a Minister may be considered by the Council of Ministers (Article 167); and

(e) reporting to the President that the Government of a state cannot be carried on inaccordance with the provisions of the Constitution [Article 356 (1)].

It is an accepted principle that in a Parliamentary democracy with a responsible form of Government, the powers of the Governor as constitutional or formal head of the State should not be enlarged at the cost of the real executive, viz., the council of Ministers. The scope of the discretionary powers has to be strictly construed effectively dispelling the apprehension, if any, that the area for the exercise of discretion covers all or any of the functions to be exercised by the Governor under the Constitution. In other words, Article 163 does not give the Governor a general discretionary power to act against or without the advice of his Council of Ministers. The area for the exercise of his discretion is limited. Even in this limited area his choice of action should not be arbitrary or fanciful. It must be a choice dictated by reason, actuated by good faith and tempered by caution.[2]

In the light of Sarkaria Commission's recommendations it is appropriate to, discuss the circumstances under which the exercise of discretion by the Governor has been called in question in S.R. Bommai V. Union of India[3] and subsequent events.

The Sarkaria Commission recommended inter alia :

(a) In choosing a Chief Minister, the Governor should be guided by following principles, viz.,

(i) The party or combination of parties which commands the widest support to the Legislative Assembly should be called upon to form the government.

(ii) The Governor's task is to see that a Government is formed and not to try to form a Government which will pursue policies which he approves.

(b) If there is a single party having an absolute majority in the Assembly, the leader of the party should automatically be asked to become the Chief Minister.

If there is no such party, the Governor should select a Chief Minister from among the following parties or groups of parties by sounding them, in turn, in the order of preference indicated below:

(i) An alliance of parties that was formed prior to the election.

(ii) The largest single party staking a claim to form the Government with the support of others, including independents.

(iii) A post electoral condition of parties, with all the parties in the coalition joining government.

(iv) A post-electoral alliance of parties with some of the parties in the alliance forming Government and the remaining parties, including independents, supporting the Government from outside. A Governor while going through the process described above should select a leader who in his (Governor's) is most likely to command a majority in the Assembly.

(v) A Chief Minister, unless he is the leader of a party which has absolute majority in the Assembly, should seek a vote of confidence in the Assembly within 30 days of taking over. This practice should be religiously adhered to with the sanctity of a rule of law.

The Governor should not risk determining the issue of majority support on his own, outside the Assembly. The prudent course for him would be to cause the rival claims to be tested on the floor of the House.

When the Legislative Assembly is in session, the question of majority should be tested an the floor of the house.

If during the period when Assembly remains prorogued, the Governor receives reliable evidence that the Council of

Ministers has lost majority, he should not, as a matter of constitutional propriety, dismiss the Council unless the Assembly has expressed on the floor of the House its want of confidence in it. He should advise the Chief Minister to summon the Assembly as early as possible so that the majority may be tested.[4]

The Sarkaria Commission recommended that it would be reasonable to allow the Chief Minister a period of 30 days for the summoning of the Assembly unless there is a very urgent business to be transacted like passing the Budget, in which case a shorter period may be allowed. In special circumstances the period may go upto 60 days.

If a notice of no-confidence motion is pending against a Ministry, the motion represent a legitimate challenge from the Opposition, but the Chief Minister advises the Governor to prorogue the House, the Governor should not at once accept the advice. He should advise the Chief Minister to postpone the prorogation and face the motion. If ultimately a viable Ministry cannot emerge, the Governor should first consider dissolving the Assembly and hold fresh elections after consulting the leaders of the political parties concerned and the Chief Election Commissioner. If fresh election cannot be held immediately on account of a national calamity or state-wide disturbances, it should not be proper for the Governor to instal a caretaker Government for the long period that must elapse before the next election is held. He should recommend proclamation of President's rule under Article 356 without dissolving the Assembly. The Commission felt that the discretionary power under Article 163 should be left untouched.

The Sarkaria Commission has aptly observed that it would be neither feasible nor desirable to formulate a comprehensive set of guidelines for the exercise of discretionary powers of the Governor. The Governor should be free to deal with a situation according to his best judgement, keeping in view the constitution and the law and the conventions of the Parliamentary system.

In *S.R. Bommai V. Union of India*[5], exercise of Governor's discretionary power under Article 356 came up for judicial scrutiny before the apex court. A majority consisting of Pandian, Sawant,

Jeavan Reddy and Agarwal, JJ has laid down the extent of judicial review permissible of the proclamation under Article 356. It is limited to examining whether there was any material at all, whether it is relevant and that it is not tainted by malafide, perverse or irrational exercise of power. All of the judges nevertheless agree that the exercise of power under Article 356 is subject to judicial review. The majority has also rightly laid down that Article 74(2) is not a bar against the scrutinity of the material on the basis of which the President had arrived at his satisfaction. The court further observed that till the proclamation was approved by both Houses of Parliament under Article 356 (3) it was not permissible for the President to take any irreversible action under clauses (a), (b) or (c) of Article 356(l). Hence the legislative Assembly of any state could not be dissolved till the proclamation was approved by both houses of Parliament. In the light of the Sarkaria Commission's recommendations the court held that if the proclamation is held invalid by the Court then notwithstanding its approval by Parliament the *status quo* ante can be restored by the Court in its discretion, meaning thereby that the dissolved Legislative Assembly and the Ministry can be revived.

On the question of secularism being the part of basic structure of the Constitution or that is a basic feature of the Constitution, the Supreme Court observed that the 42nd Amendment only made explicit what was implicit and embeded in our Constitutional philosophy. Consequently, if any political party in power in a state, supports or encourages acts which subvert, sabotage or erode secularism then, it can be said that a situation has arisen where the Government of a State cannot be run in accordance with the Constitution. Mixing of politics with religion is not countenanced by the Constitution.[6] Thus the Supreme Court has rejected the argument that 'secularism' is a vacuous word' or 'plantom concept'. So also the view to the affect that merely because a different political party is elected to power at the union, even if with a thumping majority, that is no ground for exercise of power under Article 356 (l).

The political significance of the ratio in Bommai case is that it will act as a bar on motivated and arbitry dismissal of State Governments by the centre as had happened in a number of cases in the recent past. Now that the Court could go into the circumstances of the dismissal and declare the act unconstitutional leading to the restoration of status quo ante, the Governor of the concerned state and the party in power at the centre will think twice before embarking on the adventurous course of imposing President's rule. In fact this very question was examined in some detail by the Sarkaria Commission on Centre-State relations which said that action under Article 356 would be improper if no warning or opportunity to the State Government was given to correct itself.

The discretion of the Governor in assessing the political situation in the state and determining the circumstances leading to failure of constitutional machinery still has a significant bearing on the federal system envisaged under the Constitution. The much maligned and, ofcourse the much-needed Article 356 still seems to have a purposeful role to play. The founding-fathers were certainly aware of the implications of the provisions contained in Article 356 and were only hoping that its use would be a last resort. Gujarat and UP developments are classic examples of its need and necessity, restraint being the watchword.

Now fast deteriorating political situation in India that loyalties of political parties and politicians changing with whimsical regularity, the institution of the Governor will be yet another office that could be abused by all. When principled politics has become rarity, one can hardly look for Governor's act according to the dictates of conscience or the rule book.

REFERENCES

1. Report of the Sarkaria Commission on Centre-State Relations - Part II p. 19.
2. Report of the Sarkaria Commission on Centre-State Relations - Part I p. 117.
3. (1994) 3 SCC
4. Report on Centre-State Relations (Sarkaria Commission) Part-I pp. 135 and 136.
5. (1994) 3 SCC.
6. S.R. Bommai V. Union of India (1994) 3 SCC p. 3.

CHAPTER X

Social Justice Through Environmental Protection: The role of Indian Judiciary

A. David Ambrose

The preamble of Indian Constitution in unequivocal terms says that the function of the Republic is to secure, to all its citizens social, economic and political Justice. The Directive Principles of State Policy contained in the Part IV of the Constitution which constitute a very comprehensive political social and economic programme for a modern democratic state, while setting out the aims and objectives to be taken up by the states in the governance of the country also reaffirms what has been said in the Preamble of Indian Constitution.

Article 38 (1) of our Constitution provides that the state shall strive to promote the welfare of the people by securing and protecting as effectively as it may a social order in which Justice-social, economic and political - shall inform all the institution of national life.

The word 'Social Justice' is a comprehensive term under which many rights of the society and community can be discussed. 'Social Justice' in a sense not only relates to the raising of the social conditions but also to the improvement of living conditions of the people. Thus Article 47 of the Indian Constitution provides that the state shall regard the raising of the level of nutrition and the standard of living of its people and the improvement of public health as among its primary duties............".

However, social justice in general and improvement of living condition in particular cannot be wiped away by constitutional ideals alone. If, for instance, the constitution says that the living condition of the people must be improved, the living condition of masses would not simply improved over night. The constitutional ideals found in the Preamble and in the legally unenforceable Directive Principles can practically be related only if suitable legislations are made and are effectively implemented.

But for the various reasons the legislature and the administration have lagged behind in making necessary legislations for and effective implementation of the cherished social ideals of the Constitution. When two of the three limbs of the democracy viz. the legislature and the executive have failed, the other limb namely the Judiciary had to step in and to some extent, has helped in the realisation of some of the social ideals.

The Judiciary with all its limitations has played a vital role in the realisation of certain social ideals of the Constitution. It is interesting to note that the judiciary has used and is still using the recent international and national consciousness for environmental protection for the realisation of social justice.

Since the last decade Public Interest Litigation (PIL) or Social Action Litigation has played a telling role by which people belonging to all walks of life and especially the downtrodden and unrepresented are getting social justice from the Supreme Court and other High Courts. One thing which has to be noted is that the concept of PIL was introduced by Justice V.R. Krishna Iyer in the *Ratlam Municipal Council* V. *Vardhichand*[1] which incidentally concerned with environmental protection. Justice Krishna Iyer observed that this, case is pathfinder in the field of peoples' involvement in the justicing process and it is necessary to enforce public bodies.

Since then many cases involving environmental protection have been brought before the Indian courts and Indian Judiciary has upheld the need for environmental protection. But while protecting the environment the Indian Judiciary has indirectly realised social justice. The aim of this paper is to discuss how environmental protection has been used by the Indian judiciary for the realisation of social justice.

CONSTITUTION AND ENVIRONMENTAL PROTECTION

The Constitution, as originally adopted is environmentally blind and not sensitive to the deteriorating ecological system. Eventhough at the time of framing of the Constitution, there were several central and state enactments[2] which incidentally covered a wide variety of environmental issues including pollution of air and water, protection of forests and wild life, as environmental consciousness is a recent phenomenon, it is not surprising that the Constitution, as originally enacted did not even contain the expression "environment". Nevertheless two provisions namely Articles 48A and 51A (g), having a direct bearing on environment were added to the Constitution in the year 1976 after nearly 3 decades of adopting our Constitution, by the Constitution (Forty - Second Amendment) Act, 1976, there by giving environmental dimension to the Constitution.

Article 48-A, directs that state to mould its policies to protect and improve and environment, which runs thus;

> "Thus state shall endeavour to protect and improve environment and to safeguard the forests and wildlife of the country."

It addition, article 51-A which deals with fundamental duties of citizens provides in clause (g) that it is obligatory for every citizen;

> "To protect and improve the natural environment including forests, lakes, rivers and wild life and to have compassion for living creatures".

It is of interest to note that while Article 48-A, uses the expression "Environment" Article 51-A(g) uses the expression "Natural Environment". It is not known why two different expressions have been used in the Amendment. Further it requires the state to safeguard" the forest wild life of the country" in the context of protection and improvement of environment, the latter imposes a duty on the citizens to protect and improve, among other things, "forests, lakes, rivers and wild life". On balance the difference between the two Articles relate to form and not to substance. On the whole both the Articles contain inclusive definitions of obligation in respect of environmental protection. Elevation of environmental protection to the level of a constitutional prescription is an important step towards a rational management of environment.

JUDICIARY AND ENVIRONMENTAL PROTECTION

Taking notice of the growing environmental consciousness in and around the country and also encouraged by the constitutional provisions, the Indian Judiciary, which had to decide many environmental cases, included environmental protection with in the expanding boundaries of the right to life and personal liberty guaranteed under Article 21 of the Constitution.

Starting from the *Ratlam Municipal Council* V. *Vardhichand*[3] (referred earlier) most of the cases connected with environmental protection came to the court by way of PIL. Courts by relaxing the traditional rule of *Locus Standi* paved the way for NGOs and public spirted people to move the court for the redressal of grievances connected with environmental hazards under Article 32 and Article 226 of the Indian Constitution. In Ratlam case the residents of Ratlam Municipality affected by the stench, and stink caused by open drains and nearby slum dwellers' public excretion moved the Magistrate under Sec. 133 of Cr.P.C. to compel the Municipality to do its duty towards the members of the public. The Magistrate gave directions to Municipality to draft a plan within six months for removing nuisance. In appeal, the Sessions Court reversed the order. The High Court approved the order of the Magistrate and in further appeal, the Supreme Court also affirmed the Magistrate's order. Justice Krishna Iyer observed that, "Social Justice is due to the people, and therefore, the people must be able to trigger off the jurisdiction vested for their benefit to any public functioning". He recognised public interest litigation as a constitutional obligation of the Courts.

It has been held by the Supreme Court in *Subhash Kumar* V. *State of Bihar*[4] that the right of enjoyment of pollution free water and air for full enjoyment of life is a fundamental right under Article 21 of the Constitution. The Court held that Right to live is a fundamental right under Article 21 of the Constitution and it includes the right of enjoyment of pollution free water and air for full enjoyment of life. If anything endangers or impairs that quality of life in derognition of laws, a citizen has right to move recourse to Article 32 of the Constitution for removing the pollution of water or air which may be detrimental to the quality of life. A petition under Article 32 for the prevention of pollution if maintainable at the instance of affected person or even by a group of social workers or journalists.

It has been observed by the Kerala High Court in *F.K. Hussain* V. *Union of India*[5] that the right to sweet water and right to fresh air, the right to wholesome environment are attributes of the right to life, for these are the basic elements which sustain life itself.

From environmental jurisprudence of the Indian Courts it is now clear that right to clean environment is a fundamental right under Article 21 of Indian Constitution which guarantees right to life and personal liberty.

ENVIRONMENTAL PROTECTION AND SOCIAL JUSTICE

The social mandate to raise the standard of living and the improvement of public health has been of late realized by the environmental protection because the word "Environment" has been defined by the Environment (Protection) Act of 1986, intended to protect and improve the human environment and prevent hazards to human being, to include water, air and land and human beings and other living creatures plants micro organisms and property.[6] Protection of environment which includes water, air, land etc., means, naturally improvement of the human living conditions, health and hygiene which is nothing but the social obligation of the state.

RIGHT TO CLEAN WATER

In India two-thirds of all illness are related to water borned diseases such as Typhoid, Infective Hepatitis, Cholera, Diarrhoea, Dysentery. It is rather paradoxical that with so much rivers running in India, safe water for drinking is still luxury to most of the people in India. Provision for safe drinking water to all especially the underserved villages is considered to be crucial for the health and better quality of life of our masses.

Water pollution is becoming enormous in rural regions of India. Most of the water resources are polluted by the direct discharge of community wastes from settlements and industrial effluents, thus posing great threat to public water supply systems and contamination of rivers.

In *Pondicherry Paper Ltd. V. Central Board for Prevention and Control of Water Pollution*[7] the Central Board for Pondicherry applied to a Magistrate's Court under section 33 of the Water Act seeking an injunction restraining Pondicherry Papers Ltd., from discharging effluent until the company constructed a water treatment plant as required by the Board's consent orders. The Magistrate issued an injunction. The company filed a motion to quash the injunction on the grounds that a Magistrate does not have the authority under section 33 to order compliance with a consent order. The matter came up before the Madras High Court and the High Court held : The Water Act is a social welfare legislation, enacted for the purpose of prevention of pollution of water and for maintaining or restoring wholesomeness of water. Therefore, the Act has to be strictly enforced and every effort should be made to carry out the true intent of the legislation. On these principles, the Magistrate has to act when an application is filed under section 33 and it would be for him to determine according to the circumstances of the case what order he should pass in order to give effect to the provisions of the Act and to remove the pollution or prevent it.

The Supreme Court in *Ganga Water Pollution* by *Tanneries case*[8] ordered for the closure of the tanneries which cannot set up a primary treatment plant and out weighed the inconvenience that may be caused to the management and the labour employed by it on account of closure. Thus the Supreme Court virtuously put community interest above the benefit of few.

In *M.C. Mehta* V. *Union of India*[9] another case based on the Water Act and Environment Protection Act, 1986, the allegation was that the municipal bodies have been responsible for the pollution of the water in the river Ganga by allowing sewage to flow into it. It is said that 274.50 million litres a day of sewage water is being discharged into the river Ganga from the city of Kanpur, which is the highest in the State of Uttar Pradesh and next only to the city of Calcutta with discharges 580.17 million litres a day of sewage water in the river Ganga.

The Supreme Court, after referring to the relevant provisions of the Municipalities Act and to the functions of the Central and State Pollution Board under the Water Act, lamented: "It is unfortunate that although parliament and the State Legislature have enacted the aforesaid laws imposing duties on the Central and State Boards and the Municipalities for prevention and Control of Pollution of water, many of those provisions have just remained on paper without any adequate action being taken pursuant thereto". Then, impelled by the need to activate the Government machinery to take steps to control and prevent pollution of water, the Supreme Court issued certain directions.

Finally, the Supreme Court said : "what we have stated above applies *mutatis mutandis* to all other Mahapalikas and Municipalities which have jurisdiction over the areas through which the river Ganga flows". Supreme Court by this decision not only brought out the enforcement deficit in the environment field but also supplemented and activised the existing laws by its directions.

In *F.K. Hussain V. Union of India*[10] the Kerala High Court did not permit the scheme of digging wells and pumping water on large scale from existing wells by electric pumps on the ground that it could upset the fresh waters equilibrium leading to salinity in the available water resources in Lakshadweep islands. In the instant case the court held that right to potable water is within the sweep of right to life.

It is also pertinent to note that the Supreme Court in *Subhash Kumar's case*[11] held that "Right to life is a fundamental right under article 21 of the Constitution and it includes the right of enjoyment of pollution free water and for full enjoyment of life[12].

The Orissa High Court in *Cuttack Water Pollution case*[13] directed the authorities to take immediate action to prevent and control water pollution being caused by the Municipal Committee, Cuttack and the S.C.B. Medical College Hospital Cuttack on the ground that water pollution is violative of Article 21.

In *the General Public of the Saproon valley and another* Vs *State of Himachal Pradesh*, the High Court of Himachal asserted the urgency for solution of environment problems. It held that strict proof of environmental pollution is not essential. The court can decide its own modalities for ascertaining the facts. In this case the court was convinced that the mining operation in the valley had caused damage to the fields. It had polluted the general environment and had resulted in dirtying the water, creating soil erosion of the surrounding land and had resulted in ecological imbalance.[14]

Recently in *Indian Council for Enviro-Legal Action* Vs *Union of India*[15] an environmentalist organisation filed a writ petition under Art. 32 before the Court complaining the plight of people living in the vicinity of Chemical industrial plants in India and requesting for appropriate remedial measures. The fact was that in a village Bichari in Udaipur district of Rajasthan an industrial complex had developed and respondents have established their chemical industries therein. Some of the industries were producing chemicals like oleum and Single phosphate. The respondent had not obtained the requisite licences and nor did they install any equipment for treatment of highly toxic effluents discharged by them. As a result of this the water in the wells became unfit for human consumption. It spread diseases, death and disaster in the village and surrounding areas. Because of the court's intervention, drinking water has been supplied to the people. The court further held that the respondents were responsible for all the damage to the soil, to the underground water and to the village in general. Regarding the determination of cost of remedial measures, the court held that the Union Government had power to decide it. The principle on which the liability of the respondents so defray the costs of remedial measures will be determined is, the Polluter pays, "that is, the responsibility for repairing damage is that of the offending industry."

Thus a perusal of decisions of the Indian Courts clearly reveals that where there is a lacuna in the legislation or where the administration has failed to implement the existing laws effectively, the courts have made it certain that the state shall take necessary steps to prevent and control water pollution and to maintain wholesomeness of water which is supplied for human consumption. Right to safe and potable water has now assumed fundamental Rights status and within the purview of Article 21 of the Indian Constitution.

RIGHT TO CLEAN AIR

If the air which we breath is polluted then it could lead to many diseases in human beings including some chronic ones. Air, polluted by some chemical substances can be fatal also. The Bhopal Gas leak still fresh in our minds proves this point very much. The force of urbanisation and industrialisation led to a drastic escalations in air pollution. In India industrial camplexes are localled close to residential areas without considering the consequences of air pollution. The Indian Judiciary had some occasions to intervene when town planning was done without due concern for the environment, especially for air, and rectify the defects there by safe guarding the interest of the society at large.

Thus in *Venkatappa* V.B. *Lovis*[16] which was a case relating to erection of chimney with holes emitting smoke. It was held that when smoke emanates it will also pass through the holes in the chimney and the emanating some will be injurious to the health of neighbours. It will therefore cause discomfort in the enjoyment of property and injurious to health as well. Emitting smoke thus constitutes actionable nuissance furnishing cause of action for a suit. It follows therefore that when the defendant erects a chimney with holes emitting smoke through them towards the side of the plaintiff an actionable wrong is committed by the defendant.

The Karnataka High Court in *V. Lakshmipathy* V. *State of Karnataka*[17] directed the authorities to prevent the establishment of Industries in residential area in violation of various acts. The court in the instant case held that :

> "Article 226 of the constitution enables the citizens to the High Court to enforce the performance of statutory obligation of any authority coming within the sweep of Article 21 of the constitution in particular, or for e.g. under

the anti-pollution laws of the land like the pollution control Act etc."[18]

In Murari Purushothaman V. Union of India[19] Kerala High Court issued directions to the authorities to control the air pollution created through uncontrolled and unlimited automobile emission. According to the petitioner the gaseous pollutants emitted by Vehicles plying through the streets of Kerala are highly harmful and growing day by day to monstrous levels.

In this case the court issued orders to the authorities concerned to strictly implement the legislative provisions. In this connection the court held that :

> "Human life is far more important that vehicular traffic. The pristine adage that 'Rules are for men and not men are for rules' assume contemporary relevance. Particularly in the area of environmental cleanliness. No authority, not even the state can be permitted to abide time without enforcing whatever provision is available and without exercising whatever power is commandable to protect human life".[20]

In another case involving vehicular pollution the Supreme Court came to the rescue of the helpless public exposed to the grave dangers and health hazards created by the emissions from more than 1.8 million vehicles plying in Delhi. In the vehicular pollution case,[21] the court called for every available information on the subject by various Ministries of transport, gas, environment and others. Finally it ordered the constitution of a committee under the chairmanship of Justice K.N. Saikia, a retired judge of the Supreme Court. The Committee was asked to examine details and present bimonthly reports on technologies available for vehicular pollution control low cost alternatives for operating vehicles accordingly. In pursuance of this judgement, the Justice Saikia Committee has been making regular bimonthly reports which are submitted in the Court. Simultaneously, hearings of the case have been conducted on related issues. A significant order was passed by the Supreme Court on 8.1.92, directing that if any Delhi Transport Corporation (DTC) bus or any private bus on the fleet of DTC is found emitting excessive smoke, that fact may be brought to the notice of a DTC officer to be named, under the intimation to the Registrar of the Supreme Court and on receipt of the information from any member of the public, the DTC officer concerned will immediately have the bus checked and intimate the action taken to the Registrar of the Supreme Court.

Noise pollution is another dimension of air pollution. India is one of the many countries which do not have effective laws to prevent pollution of environment by automobiles, loud speakers and other innumerable sources of noise. Noise pollution due to use of loud speakers is restricted by the court in *P.A. Jacob* V. *Superintendent of Police Kottayam.*[22] Sound levels generally caused by loudspeakers exceed safe limits by a wide margin. Loud speakers have become part of political, social, religious and cultural life of this country. The Court in the instant case held that :

> Compulsory exposure of unwilling persons to dangerous disastrous levels of noise would amount to a clean infringement of their constitutional guarantee of right to life under Article 21. Right to life, comprehends right to a safe environment, including safe air quality safe from noise".

The court further held that;

> Apart from the right to be let alone, freedom from aural aggression- Article 21 guarantees freedom from tormenting sounds. What is negatively the right to be let alone, is positively the right to be free from noise[23].

In *Subha Rao* v. *State of Himachal Pradesh*[24] the court accepted a PIL and directed the colsure of a bone factory that was polluting the environment by its pungent smell and making the life of the people miserable.

From the decisions discussed above it becomes clear that the judiciary has accepted the right to wholesome environment is implied in right to life guaranteed under article 21 of the Constitution. The judicial interpretations further ensure that environmental laws and their administrative implementation shall comply with constitutional standards including the social standards spelt it out.

LAND AND ECOLOGY

Land conservation and protection of ecology is very much important for the human living conditions. In *Damodar Rao* v. *The*

Special Officer of Municipal Corporation of Hyderabad[25] the Andhra Pradesh High Court has gone as far as to interpret environmental pollution as an infringement of Art 21 of the Constitution which enshrines the right to life as fundamental right. An attempt was made by some government departments to build residential houses in an area reserved under the master plan for parks. The Court held that "the enjoyment of life and its attaintment and fulfilment guaranteed by Article 21 of the Constitution embraces the protection and preservation of nature's gifts without which life cannot be enjoyed. The slow poisoning caused by environmental pollution and spoilation should also be regarded as violation of Article 21.

In *Bangalore Medical Trust* v. *B.S. Muddappa*[26] an open space which was reserved for public part was allotted to a private person for the purpose of constructing a hospital by the Development Authority Bangalore. The residents of the locality challenged the allotment on the ground that it was contrary to the object of the Act. It was held that the residents of the locality have locus standi to challenge the allotment under Articles 21 and 226 of Constitution. A private nursing home could neither be considered to be an amenity nor it could be considered improvement over necessity like a public park. A park is a necessity not a mere amenity. For maintaining ecology in urban areas open space and park is necessary.

In *D.D. Vyas and others* V. *Ghaziabad Development Authority*[27] the court held "failure to develop public parks earmarked in the development plan amounts to failure in discharging its (GDAs) responsibility under clauses (g) and (j) of Article 51-A.... in crowded town the residents do not get anything but an atmosphere polluted by smoke and fumes emitted by endless vehicular traffic and factories --- parks are the lungs of human beings. It is the verdant cover provided by the public parks and green belts in towns which renders considerable relief to the public..... Looking at the importance of the environmental issues we permit petitions for its improvement and preservation to be filed by environmental activists living in the concerned locality or even outside.

The urgency which our courts are attaching to environmental problems relating to land conservation and protection of Ecology and strictness with which there are issuing directions after directions to state instrumentalities for conservation and improvement of ecology shows not only our courts' concern for conserving the environment but also for improving the standard of living.

INDUSTRIAL HAZARDS

If there is one area in which the Indian Judiciary has played a major role in environmental protection and improvement of human living condition then it is in protecting the human being from industrial hazards. The Courts have clearly put human interest ahead of Industrial development.

For example in *R.L. and E. Kendra Dehradun* V. *State of U.P.*[28] the Supreme Court ordered the closure of some of the limestone quarries on the ground of causing imbalance to ecology and hazards to healthy environment. In this case the court agreeing, that closing down of queries which polluted the environment would undoubtedly cause hardship to the owners of those quarries, held that "It is a price that has to be paid for protecting and safeguarding the rights of people to live in healthy environment".

In *Ambica Quarry works* V. *State of Gujarat and others,*[29] the Supreme Court recognised the right of the people to live in hygienic environment. Environmental balance was weighed by the Court against the need for limestone quarrying for industrial purposes. The case dealt with the prevention and deforestation and ecological imbalances resulting from deforestation. The Supreme Court observed :

> "Deforestation and ecological imbalances as a result of deforestation have become social menaces and further deforestation and ecological imbalances should be prevented. The primary duty was to the community and that duty took precedence. The obligation to the society must predominate over the obligation to the individual".

It is highly relevant to mention the historic Judgement delivered by the Supreme Court in *M.C. Mehta* V. *Union of India*[30] which is popularly knows as Delhi gas leak case. In this case the Supreme Court laid down revolutionary new principles. The petitioner had alleged the infringement of right to life of several thousand people due to severe pollution and hazardous activity of Shri Ram Food and Fertilizers, manufacturing petroleum and chlorine, situated in the heart of the city, Delhi. While delivering its judgement, the Supreme Court laid down two substantial principles of law : The power of the Supreme Court to grant remedial relief for a proved infringement of a fundamental right (in this case Article 21) includes the power to award compensation, albeit in exceptional cases. Thus the Court not only widened the scope of Article 21 (by including in its protection of environment) but also included a liability in tort for those harmed by pollution.

Secondly the court declared boldly "the principles of common law liability for compensating the victims of pollution have become grossly inadequate to meet such contingency created by hazardous and inherently dangerous industries. Creating a new indigenous Jurisprudence of absolute liability the court said "the application of the exceptions of *Ryland* V. *Fletcher,* were not applicable. Thus any industry which carries on hazardous or inherently dangerous activities that are threat to the security of those living around it, owed a strict and absolute liability and a "non-delegable duty" to the community that no accidents occur which may cause harm to people. If such a harm should occur, the enterprise has an absolute liability to compensate those affected by it and the plea that all possible case was taken will be no defence. The 'Social cost' for carrying on such hazardous activities for profit was a legal presumption that the industry will compensate. Thus the standards of liability now laid down by the Courts are in consonance with the constitutional norms and social mores.

In *Mahila Udyog Sangathan*[31] case (the Bhopal case), Indira Jaisingh, the learned counsel for the petitioners exposed the governmental inaction and also the hopelessness and haplessness of the victims for whom the relief measures were including providing the essential commodities and stables, which commenced from the year 1985 but were subsequently now discontinued. She claimed that the interim relief measures should continue immediately. The court activised the Gas Relief Department who prepared a detailed scheme and until its implementation, the order directed the authorities to continue with the relief measures. The order of the court instead of leaving the victims to their fate, gave some hope of relief.

CONCLUSION

The Constitution of India seeks to all citizens social justice. The term 'Social Justice' also includes various welfare measures taken by the government for the improvement of the living condition of the people. Improving the living condition of the poor is one of the social obligations of the State. The State has a social duty to provide better human living conditions in order to enforce the constitutional social mandates. However, when the State failed to enact suitable laws or when the administration failed to implement effectively the laws enacted to fulfil this social obligation, the Indian Courts are extremely instrumental in enforcing the constitutional social mandates and the social legislative policies.

As if following the principle "do good in whatever means", the Indian Judiciary has made several significant contributions for the improvement of the living conditions of the people a social obligation of the State, but unilaterally and also incidentally choose environmental protection for this purpose.

In fact in the guise of environmental protection the Indian Courts have indeed contributed significantly for the improvement of living conditions. It was possible for the courts to realise some of the social obligations through environmental protection, because of the fact that the working environment is an all embracing one under whose umbrella many rights such as right to clean water, air, conservation of land and ecology etc., important for the realization of social justice can be effectively and properly discussed.

The Courts greatly expanded the rule of *locus standi* under Articles 32 and 226 of the Constitution and provided opportunity to the NGO's and individuals to move the court for the protection of the living condition i.e., environment. The courts, as seen above, in a series of cases included the right to wholesome environment within the ambit of life under Article 21 of the constitution. The courts consistently held the entitlement to a clean environment i.e., air, water, land etc., is one of the recognised basic human rights.

The host of decisions rendered by the judiciary on the subject discussed above clearly establish the fact that neither person nor industry can be permitted to injure or impure the water, air, land, and ecology. Not yielding to the pressure groups belonging to giant industrial houses and multinational corporations the courts have delivered speedy judgements and adjusted the concept of social justice with the changing times to suit the larger interests of the society. The inescapable conclusion is that the judiciary has performed its part of realising social justice through environmental protection, well, boldly and with innovative zeal. It will not be an exaggerated statement to say that the social goal of providing better living conditions to Indian masses will be realised soon, if the legislative and executive authorities being encouraged by the role of the judiciary rise up to the occasion. Another factor that influences the speedy realization of social justice environmental protection if public through participation and awareness, without which it will be impossible to realise the social goal of providing clean environment for better living.

REFERENCES

1. AIR 1980 SC 1962
2. Indian Fisheries Act 1897; Indian Forest Act, 1927, Poison Act 1919; Factories Act, 1948 are some of the examples of the Central Acts. Some examples of State Acts are Bengal Smoke Nuisance Act, 1905; Andhra Pradesh - Agricultural Pest and Disease Act, 1919; Bihar Waste Lands (Reclamation, Cultivation and Improvement) Act, 1946.
3. Supra note 1.
4. AIR 1991 SC 420.
5. AIR 1990 Ker 321.
6. See Sec 2 (a) of the Act.
7. Reported in Armin Rosenerany et al, *Envrionmental Law and Policy in India Cases Materials and Statues* (Tripathi, 1991) at p. 158.
8. *M.C. Mehta* Vs. *Union of India* AIR 1988 SC 1037.
9. AIR 1988 SC1115.
10. *Supra note* 5.

11. *Supra note* 4.
12. *Ibid* at p. 424.
13. *M.C. Mehta* v. *State of Orissa* AIR 1992 Orissa 225.
14. AIR 1993 H.P. 52.
15. (1996) 3 SCC 212.
16. AIR 1987 AP 239.
17. AIR 1992 Karnataka 57.
18. Ibid at 67.
19. AIR 1993 Kerala 297.
20. Ibid at 299.
21. AIR 1991 SC 1132.
22. AIR 1993 Kerala 1.
23. Ibid at p. 9.
24. AIR 1989 SC 171.
25. AIR 1987 AP 171.
26. (1991) 4 SCC 54.
27. AIR 1993 All 51.
28. AIR 1985 SC 652, at 656.
29. AIR 1987 SC 1973.
30. AIR 1987 SC 965.
31. *Union Carbide Corporation* V. *Union of India*. AIR 1990 SC 273.

CHAPTER XI

Fifty Years of Indian Industry

K. Chandra Sekhara Rao

Indian industry has undergone a vast transformation since Independence and has progressed from household industry to Modern industry. The successive Five Year Plans and the Industrial Policy Resolutions greatly played a vital role in bringing industrialisation in India which in turn accelerated the Economic growth.

The First Year Plan (1951-56) aimed at providing a base for industrial growth through adequate availability of agricultural raw materials and industrial facilities. It is aimed at building up basic services like power and irrigation, so that industrialisation may be facilitated. The fuller utilisation of capacities particularly in agro based industries like sugar, cotton and jute, replacement of old plant and machinery and setting up of some core projects has been the basic aim of this plan. The Public Sector outlays on power and transport as well as in Communications were Rs. 260 crores, Rs. 520 crores and Rs. 120 crores respectively. Several new Public Sector undertakings were set up, e.g., Sindri Fertilisers, Chittaranjan Locomotive works, Integral Coach Factory, Indian Telephone Industries. However, the actual growth of industry is rather slow in First Year Plan recording a rate of 6.5 per cent per annum (Base 1956=100).

The Second Five Year Plan could be truely called as the Industrial Plan. The foundations for building up the heavy and basic industries have been laid. The Public Sector outlay in the second Five Year Plan (1956-61) was the order of Rs. 1080 Crores. The Industrial Policy Resolution has set the pace and direction of industrial growth in India. A Spectacular achievement of Second Five Year Plan was the remarkable expansion of Iron and Steel Industry. Appreciable expansion of some Heavy industries like Heavy engineering and Machine tools; Producer goods industries like Aluminium, Cement, Fertilisers and Chemicals is observable in this Five Year Plan. Modernisation of important industries like Cotton, Jute and Sugar and expansion of consumer good industries given importance. Manufacture of new industrial items like boilers, motor cycles and scooters was another achievement. Programmes of development of atomic energy were launched and that of oil exploration and coal were strengthened. Industry was diversified on a broad spectrum and many new items of production takenup in large scale. Newer Public Sector enterprises are established such as Steel Plants at Bhilai, Durgapur and Rourkela, Fertiliser Plant at Nangal and Hindustan Machine Tools, Hindustan Shipyard. The industry in toto recorded a growth rate of 7.3 percent during this plan.

The main emphasis of third Five Year Plan (1961-66) was on Machine building and on the acquisition of related skills. Development of power and transport was accorded top priority along with industry. The Public sector took upon the role of self-sustained growth in producer good industry with an outlay of Rs. 1970 crores. The performance of basic and capital goods far exceeded the targets. The electricity generation achieved a spectacular growth of 13.5 per cent during this plan. Engineering goods, Petroleum products, chemicals, cement and mineral-based industries registered a significant growth. The performance of sectors like special steels, aluminium report a growth rate of 8.2 per cent (1960 base) per annum.

During the period of 1966-69 the economy witnessed a plan holiday. Severe drought in 1965 and declined investment in 1966 has put down the growth of Industry to a negligible figure of 0.2 per cent in 1967-68. The basic and capital good industry has faced a set back. However by 1968-69 there is a gradual recovery in the manufacturing sector and the industrial output went up by 6.9 per cent.

The Fourth Plan (1969-74) has emphasised the need for the achievement of self-reliance in industry. It has proposed for expansion of industries producing capital equipment, petroleum products, chemicals and metals. Further the plan has emphasised for developing indigenous technologies, design and engineering skills and reduce the import of foreign technologies. It has laid particular emphasis on backward area development and prevention of concentration of industrial activity in the existing urban areas. However, a severe resource constraint in the Fourth Plan resulted in shortfall in financial investments. The inadequate investment reduced the demand for machinery and the capital good industry is adversely affected. Although a bulk of investment was envisaged in the core industries, production did not pick up due to Coal and Power shortages, unsatisfactory industrial relations in Steel plants and Operational problems in Fertiliser projects. As a result the actual growth in industrial output during the Fourth Plan averaged at 4.2 per cent (Base 1970:100) as against the target of 12.0 per cent.

The Fifth Plan is assigned with the task of achieving self-reliance and social justice. In view of slow industrial growth in the Fourth Plan, the Public Sector outlay is almost trippled from Rs. 3,630 to Rs. 9,700 in Fifth plan with about 50% outlay for power generation. Industrial Production has recovered to 6.2 per cent per annum during this Plan (1974-79) due to spurt in investment and relaxation of restrictions on the growth of capacity by Monopoly undertakings in November 1975. However this plan has ended with shortages in Power and coal, transport bottlenecks disturbed industrial relations, unremunerative administrative prices. The second Oil shock of 1979 seriously crippled the industrial growth and it is recorded only 1.4 per cent in 1979-80.

The Sixth Plan (1980-85) is designed to achieve optimum utilisation of existing productive capacities in addition to expansion of capacities in a wide range of industries. The emphasis is on dispersal of industrial units to backward areas. A larger public sector outlay is envisaged with Rs. 23,000 crores for the development of infrastructure industries like Steel, Coal and Petrochemicals. However, the problems faced by industry in the fifth plan continued in the Sixth Plan. Shortages were observed in basic good industries and agro based industries. In the consumer good sector the passanger cars, motor cycles, scooters and electronics made considerable progress. The overall growth rate in sixth plan is 6.4 per cent (base: 1980-81) against the target of 8 per cent.

The Seventh Plan (1985-90) has envisaged for removal of infrastructural constraints, technological upgradation of textiles and sugar, raising the productivity in basic and heavy industries, giving a lift to the modern industries like Computers, electronics, telecommunications and bio-technology. A total outlay of Rs. 19,700 crores is planned in Public Sector. To give a fill up for the expansion of capacities, the asset limits of MRTP companies raised. Non-FERA and Non-MRTP companies were delicensed for 31 industry groups and industrial units undertaking investment upto Rs. 50 crores in backward areas are exempted from Licensing. Thus a begining is made towards Industrial Liberalisations. Liberalisations in imports of capital goods and technology, diversifiacation and broad-banding of products in number of industries helped in expansion of capacities in several industries. All these measures helped the industries to record a growth rate of 8.5 per cent per annum in Seventh Plan.

A series of Liberalisation measures have been intiated since the beingings of 90's. The Eighth Plan framework (1992-97) was prepared in the context of these economic liberalisations. These economic reforms covered a wide variety of areas, which include:

- Elimination of Industrial Licensing, Capacity controls and capital issue restraints
- Relaxation of MRTP regulations on the growth of big business houses.
- Removal of administrative control on prices and distribution of commodities, public utilities and
- Reforms of credit and financial system calling for liberalisation of financial institutions from interest rate regulations.
- Fiscal reforms aim at elimination of deficit financing and inflation along with rationalisation of Tax structure.

- Price reforms through Tariff structure.
- Import Liberalisations by elimination of quantitative restrictions, imported inputs for exports and managing exchange rates and relaxation of exchange controls.
- Opening up of the domestic capital markets to allow flow of international capital flows.

These initiaties constitute a regime change for the Indian Corporate Sector. Several policy initiatives like delicensing of industries and simplification of procedures, easy flow of capital helped the industry to record an accelerated growth of 11.6 per cent in 1995-96.

Economy: A Six-fold Increase

(GNP at Factor Cost, 1980-81 prices, Rs. crores)

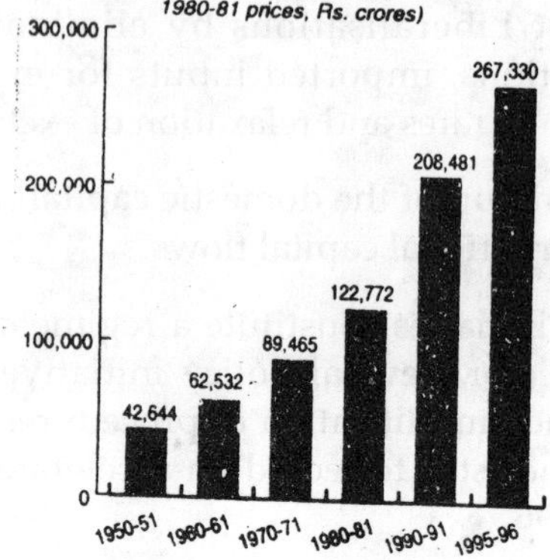

Per Capita Income: Limited Rise

(At 1980-81 prices, Rupees/year)

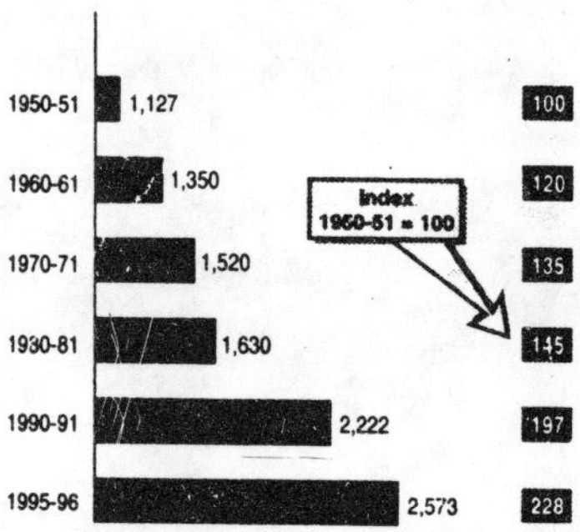

Saving and Investing More

(As % of GDP at Current Market Prices)

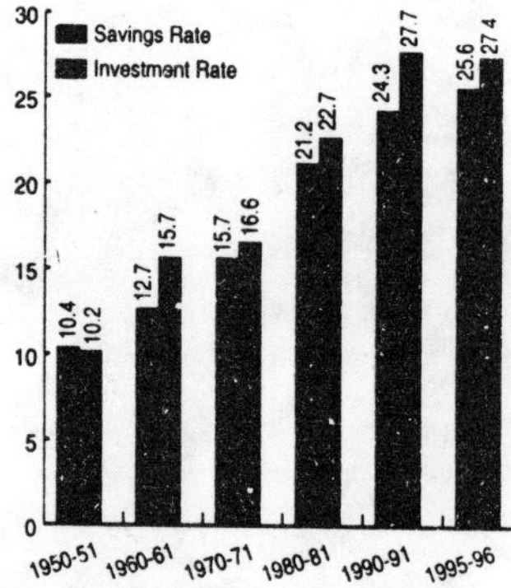

Erratic Growth in a Planned Economy

(Annual Compound Growth Rates, %)

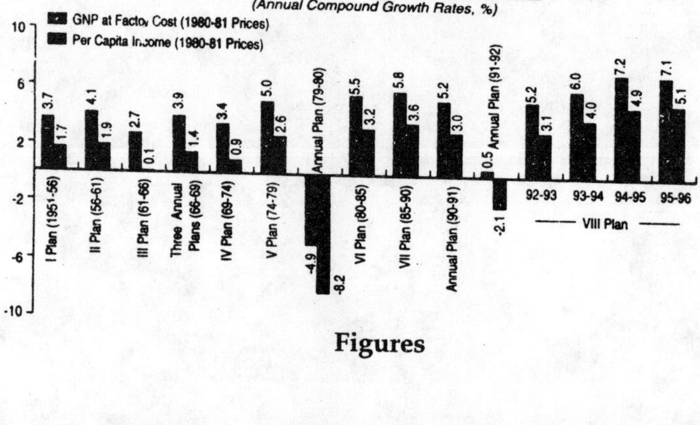

Figures

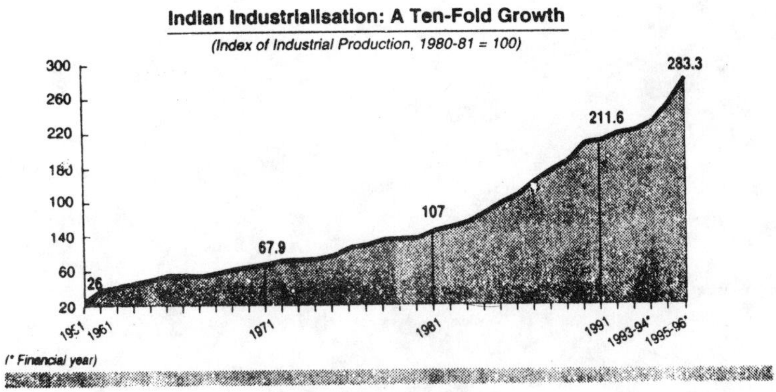
Indian Industrialisation: A Ten-Fold Growth
(Index of Industrial Production, 1980-81 = 100)
283.3
211.6
107
67.9
26
(* Financial year)

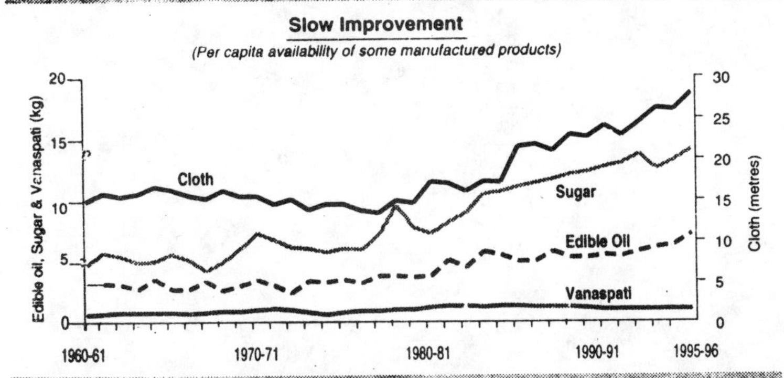
Slow Improvement
(Per capita availability of some manufactured products)
Edible oil, Sugar & Vanaspati (kg)
Cloth (metres)
Cloth
Sugar
Edible Oil
Vanaspati
1960-61
1970-71
1980-81
1990-91
1995-96

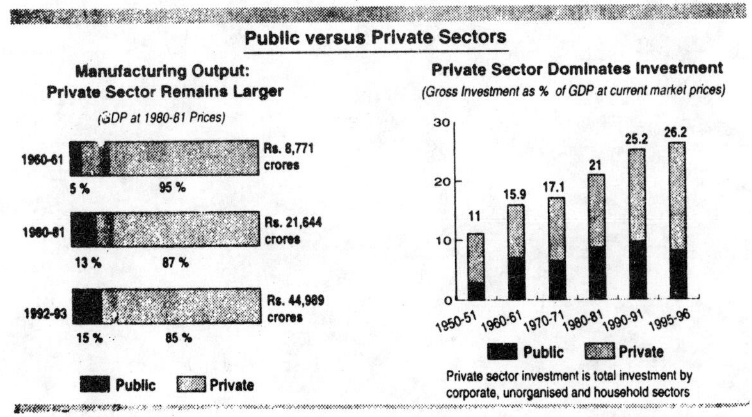
Public versus Private Sectors
Manufacturing Output:
Private Sector Remains Larger
(GDP at 1980-81 Prices)
1960-61 5 % 95 % Rs. 8,771 crores
1980-81 13 % 87 % Rs. 21,644 crores
1992-93 15 % 85 % Rs. 44,989 crores
Public Private
Private Sector Dominates Investment
(Gross Investment as % of GDP at current market prices)
11 15.9 17.1 21 25.2 26.2
1950-51 1960-61 1970-71 1980-81 1990-91 1995-96
Public Private
Private sector investment is total investment by corporate, unorganised and household sectors

Figures

CHAPTER XII

Market Economy and the State : A Retrospect

K. Uma Shankar Patnaik and S. Bhravamurthy

The controversy between the two economic systems, viz. market economy and State controlled one became prominent during the great depression period i.e. 1930s and thereafter. The whole World had been witnessing the failure of the market economies and the concept of laissez-faire and surrendering to the marxian path of transformation of capitalism/imperalism towards socialism. Capitalists were unwilling to surrender the means to the State. At that juncture, J.M. Keynes had rescued the capitalists and the market economies by providing an alternative model the violating laissez-faire principle of the classicals and suggested that government involvement is inevitable in raising the aggregate demand. The protection of the capitalists who need not surrender the means of the production, but rather government involvement particularly in the welfare activities of the people/ workers, had greatly relieved the capitalists with such a revolutionary theory of the Keynes. Such protectionism to capitalism is today named as the protectionism to the labourer, thereby such economies are called as "Welfare State Economies" rather market economies. On the other, the State economies do lose its identity by transforming themselves as market oriented socialist economies.

The dichotomy of the two economic systems is reviewed further under the following economic activities.

1. Planning, 2. Price Determination, 3. Regulations, 4. Income and Employment Aspects, 5. Surplus Value and Capital Accumulation, and 6. Growth Aspect.

PLANNING

In a market economy, where market mechanism prevails under free trade conditions, the constitutional provisions are made with respect to the free trade, commerce and intercourse throughout the territory of the particular state. Hence, planning would be only a directive which would help in regulating free trade. Law would take its course of action, in case state involves in the creation of obstructions to free trade. In case of State controlled economies, the planning would be rigid, the enterprises are known their physical targets to be achieved. The trade is completely controlled by the State. The incentives exist only in case of the enterprises reaching targets. However, due to the emergence of welfare state economies in the World, the state should enforce planning with a fixed targets for all the sectors. Hence, the fiscal policy is a by-part of the planning both in welfare state and state controlled economies. However, the degree of the fiscal involvement varies between them.

PRICE DETERMINATION

In a State economy, the price of a factor is fixed according to the marginal productivity of it, i.e. the reward is based on the contribution made. Contrarily, the price fixation is based on the degree of the scarcity, i.e. supply and demand conditions in a market economy. Due to the imperfections in the market economies, and the state's inability to regulate the market, the prices are either undermined or overvalued the resources and goods. On the other hand, in case of State economy, the goods irrespective of its use or exchange values, will always be valued on a standardized basis, i.e the value of the marginal products. Hence, irrespective of the nature of the use and exchange activity, the good will always be undervalued.

In such cases, in the international trade arena, the state economies would lose substantially compared to the inflationary nature of imperfect market economies. In the long run, opening up of international trade by the state economies with the market economies, there is a possibility of vanishing of the state economies in the World due to the capitalist pricing menace.

REGULATIONS

The enforcement of the state regulations in a market economy to eliminate imperfections in the market is an eye-wash to small producers in agriculture, industry and service sectors. The giant capitalists always dominate the market and the survival of the small is governed by the social factors as well. For instance, the caste, creed, religion, etc. act significantly for providing trade support to the small producers by the giants. Hence, regulations by the state is only to reduce the imperfections but not to eliminate completely in the market. In the state economy, the regulations would not exist. But the input-output relationships between and within the enterprises are well defined. Any break-down of such relationships at any enterprise level would result in the overall failure of the economy. Hence, such state economies would always provide controls/cushions for absorbing the failures at any level.

INCOME AND EMPLOYMENT

In case of welfare state economies, the state sets on the lines of state controlled economies in the provisions of welfare activities, viz. insurances, pensions, accident and gratuity benefits, etc. Hence, the determination of employment/unemployment is, more or less, governed by the growth of the gross domestic product and capital accumulation in both the economies. However, the income distribution seems to be adjusted by the welfare activities run by the state in the market economies. However, such equality to the nature of work is an in-built system in the state economy.

SURPLUS VALUE AND CAPITAL ACCUMULATION

The marxian concept of surplus value is derived from the labour hours. The surplus value is generated after paying the socially necessary time hours to the labourer from his total hours of contribution. In a capitalistic/imperialistic mode of production, the organic composition of capital would be on rise and the rate of surplus value or profits would tend to zero. Hence, capital accumulation in a monetized market economies is possible when the surplus is generated in terms of monetary value. In other words, the surplus is generated when the capital value for replacement is lesser than its contribution. This is, infact, possible in case of inflationary economies where every economic variable seems to be growing positively. However, in the state economy, the marxian surplus value is possible only due to the physical unit of measurement.

ECONOMIC GROWTH OF THE STATE VS. MARKET ECONOMIES

The growth of the market economies would be faster in case of the rate of induced investment is larger than that of the autonomous investment. That is if the capital accumulation or reinvestment process takes place from the rise in the output, sales or profits at a faster rate, the economies would obviously grow faster. This would, however, lead to self-sufficiency. According to Karl Marx, the rate of profits tend to zero in such cases, hence induced investment would tend to zero.

The technological progress and resource discovery call for further investment which is called as autonomous investment. The rate of autonomous investment would be high where competition among the enterprises high. Hence, the state economies should plan for technological development within the economy. Whereas in the market economies, the market mechanism takes care the aspect of specialization and technological innovations.

CONCLUSION

To conclude, the general attitude of the human-being is to change. Hence, it is inevitable for the market economies converting themselves into welfare economies where socialism on different foot prevails. Similarly, the state economies are now transforming themselves into market oriented economies. Thus, there is no end to change in the economic systems subject to the changing socio-politico environment. The growth of the economy depends upon the economic system which should suit the attitude and environment of the prevailing societal system.

CHAPTER XIII

Courts in the Indian Polity

Justice David Annoussamy

Polity consists of three kinds of public activity : legislative, executive and judicial. Courts are not extraneous agents, but are an integral part of any system of government. In this perspective the aim of this paper would be to review and assess the role played by the judiciary in protecting the rights of the citizens and promoting their welfare for half a century after independence. The activities of the judiciary were clearly of two kinds : one of traditional nature and another of extrajudicial nature, which we shall scrutinize one after the other.

JUDICIAL FUNCTION

Interesting Developments

Extension of fundamental rights

The most striking feature is the expansion of the area of action of the judiciary after independence. This results from a mandate from the Constitution itself embodied in Articles 32 and 226.

The Supreme Court was empowered to issue directions or orders or writs of any kind, including the writs of habeas corpus, mandamus, prohibition, quo warranto and certiorari for the enforcement of the fundamental rights. High Courts have been empowered by Article 226 to issue similar kinds of writs for the same purpose and also *for any other purpose*, the orders of High Courts being appealable to the Supreme Court. Orders can be issued to any persons or authority, including the Governments both of the Union and of States. In this way superior courts have acquired a vast jurisdiction in respect of the kind of orders (the purpose for which) and the persons to whom they can issue orders.

These courts have exercised their powers fully, even to an extent which was not contemplated by the Constitution makers. Fundamental rights as enumerated in the Constitution are only five in number; they consist of the most important of human rights of first generation. Courts have extended their power to cover the human rights of second and third generations by interpreting in a liberal manner the rights as enlisted in the Constitution. For instance, Article 14, affording the right of equality, has been understood to include any form of injustice so that it became available for any person who felt aggrieved in any manner. Similarly Article 21 regarding protection of life and personal liberty was construed as including the right to health and right to education etc.

On the other side political propaganda and a plethora of social legislation have made people aware of their rights. When they felt that their claims could not be satisfied promptly by legislative or executive action they have taken the habit of knocking at the doors of Courts. In this way, even matters which prima-facie do not violate a human right as understood in other countries are brought directly before higher courts. So a writ petition which should have remained an ultimate remedy has become the ordinary way to agitate any claim by those living in State capitals. Parties have a marked preference for this kind of petitions through which they can get a quick relief with the help of an affidavit in lieu of formal evidence. Even complex matters happen to be dealt with in this summary way. So a defendant in a civil suit is tempted to rush to the High Court to move a writ petition of some kind or other in order to defeat the purpose of his opponent. Higher courts in the eagerness to render justice to those who approach them entertain those petitions liberally. No doubt some of their decisions have attracted universal applause. A new mode of settlement of disputes has thus emerged; we are witnessing the development of a writ law in all fields parallely to the statutory law.

If this mode of settlement of disputes has some advantages it has also its drawbacks. First, higher courts are burdened with matters of minor importance. Secondly, for the same relief there are now two sets of courts and two sets of principles of law and of procedure, one for the poor and another for the rich. Advocates have also a marked preference for recourse to higher courts directly because they can get for their clients quickly a final relief and for themselves higher fees for a less time consuming work.

Resolution of political conflicts

The Constitution has created a set of full fledged political bodies both in the State and at the Centre. Disputes in respect of their functioning constitute a new set of cases which the higher courts had to deal with. We shall give a few instances of this kind of work for the purpose of illustration. In the State of Manipur, the Speaker of the legislative Assembly dismissed at one stroke, 12 members out of 60. This, of course, had an impact on the majority of the Assembly and disturbed the political life of the State. The dismissed members approached the High Court which set aside the order of dismissal. The Speaker appealed to the Supreme Court. When the appeal was being heard, the Chief Minister was facing a no-confidence motion. The Supreme Court decided the matter just in the morning of the date fixed for the vote of the motion of no-confidence. One can easily guess the suspense created by such a situation and the importance of the higher courts in the political life.

Another instance is in respect of identity cards which were ordered by the Election Commission in its attempt to avoid fraudulent practices in elections. The Commission warned the States that no election could be held without identity cards. Issuance of identity cards for large electorates involved much money. State Governments attempted feverishly to issue identity cards but felt that they could not complete the work before the deadline fixed by the Commission. So they brought the matter before the Supreme Court. The Election Commission resiled and submitted to the Supreme Court that it would not insist on identity cards for the impending elections. The crisis was thus solved.

Another recent intervention of the Supreme Court is in respect of proclamations issued under the most misapplied Article

356. Cabinets of the States ruled by the Bharathia Janatha party which were dismissed under the article approached the Supreme Court which held that any action taken under Article 356 was subject to judicial scrutiny. It however rejected the petitions in holding that secularism formed part of the basic structure of the Constitution and that the Bharathia Janatha party threatened to destroy social harmony in promoting Hindu integrism. These few examples show to what extent the very existence of Governments depends on judicial decisions and this is an ever growing area of jurisdiction for courts.

Proliferation of tribunals

The third feature clearly noticeable after independence is the proliferation of specialised tribunals. Of course, even during British rule, tribunals were created whenever there was no machinery available all over the country for settling disputes arising on account of rights and obligations created by an Act. The trend has gained momentum after independence. There are special tribunals for almost all matters : land reforms, rent control, public estate, land acquisition, insurance, co-operation, land survey, forest, irrigation, plantation, press, refugees, family matters, service matters, consumer disputes, taxes, labour etc. In respect of the last matter there is about a dozen tribunals dealing with each aspect of labour law. Tribunals received constitutional recognition by the insertion of part 14-A, "Tribunals" through the 42nd Amendment. In this way many of the tribunals have been conferred jurisdiction constitutionally and the jurisdiction of ordinary courts on those matters has been ousted.

Consequently the judicial function is now performed by two sets of institutions, courts and tribunals, the first bound by strict rules of procedure and evidence and the second not fettered by such rules but intended to deliver speedy justice according to real situations. The avowed purpose of such a policy is not to burden further the courts. But there was also some mistrust of courts, and even a dislike of High Courts. The main advantages are speedy justice and equitable decisions by persons having sound knowledge in the field. But there are also drawbacks. Since each specialised tribunal deals with a limited matter it will not have a great number of cases to deal with and therefore it can be established only important towns, depriving people living elsewhere from the advantage of easy access to justice. Secondly whenever a matter is brought before a tribunal the defendant is invariably tempted to dispute the jurisdiction of the tribunal and protract the proceedings, defeating thereby the objective of quick disposal. Thirdly, the litigant is at a loss to know which is the door to knock at and where it is situated. Some times the presiding officer himself, who is holding another absorbing office and is ex-officio chairman of a tribunal, is not aware of the jurisdiction vested on him.

Evolution from Common law to Enacted law

The fourth important change in judicial action is in respect of codified law. Common law as it was in vogue in England happened to be introduced in India. At that time in England under the influence of Jeremy Bentham there was a movement to codify the law as followed by Courts. But there was a strong opposition to it from judges and lawyers. So, the disciples of Bentham thought it should be possible to codify the common law in India and later to re-import it to England. This is what was done. Though almost the entirety of common law was codified and made available in that form, judges and lawyers used more law reports than codes.

After the advent of independence a large number of new Acts especially in socio-economic fields have come into existence. There were no corresponding provisions in the common law. Therefore lawyers and judges were led to interpret and implement codified law. In the beginning there was some uneasiness and people were under the impression that courts were reluctant to implement the progressive legislation. There was of course among some judges, especially, among judges of higher courts, some reservation about the new progressive legislation. But the cause for resistance was deeper: Indian judges were not trained to implement codified law. They were at ease only when they found a proposition of law in a decision. The first attempt was to find a decision on a similar or analogous section in some other Act. When there were no such decision, courts were compelled to read the Act and cull out therefrom the proposition of law. So in the course of the last 50 years there has been a slow evolution of Courts in India from case law to codified law even though the practice of referring to decisions for getting the feeling of being right and playing safe is still lingering. As a result of this trend, Acts are now published with court decisions under each sections of Acts. This has become an important tool for lawyers and judges. But unfortunately those decisions are reproduced crudely, without any logical order, even when they contradict one another. The analysis of those decisions presenting the emerging trend is still to be achieved.

Protective Role

New Acts especially in the field of labour, consumption or environment takes the judge beyond its traditional role of neutral umpire. He is enjoined to extend a helping hand to the promotion of the goal contemplated in the Act. In fact, in some of these Acts the word "protection" is included, for instance Environment (Protection) Act, 1986, the Consumer (Protection) Act, 1986. In the field of labour as well, one party namely the employee is found to be weak and exploited and unable to vindicate his rights according to the rules of civil litigation. So the courts are assigned the duty of restoring the balance in giving the labour its due. This tends to bring about a change in the attitude of judges to administer justice not according to establish legal norms treating both the parties as equal, but to take into account the inequality between the parties in all respects and to decide in keeping that factor in mind.

Regrettable Shortcomings

Delay

The above developments in the administration of justice clearly go to the credit of courts. But a single factor has considerably eroded the confidence of the litigant, viz., the long delay taken for the case reaching finality. There are 3900 cases pending before the Supreme Court. Out of that 2000 are awaiting for decision for more than five years. Accumulation of the same magnitude is recorded in High Courts. A civil suit filed before the sub-court takes sometime more than 20 years to reach finality. So people hesitate to bring matters before courts and are often advised not to do so, even by advocates. On account of this huge pendency which the courts are unable to clear, interim injunctions or interim stays given by courts are allowed to last for many years. In this way, even if ultimately just decisions are rendered by courts, gross injustice is perpetrated by the effect of these interim orders. This is also a propitious area for corruption. Interested parties are aware of the advantage they can draw from those interim orders and therefore file appeals in even undeserving cases, for the sole purpose of getting a stay and perpetuation of their injustice.

There are several reasons for this accumulation of cases. Population has grown and has become more aware of its rights and more prone to seek justice in courts. So the number of cases has swollen without corresponding increase in the number of judges.

Secondly, the monetary jurisdiction of courts are fixed in terms of rupees and no prompt revision of ceilings is made taking into account the fall in the value of the rupee. So suits which were within the jurisdiction of District Munsiff Court are now filed before the sub-court; appeals which should be dealt with by District Courts are brought before the High Court encumbering unnecessarily the latter. At present there is room for multiplicity of appeals in spheres where they are totally unwarranted; for instance in rent control or sales tax matters, a case may be brought successively before five courts if one party has interest to do so in quest of stay orders to perpetuate his unjust position.

Uncertainty of law is also one of the reasons for a great number of litigations. Though lower courts are bound by decisions of higher courts, they are some times at a loss because the proposition of law as laid down by the higher courts are not always clear and is to be gathered from judgements which are prolix and much longer than necessary. Further the Supreme Court does no longer feel bound by the rule of *stare decisis*. Judgements are reviewed within a short span of time. Even contradictory judgements are delivered. For instance section 309 of the Indian Penal Code punishing the attempt of suicide was struck down by extending with much jugglery the ambit of Article 21 of the Constitution; three years later, the Supreme Court made a volte face and held that section 309 of I.P.C. was valid and that attempt for suicide was punishable.

Lastly, new laws are hastily drafted and therefore give room to different interpretations. Old laws have not been revised timely to put them in tune with the need of the day, compelling the courts to stretch the provisions of law in their eagerness to render justice. The whole process requires a new turn. Law, which every one is deemed to know, cannot afford to be in a language unknown to the people. At present even lawyers, especially the younger generation, are at pain to understand the legal provisions expressed in English. Confirming in flowery English the death sentence of a person not knowing that language is a blatant violation of human rights, which should at least in this year of golden jubilee of independence be put and end to.

Parallel Courts

The alienation created by a foreign language and the huge accumulation of cases in courts have led to several attempts to divert cases from courts. Some of them are in the right direction, like the lok adalats under the aegis of legal aid agencies, or conciliation or arbitration in respect of which new provisions have been made by a recent act of Parliament. All steps for the effective implementation of these provisions are to be taken earnestly. But there are also some unhealthy developments created by delay in courts. In the first place religious courts in respect of which the Muslim community has taken the lead. As long as the jurisdiction of those bodies are wholeheartedly accepted by both the parties and their decisions do not offend any provision of the Constitution or the fundamental laws of the country, there is no harm. But there may be temptations to force one of the parties to accept the jurisdiction of such bodies or to have the verdict of those bodies implemented by way of ostracism or even more seven penalties. Therefore this development deserves to be watched carefully.

Political feuds flattered by their sycophants and having no idea about the limits of their powers like to play at holding sittings. When approached by a person friendly to them, they call the other party before them and give a verdict after a semblance of hearing and have it executed with the help of their henchmen. Some police officers also attempt to emulate the examples of the local political feuds. Quite often they both act in collusion.

Slumber of criminal justice administration

Another important failure of the judiciary is the downward efficiency of criminal justice administration. Several cases where important persons were involved were not taken up by the police for investigation. Others were stalled with the help of stay orders by higher courts. Criminal law both substantial and evidential has been in the course of time distorted. Only cases in which there is direct evidence are accepted. Circumstantial evidence is hardly taken into consideration, so cases in which such evidence alone is possible go often unpunished. An appeal against acquittal is not treated as a normal appeal in which the matter is at large before the appellate court; the role of the appellate court has been reduced by pronouncements of the Supreme Court so that it can interfere only in cases where the decision of the trial courts is utterly unacceptable.

While poor people are langishing behind the bars awaiting for trial for years for offences for which they can be meted out punishment of hardly three months of imprisonment, all those who possess money or wield political influence have succeeded to tamper with the system and make it ineffective. This has created a sense of impunity among those having money or influence and has led ultimately to a strong nexus between crime, power and money. Alarmed by the situation the Supreme Court decided to interfere to prevent total collapse. It liberated the C.B.I. from the fetters of the Government. It discouraged indiscriminate and mechanic release on bail. It remains to be seen how far this new tendency can be sustained without a statutory overhauling of the whole criminal justice administration system.

Lack of impartiality

The calibre of judges has progressively come down as their conditions of service have deteriorated. For instance the emoluments of a District Judge, in terms of purchasing power, is only 1/5 of what they were at the time of independence. Therefore it is more and more difficult to judges to keep their integrity and dignity intact. Some of them are prone to yield to temptations. Though the majority of judges are still immune to any kind of crude influence yet the fact that a few of them have fallen victim of temptations has eroded the prestige of the whole judiciary. There is at present no effective system of removing the black sheep quickly.

The practice of appointment of judges to the High Court mostly from among the government pleaders, who are nominees of the Government, is a blow to the cardinal principle that justice should appear to be done. In fact the same government is often a party before them; their juniors and even seniors appear before them. On the other side the threat of transfer and the prospect of post-retirement appointments in various positions make also some of the judges to curtail there independence.

There are also other tricks through which the interested parties can bring their case before the judge of their choice: creation of special courts, transfer of cases, change in the distribution of work among judges. Parties get also cases adjourned till a favourable bench becomes available.

Loss of prestige

A fall in the emoluments of judges and their relative loss of impartiality have brought down their authority. It has changed the attitude of the Bar towards judges. Gherao of judges and systematic boycott of courts are not rare. Lawyers throwing a chair on a judge, or shouting slogans against the judge sitting in the court have also happened. The Bar has also succeeded in obtaining transfer of judges from one place to another; they practically compelled some judges to resign. If advocates sit in judgement on the conduct of judges and adopt resolutions against them and give publicity to their resolutions, faith in justice will fade away and the whole system will crumble.

Police have always been subordinate to the judiciary. A stricture by the Magistrate, in respect of a lapse in investigation used to affect the career of the police officer. For various reasons, fear of the judiciary have given place to a mere formal respect. Sometimes, police officers have gone to the extent of taking criminal action against judges by way of retaliation. A Police inspector in Gujarat annoyed by a decision of the Chief Judicial Magistrate withdrew constables from his court. It exploded in major conflict in which the Chief Judicial Magistrate was arrested, handcuffed, tied with rope, exhibited; his photograph in such a position was given wide publicity. The Supreme Court had to step in to set right things. This incident should be an eye opener and lead to a re-definition of the respective position of the judiciary and police, so as to restore the authority of the former.

EXTRA JUDICIAL FUNCTION

Area of action

Public interest litigation

Even though the judiciary is crumbling under a huge backlog of cases the higher judiciary has ventured to take up some kind of cases which will normally do not come under its purview. The most note-worthy of this venture is what happened to be called "Public Interest Litigation". Dispensing with the locus-standi in respect of the parties courts have taken on their file matters without a petition in proper form, just upon a letter or a telegram or even an article in the press. Journalists, advocates, law-teachers have given the lead; associations, parents and friends of concerned persons have followed. This kind of litigation dealing with social evils, upon which no action was taken by the concerned authorities, was followed with great interest by foreign jurists. But the Government is sore about the development and bent to curb it. The Bar on the contrary was happy about the court extending its tentacles and the horizon of its action further and further.

Problems which were brought to courts in that manner were of various kinds, traffic of women, rape, medical negligence, torture on detenus, removal of huts on the pavements during the monsoon, TADA excesses, apathy of the police, erection of a statue, lengthy deliberation of a municipality on trivial matters etc. Even though this kind of action gets wide acclaim and enhances the prestige of judiciary, there are reservations. Firstly, among the numerous problems which come to the knowledge of the judge he picks up some. In ultimate analysis, he goes on search for cases palatable to him, instead of deciding only cases which are submitted to him, which attitude is against a basic judicial principle. Secondly the absence of real parties is a great handicap for courts. In fact the value of a judgement depends on the hearing of the conflicting views, pointing out their justifications and other reasons. When both sides are represented by motivated and competent advocates, the problem revolves fully before the judge and a good judgement on the matter emerges spontaneously in his mind. In the case of a public interest litigation the judge is deprived of the benefit of hearing really interested parties which is indispensable for judicial wisdom. Thirdly most of the orders on matters of public interest take the shape of a scheme. Some of them relate to matters simple in nature not involving huge financial outlay and found deserving by the Government as well; they end in success. Otherwise the scheme is criticized. For instance, the scheme instituted as the Child Welfare Re-habilitation-cum-Welfare Fund by way of contribution of Rs. 25,000/- by employers for each child employee, was found non-practical and not really beneficial by the International Working Child Meet in Delhi which took place almost immediately it was framed. In fact courts do not have the required administrative expertise to deal with social problems, nor do they have the full knowledge of facts. When courts take the initiative of swinging into action there is always risk of committing mistakes and necessity of reviewing the scheme again and again arises. Thus the authority attached to a res-judicata receives a serious set-back.

Law Making

Another area of judicial venture outside its domain is law making. Courts possess already a vast power of residual law making by way of interpretation. In fact they have made use of that possibility to extend their range of action by giving a wide content to fundamental rights. In other cases, higher courts under the guise of interpreting law twisted it. For instance, the word "consultation" in matter of appointment of judges was held to mean "concurrence". It is true that the government attempted to reduce consultation to mere information.

They have gone further and jumped into law making without any legislative text as basis. A good example of full-fledged legislation can be found in the matter of international adoption. In the wake of large scale export of abandoned children to foreign countries, everyone became aware of the need of guidelines. The Government brought a bill covering the whole field of adoption including the international adoption and applicable to all Indians. The attempt of the Government was thwarted twice by Muslim reactionaries who contended that their personal law was averse to adoption. Thereupon the Supreme Court seized of the matter gave elaborate guidelines which were in all respects a piece of legislation. The Judgement of the Supreme Court was forwarded for implementation to all concerned, including State Governments by way of a resolution to the Home Ministry.

It is to be stated, to absolve to a certain extent the judiciary for its extending its limits, that it was invited to do so by way of a vacuum created by the legislative or executive. The legislative deficiency can be gauged by the fact that the amendment bill of Indian Penal Code which was prepared by the Law Commission 10 years back has not yet been enacted because Parliament does not find time for such a purpose. In some cases the Government has even taken the initiative of transferring its responsibility to courts, as it was evident in Ayodhya case. It asked the Supreme Court its opinion on the point whether a Hindu Temple existed on the site where the mosque of Babri masjid was erected. The Supreme Court wisely refused to give its opinion on this point of fact dating back to several centuries.

Reaction by the other limbs of power

Even though the Government finds it at times convenient to have a ticklish matter decided by courts to avoid unpopularity, they are in general averse to the extension of powers by the judiciary and conflicts arose on that score. The most noteworthy and the longest tussle between the judiciary and the Parliament was in respect of the fundamental right to property. The Government in its eagerness to achieve better distribution of wealth has undertaken several land reforms. Persons affected by the reforms prayed the courts for the protection of their fundamental right to property. Acts passed by the Parliament were set aside by courts. Parliament responded by amending the Constitution and placing the acts in the IX Schedule meant to shield them against court erosion. When modifications to the Constitution were also set aside by the Supreme Court for violation of the basic structure of the Constitution, the Parliament by the 42nd Amendment, 1976 asserted its unfettered power to modify any provision of the Constitution. During the debate the minister of law piloting the bill went to the extent of warning the judiciary against any temptation to tamper with the Amendment. The position of the Parliament was that it was paramount as it represented the will of the people. The opinion of the Supreme Court was that the Parliament had no power to destroy the basic structure of the Constitution under which the Parliament also was holding its power. Of course the Supreme Court was of the view that it had as per the Constitution the last word to state what any provision of the Constitution meant.

Occasions for this kind of confrontation are embedded in the Constitution itself. In one side the Constitution proclaims fundamental rights of liberal inspiration and courts have been entrusted with the responsibility of upholding them. On the other side it contains directive principles of State policy which are of socialist inspiration and which the Government is enjoined to promote. It is also to be said that the Parliament represents the mass of poor people; judges on the other side belong mostly to upper classes; their respective perception of problems and solutions to the problems are not similar though the concern for the poor people is the same.

The assertion of powers by judges necessarily invites reaction from the Government. One primary form of reaction is the inclusion of "fundamental duties" to express the aversion created by the decisions based on "fundamental rights". Another form of reaction consists of undoing the rulings of the court by legislation to the contrary. This process is still now continuing. Attempts are being made to reverse the rulings of the Supreme Court on appointment of Judges and out of turn allotments.

The Government went even a step further; punitive transfers of High Court Judges were effected, Supreme Court Judges were superseded, the Government flouted openly the courts. The most contemptuous act is the one regarding the election of the then Prime Minister, Indira Gandhi. When the election was set aside by the High Court, the candidate obtained a stay upon filing a petition before the Supreme Court and stating that she had a very good case. Then the Parliament rendered the court proceedings infructuous by validating retrospectively the election by way of an amendment to the Constitution. The Judiciary was at its lowest ebb at that time. The word of the day was "committed judiciary".

Regulating factors

In the tussle between the Government and the Judiciary the people are ultimately the final umpires. In the general elections held in 1977 after the 42nd Amendment to the Constitution and threats to the judiciary, the party which adopted such an attitude lost power. The principle of judicial review as asserted by courts got impliedly the approval of the people. It is thus clear that when the judiciary treads on new fields it has to be attentive to the sentiments of the people. It has to take into account not only the enlightened opinion appearing in the press in the English medium but also the popular opinion. It cannot forget that in the matter of privy purses and nationalisation of banks the public opinion was in favour of the Government. It cannot also ignore that effigies of judges were burnt in respect of orders on reservation matters, though in this matter judges were well with their domain. Certain questions which defy political solution can be solved by judicial wisdom and other not. Before independence jurisdiction of courts was clearly delineated by law. Now the boundaries have become elastic with powers to courts to fix their own boundaries. Judges have necessarily to keep in their mind their limitations and refrain themselves whenever necessary inspite of their genuine urge to do justice. When jurisdiction is pre-determined, the legitimacy of judicial orders is ensured by law. When new areas are conquered, legitimacy has to be acquired by the merit of orders through a tacit approval of the Parliament or the people.

When the judiciary exceeds its normal powers that would mean that it encroaches upon others powers. On account of the arrangement made in the distribution of powers the extra activity of the judiciary is also dependent upon the performance of other limbs of power. The capability of the judiciary is almost constant. The strength of the Government is subject to great variations and the role of the judiciary may vary accordingly.

After the people's verdict in 1977 the judiciary started reasserting itself. The Bar which stood by its side during those dark days solicited more and more the intervention of the judiciary and the latter wanted to satisfy the public opinion which manifested itself in its favour. When during the last period the Government turned weak and disinclined to take decisions, court intervention has necessarily increased. The way to protect judiciary from great variations in its activity is to have a steady government exercising all its constitutional powers and in a constitutional manner. If such is the case there will not a spurt of activity by the judiciary which in fact is a strain on it and may affect its character.

It is worth remembering that judiciary is at the end of the power process. Its glory and limitation reside in that fact which should never be lost sight of. Being at the end of the power process, courts receive all matters which cannot be settled properly by others, therefore difficult to handle. At the same time courts have the benefit of the mistakes by others in their unsuccessful efforts and are in a better position to find a proper solution. Parties which are also exhausted by their long battle are more prepared to accept a compromise. When the judiciary moves to the solution of social problems, its success is far from being assured.

SUGGESTIONS FOR IMPROVEMENT

The above bird's eye of the performance of the judiciary during the last 50 years reveals two trends contradicting each other. In one side inability to cope up with the increasing amount of cases of traditional nature and in another side appearance of new fields of judicial work and venture in parajudicial field. Performance in the second sphere has compensated to a large extent for the loss of prestige caused by shortcomings in the former. But on account of the considerable increase of the volume of work the judiciary is under stress and may loose further prestige and be unable to fulfil its salvaging role in the society if remedial steps are not taken immediately to keep it in good stead.

The first area in which steps are necessary is the improvement of the image of the judge. The pay and the conditions of service of judges right from the start have to be considerably improved. At the initial stage recruitment of the best talents straight from the law college and appropriate training for judicial work should become the general rule. To attract the best talents, they should be allowed to move up the Supreme Court. Lateral recruitment may be resorted to till the new brand of directly recruited junior judges are mature to fill up offices of higher ranks. That lateral recruitment should never be beyond the level of District Judges. High Court judges should necessarily be drawn from the category of District Judges. In case of absolute necessity, High Court judges may be drawn from the Bar of other States directly, with avoidance of transfer. A person belonging to a Bar of the High Court should not be elevated to the Bench of the same High Court.

People cannot tolerate failures or corruptions in the ease of judges to the extent they do in respect of other officers. On the other side respect for judges and courts has to be kept intact for the acceptance of judgements. Therefore, the system of discipline for judges cannot be the same as for civil servants. One can conceive only of the following measures : Confidential admonition by the Chief Justice for small mistakes or removal from service in case of misconduct impairing the reputation of the judicial officer.

The second factor on which a considerable amount of work is necessary is the statement of law. Acts and rules have to be drafted not in the present cumbersome and clumsy way, but the statement of law should be direct, brief, clear and simple. It should be available in State languages, even in respect of Central laws which should come into force only from the time of its publication in the State Gazette of the State in the official language of that State. The bulk of the existing law has to be also re-enacted on the former lines. Computerisation of statutory law and case law should be prepared straight in State languages in order to avoid double work and perpetuation of the dominance of English in this field which is unwarranted.

The judicial hierarchy should be re-structured with jurisdiction well-defined in respect of all courts including the Supreme Court, and not left to the discretion of courts. The inherent power of the court should be only in respect of the exercise of the powers necessary to fulfil the mission entrusted to it. The jurisdiction should be defined in respect of the nature of disputes as well as the importance of the disputes. Tribunals should be rationalised so as to reduce their number. For instance, there may a tribunal for all taxes, and only one forum for all labour matters. As far as possible the jurisdiction of the fora of first instance at the early stage of the proceeding should be general so that a forum is available as near as possible to the litigant. The fora may be specialised in the middle stage in order to take full care of the particular nature of the matter when points of fact are settled finally. Again the fora should be general at the last stages namely the High Court and the Supreme Court so that general principles of law are not shattered unnecessarily and get evolved and refined smoothly to respond to all the requirements of the modern world. The composition of the court should be collegial right from the District level, at least when the court listens to arguments and passes judgement. The trial may conducted by a single judge.

The law of procedure and evidence should be fully stated by Acts of Parliament or of legislatures of States. Even in respect of tribunals, it should not be left to the discretion of the Presiding Officer. There should be three sets of rules of evidence and procedure according to the nature and importance of cases and they will have to be scrupulously observed. The jurisdiction should be fixed in harmony with these three sets, so that cases of the same nature and importance have the same set of procedure and evidence and each court should have only one set of procedure and evidence to follow so that it can master it fully and avoid making mistakes.

Cases should reach finality within a reasonable period. Even important cases should reach finality within three years. Of course there may be urgent cases which have to be disposed of within three weeks finally, and even earlier. For very small matters there should be only one court, for medium size cases one trial court and one revisional court and for important cases one trial court, one appellate court and one revisional court and never more in whatever form it may be.

CHAPTER XIV

The Apple Cart of Separation of Powers and Judicial Activism

R. Venkata Rao

The absolutist notion of the law as to will of the sovereign came first. When the emperor-whether he was Roman, German or French-had spoken, it was the task of all citizens including magistrates to obey, not to add or substract from his words as embodied in the law. Later, when democratic ideas were in ascendance, as in France after the revolution, the same argument was made in relation to the will of the people as expressed through their elected leaders. Judges as appointed officials had no authority to amend the decision of chosen representatives of the citizenry[1]. But at the heart of the civil law system was a concept beyond both the democratic and authoritarian ideologies : law was precisely what that term meant, a system, closed, self-contained and self-restrained, a nearly ordered body of principles hierarchially arranged, with less fundamental principles logically deduced from the more fundamental.[2] Any judicial tampering with this system, even if only a charitable effort to earn the law's commands in a particular case, was bound to do more harm than good in the long run by destroying the intellectual integrity of the entire corpus. Of course, over the years, civil law judges exercised a great deal of discretion in making law and policy and indeed they continue to do so today. In fact one of the forces behind the whole movement to codify the law was aimed at curbing judicial law making. The moot point here is that the official doctrine of the civil law prescribed an exceedingly narrow ambit for the exercise of judicial power and discretion.

If the hero of the civil law had been the scholar, the hero of the common law has been the judge and his squire, the practising attorney. Whereas the civil law was formulated in the antiseptic atmosphere of the university and was dependent upon abstraction, deep learning and cool, taut logic, the common law grew out of the muck and mire of the courtroom battles[3]. Its rules were efforts to settle immediate human conflicts with a resultant emphasis on practical results at the cost of conceptual purity or logical symmetry. At bottom common law is judge made law. Yet the idea of judge made law failed to be universally acclaimed. Though no sane man could deny the influence of the judges in the common law world, jurists like Balackstone[4] attacked the notion that these wise, just and virtuous men exercised any real degree of discretion. The function of the judge, he explained, was only to declare the law, judges were "the depositaries of the law : the living oracles who are bound by an oath to decide according to the law of the land." They could "take no active resolution whatever." They had "neither force nor will but merely judgement."

Thus the mechanical theory of judicial decision-making, whether created within the civil or common law system, located the judges within a network of universal and permanent principles. In the civil law, the judge found his rules in the code or, where there was not yet such complete corpus, in general principles scholars had discovered to underlie Roman Law. In the common law system, a few statutes but mostly a large number of previous judicial decisions announced the fundamental principles. But this Blackstonian Declaratory Theory was subject to attack by subsequent events and subsequent scholarship. Jeremy Bentham (1748-1832) felt that it was obvious that judges do make law and exercise private judgement in deciding cases brought before them. In the United States Oliver Wendell Holmes Jr(1841-1935) also accepted fact of judicial law making. Indeed he contended that the law had no existence apart from the decisions of the courts. He wrote "The prophecies of what the courts will do in fact and nothing more pretentious, are what I mean by Law." Nor were judges moved merely by logic", he explained in his treatise "The Common Law."

"The life of law has not been logic; It has been experience. The felt necessities of the time, the prevalent moral and political theories, institutions of public policy, avowed or unconscious, even the prejudices which the judges share with their fellowmen, have had a good deal more to do than the syllogism in determining the rules by which men should be governed."

Like Holmes, Roscoe Pound (1890-1964) stressed the critical significance of the judge. Although Pound concluded both statutes and judicial decisions were law, he regarded the judicial activity as the really creative element in law. Historically, legislation has failed to meet the requirements of change : given the complex conditions of modern life, it was inconceivable that legislators could write law that would foresee and provide for all eventualities. Judges would be in a better position than legislators to achieve the continual adjustment needed in the legal system. Pound wanted judges to be social engineers who would keep law and life in harmonious balance. Benjamin Cardozo (1870-1973) agreed with Pound on the sociological view of law and the creative task of the judges. In his book, "The nature of Judicial Process", he points that where law is less definite, the judge must create his own rules, for making this creative choice, he outlined four methods-the method of philosophy which emphasizes the element of logic; the method of history which seeks developmental explanations, the method of custom which accepts guidance for past or present practices of the community; and the method of sociology of which he meant conceptions of social welfare or social justice[5]. Thus, there has been a shift in the thinking of the jurists about the functions of the judges-from that of mere declarers of law to active involvement in social engineering in both the legal systems.

To a considerable degree judges do the same thing no matter what court they serve on, no matter where it stands in judicial hierarchy, regardless of what country it is in. They find facts in controverted situations; they interpret and apply legal rules, and they issue orders with enforceable sanctions. But there is one major respect in which some courts differ from others. The distinction is between the courts or judicial systems which have authority to interpret, declare and enforce the basic constitutional law of the regime upon the political organs and those who lack the power.

Indian and American courts are in the first category; English courts illustrate the second. Indian and American courts have the power to refuse to enforce duly enacted legislation on the ground that it conflicts with the constitution. No English courts have this power. They can interpret but they cannot question the legitimacy of parliamentary legislation. The power of the courts to decide whether or not laws (or procedures adopted by government in the enforcement of laws) are constitutional is called judicial review.[6] Two possible meanings are given to this phrase "Judicial Review." Firstly it may refer to review by judges of acts by government officials to determine whether the officers are acting under the Authority of law or exceeding their powers (*Ultravires*). This type of review is available to courts in all systems. Secondly, there is a kind of judicial review, provided for in federal systems, for policing the distribution of power between the states or provinces and the central government. This sort of adjudication forms an important aspect of the work of the Supreme Court in such federal polities as Australia, Canada, India and the United States. It fell to John Marshall, third Chief Justice of the United States, to first claim the power of Judicial review for the Supreme Court in the famous case of *Marbury* V. *Madison* (1803).[7] His reasoning was syllogistic. His major premise was that the constitution is supreme law of the land and judges take an oath to support the constitution. His minor premise was that it was the province of the judiciary to interpret the law. His conclusion was that judges must not enforce a statute that they believe to be in violation of a provision of the constitution. Since then, *Marbury* V. *Madison* has become the cornerstone of the doctrine of judicial review.

Since the doctrine of judicial review enables the court to review the acts of the lelslative bodies "which are essentially political, it would be mere wishful thinking on any one's part to conceive the notion that the court would be acting in air tight chambers free from the din and bustle of the world of Politics. As such, attention is to be focussed on the operation of the Supreme Court in these chambers not free from the influence of politics.

At one time "politics" was a dirty word and to suggest that courts and judges were involved in a political arena was heretical. Judges were entitled to respect precisely because they lived in a clean world of the law, not in the sordid neighbourhood of politics.

Judicial decisions were believed to be the products of rational processes, supported by logic and precedent in contrast to the irrationality, the compromising, the influence peddling and the propagandizing that characterise political decision. But now the word 'Politics, has lost its indecency by its all-pervasive influence in all the activities of mankind and judiciary is no exception. By their special obligation to interpret the constitution, the political importance of the judges increased. The Supreme Court cannot operate in a political isolation chamber; it functions in the real world of political action and reaction. The Supreme Court does not do its work in vacuum. Its decisions on important constitutional questions can be understood in their full significance only when viewed against the background of history, politics, economics and personality surrounding them and, out of which they grew[8]. The judiciary has always been an instrument of the government, actively involved in politics, "not a unique body of impervious legal technicians above and beyond the political struggle."[9] It should also be remembered that every power by which one organ to government is enabled to control the other[10] is inescapably political. As such, any approach to judicial process should place judging at all levels within the mainstream of political relationships. It should be a study in what Martin Shapiro has called "Political Jurisprudence."[11]

The interaction between the political and judicial forces has given birth to different schools of thought as regards the responsibility of the judges and at the risk of over simplification, these schools of thought can be reduced to two; activism and self-restraint. We shall discuss in brief the doctrine of self-restraint before delineating the doctrine of judicial activism.

The proponents of the doctrine of self-restraint espouse the claim that the doctrine of separation of powers has envisaged a system of mutual checks and the balances as its primordial concern and not one of mutual encroachment. They opine that the judiciary, one of the organs of the government, should leave policy making to the initiative of others. "Problems of policy are for politicians and not judges to decide."[12] says Justice Frankfurter who enunciated the doctrine of "political thicket." The basic changes needed in the society are best left to the political processes and should not be undertaken by judges who, as they should be because of their office are beyond the reach of political considerations[13]. The judiciary should not be political "after the fashion of legislative or executive." The approach of the judiciary should be "to go slow as not to offend any one." They argue further that activism is constitutional, unwarranted. In drafting the constitution, the framers had not intended that court should initiate prompt changes in basic policy, the legislative powers had been vested in another organ. They say activism is morally insupportable as judges are not elected by the people. Nor is court directly responsible to the electorate in the same sense as the parliament. Activism in the long run is self-defeating-it opens up the dangerous question of judicial "legitimacy" and subjects the court to attack which can weaken the whole fabric of respect for the court and for the rule of law[14]. Keeping an eye on socialist legislations, they say, the court is made a reliable bulwark of activist defence for business interests against regulatory and welfare legislation. They charge that excessive judicial activism is primarily responsible in striking down law to improve social conditions and bring business under public regulation. They believe that the constitution authorises the legislature to exercise wide discretion in ordering the social and economic institutions of the society. The court must not presume to be a "legislation and constitution making body, enacting into law its own predilection."[15] They feel that judicial prestige would be endangered and judicial image would be damaged if judges become entangled in debates over public policies. The continued acceptance of judicial authority it is argued depends on the maintenance of a mystique of judicial aloofness and non-involvement in political matters.

The proponents of judicial activism, which can be defined as the shaping of the basic law through bold court initiatives[16], on the other hand, opine that the court should provide the moral leadership and clarify the values and ideals for a country that had shown itself to be really in need of such guidance.[17] They feel the court should willingly play an "affirmative role." Instead of restricting itself to exercising a negative check of actions improperly taken by government, the court should assume the more positive role telling the government what it must do. They insist that the activist judge is goal oriented. Hit interest in achieving the 'right' result in the controversies that come before him is stronger than his interests in the process by which the court arrives at the result. His tests for the rightness of a decision are whether it is politically and morally acceptable and whether its effects will be beneficial to society. Since he views law as one form of social control, he will be more creative in developing new legal doctrines to support his conclusions about public policy and more willing to overrule precedents that stand in the way of desired results. He is less hesitant to challenges to political breaches and less fearful of becoming involved in controversy.[18]

The activists claim that the Supreme Court should share with political organs of the government an active and creative role. It should stand ready to bring about the needed basic changes in society which for one reason or other have failed or lagged in their accomplishment by other means.[19] The logic is like this. Judges are relatively immune to popular pressure. Somehow or other, men link the idea of justice with that of the judge. Other governmental agencies more readily and more freely yield to the pressure of numbers, the so called demand of the majority. Not so the judge. He, knowing that nothing can disturb his position does not hesitate promptly to lay judgement. Unless majorities in the legislature and at the ballot box were thus restrained, Justice Brewar-foresaw the departure of the government of the people, by the people and for the people. Justice Brewar comments, the courts hold neither-purse nor sword, they cannot corrupt nor arbitrarily control. They make no law, establish no policy, they never enter the drain of popular action. They do not govern. Their functions in relation to the states are limited to seeing that popular action does not trespass upon right and justice as it exists in written constitution and the natural law. These ideals of right and justice can be best preserved by the judiciary when the legislature is tempted to take away these ideals in an euphoria. In this connection Justice Sutherland implored fatalistically. "If the provisions of the constitution be not upheld when they pinch as well as they comfort, they may well, be abandoned."[20] The oftquoted criticism that judicial activism is a paradox in a democratic society as the judges are nominated and not elected is decried on the ground that judicial activism would prevent the government from profiting from its lawless behaviour[21]. They say judicial review is an essential of the free government, an attempt by the democracy to cover its own bet.[22] Judicial review is neither a deviant institution nor is it an interloper[23] and a fear of popular majorities lies at the very basis of the whole system of judicial review. Madison in the Fedarlist No. 51[24] correctly observes : 'In framing a government which is to be administered by men over men, the great difficulty lies in this : You must first enable the government to control governed : and in next place oblige it to control itself. A dependence on the people is no doubt, the primary control of the government, but experience has taught mankind the necessity of auxiliary precaution. Hence, they say, the court should not lead an isolated ivory tower existence refusing to enter the 'Political thicket'. The case for an active intervention becomes more pronounced where the sacrosanct freedoms are to be protected. Justice Jackson remarks, "The very purpose of a Bill of Right was to withdraw certain subjects from the vicissitudes of political controversy, to place them beyond the reach of the majorities and officials and to establish them as a legal principles to be applied by courts."[25] Jefferson remarks pithily, "One hundred and seventy-three despots would surely be as oppressive as one."[27] In a democratic process, though voting is the prima donna, the judiciary has to ensure that equal opportunity be provided to all. This can be ensured if the judiciary actively intervenes. Mason observes : 'Voting is patently basic, but without equal opportunity to utilise the crucial preliminaries to constituent choice-speech, press, assembly, petition and right of association-government by consent becomes an empty declaration. Where these basic rights are involved, judicial self-restraint is defensible only if one assumes the reliability, rationality and availability, of the political process as a recourse against abuse of power'. The activists hold that the goal of the constitution is not only the preservation of democratic process but also protection of certain freedoms from the majority's will, success in establishing the second goal is necessary to full achievement of the first. By actively protecting the freedom the court saves the democratic government from destroying itself by excess of its own power. By providing, the-disgruntled individuals a peaceful forum in which they can air their grievances and perhaps win vindication, the court, remembering that those who make peaceful revolution impossible, will make violent revolution inevitable[27] domesticates revolution through judicial review. Changes can be accomplished without the subversion of the constitution and the Supreme Court through judicial review can prevent the subversion of the constitution[28]. Speaking about the role of the judiciary where constitutional rights hang in balance, Justice Wright observed : "It would be far better indeed for these great social and political problems to be resolved in the political area by other branches of government. But these are social and political problems which seem at times to defy such resolution. In such situations, under one system, the judiciary must bear and accept its responsibility to assist in the solution where constitutional rights hang in the balance."[30] Cox observed "The judiciary, it is oftensaid, should concern itself with law and leave policy to the legislatures. Such a course has much to commend it, but surely rigid adherence to this implies too narrow a view of both the function of the law and the role of the court. Constitutional law must grow and change in response to the needs of the society."[30]

II

Judicial Activism, which is certainly the best bet of democracy, should not be unbridled. Judicial activism should not lead to judicial tyranny as the judiciary is vulnerable in certain important respects. The executive can always change its constitutional views by nomination of persons having different ideas to court when vacancies occur.

Or alternatively there might be moves to increase the strength of the court. Or as in America, even the public opinion can be organised against the court.[31] Judicial activism should not lead to judicial usurpation as the alternative means available for reversing the doctrines of the Supreme Court would be adopted. These means form the part of the context in which the judges must act. Such factors which form part of the political realities that surround every major court decision have led Alexander Pekelis to observe that the Supreme Court is infinitely powerful and at the same time frightfully defenceless. Though the Supreme Court determines the precise nature and extent of the individual liberties guaranteed by the constitution, its role is a matter of degree because if the elected officials that they appoint (including the police and the other public agencies) should systematically resist the mandate of the court, the court's influence and real power are seriously limited. Even when the Supreme Court approves the individual claims, officials of the government or other institutions of the society might continue to behave towards other individuals in precisely the same manner as before the case went to the court. If the respect for the Supreme Court is sufficiently lacking in the society at large, voters will elect and re-elect officials who defy the court in that way. In that event, the constitutional 'Guarantees' as the court has interpreted them are of little practical value. These are not mere abstract speculations.[33] This might ultimately weaken the stature of the court. Keeping this in view, the court, while taking recourse to activism, should not dwarf the political capacity of the people. Though the judges should play an active role remembering that the constitution is a "a living organism and not a strait jacket,"[34] they should not forget that "they are not final because they are infallible but they are infallible only because they are final."[35] The protagonists of judicial restraint should remember that "We are under the Constitution but the constitution is what the judges say it is."

It is also fallacious to think that an active court per se would ensure justice. As Warren has remarked "the Supreme Court standing alone cannot ensure justice for all citizens. Such a goal will be accomplished only if all elements of the legal system, the law makers,' the practising attorneys, legal scholars and judges worked in harmony to apply the principles which are fundamental to freedom."[36]

III

The Supreme Court of India may not have the purse but its nascent jurisprudence has been rich, the Court may not have the sword, but its recent jurisprudence has been sharp. The Supreme Court of India has been in the centre stage in the recent times because of its forays. The hyper activistic tendency - of the Court has been the subject of discussion in different fora. Though in a way judicial activism can be said to have started in the year 1893 itself when justice Mohamood of Allahabad, High Court in dissenting judgement sowed the seeds of activism, by and large, it can be safely stated that the activist era of the Supreme Court has started only after 1975. The advent of judges like Justice Krishna Iyer, Justice P.N. Bagawati and Justice Chinnappa Reddy among others has opened a new leaf in the jurisprudence, so much so, that Prof. Upendra Baxi pithily observes that India might have become Republic in 1950, but the Supreme Court has become Republic only in 1975. The Apex Court with its activism has opened new vistas and new principles of administrative law have been enunciated. One can say that for the first 25 years of its existence from 1950 to 1975, the Courts in India have been looking to the Courts from across the frontiers for principles of administrative law. But the post Menaka[37] Scenario has totally transformed the scenario and the Indian Supreme Court is now looked with awe and admiration for evolving new principles of administrative law. Its contribution in the areas of prison jurisprudence, emanicipation of bonded labour, in spreading human rights culture in crusading the cause of environmental protection, and in providing right to live with dignity for pavement dwellers, has been seminal. The very recent pronouncement of the Supreme Court in Noor Saba Khatoon's case where a Muslim father was asked to pay maintenance to the children is another feather (Shabano and Sarala Mudgal were the forerunners in this line).

The activism of the Indian Supreme Court has produced considerable gains, but it was not without pains. The former Chief Justice of Supreme Court of India Justice A.M. Ahmadi has stated that it is not the Supreme Court which has become active but the common man who has become active. He expressed the belief - that activism would be only a temporary phenomenon and that the executive and legislature would sooner than later perform their constitutionally ordained functions. The former Chief Justice J.S. Verma observed that the judicial activism is like a sharp-edged tool which has to be used as a scalpel by a skilful surgeon, to cure the malady and not as a Rampuri knife which can kill.[39]

The activism of the Court sometimes bordering on the judicial usurpation of powers of other organs has been causing ripples. The misuse of Public Interest Litigation, the Court's directives in the matters pertaining to the organisational elections of recognised political parities (which matter squarely falls in the domain of internal affairs of the political party) have made some to observe that the judiciary by adopting the holier than thou attitude has been arrogating to itself the power not visualised by the constitutional scheme of things. These people argue that among the five modes of peaceful settlement of disputes viz., negotiation, mediation, conciliation, arbitration and adjudication, judicial settlement is the last resort. But the activist rather hyper activist role of the Court has made people to take recourse to the Courts as the first-resort. They, therefore, state that there is a need for rethinking on the executive to restore the supremacy of the executive. In fact, this is a very disturbing trend.

The judiciary has been harping on the theme of making strong the long arm of law, whereas the executive and the legislature have been debunking the judiciary on the ground that the excessive and hyper activistic tenor of the judiciary has been making the long arm of law a wrong arm, thus upsetting the delicate apple cart of separation of powers.

The role of the three organs of the State is complementary but never conflicting. Each should not try to clip the wings of the other organs. Let us all remember in the Golden Jubilee Year of Independence that we have become independent not without becoming accountable, judiciary not excepting.

REFERENCES

1. Walter F. Murphy, C. Herman Pritchett : Courts, Judges and politics : An Introduction to the Judicial Process (Random House, 1974), P.9.
2. Ibid.
3. Ibid, page 10.
4. Sir William Blackstone was an eighteenth century English Jurist whose commentaries on the laws of England (1765-68) became one of the most influential writings in Anglo-American Legal theory.
5. Cardozo gave priority to the last method-the method of sociology.
6. Thomas T. Lynos : The Supreme Court and Individual Rights in contemporary society (Addison-Welsely) Publishing Company, 1975 page 14.
7. I. Cranch 137 (1803).
8. Robert E. Cushman quoted in Walter F. Murphy and Joseph Tamenbans. The Study of Public Law (New York, Random House, 1972), pages 13-15.

9. M. Shapiro : Law and Politics in the Supreme Court (1964), page 15.
10. Eakin V. Ramb (12 S. & P. 330-348, pa-1825) (Gibros, J. Dissenting).
11. Martin Shapiro, Supra note 9, page 15.
12. Felix Frnakfurter, J : Dennis V. United States 341 U.S. 494 (1951).
13. Harlan, J : U.S. News and World Report, December 18, 1967 page 36.
14. Anthony Lewis : War and the Court (The New York Times, November, 21, 1970).
15. Stone quoted in Mendelson Supreme Court, page 136.
16. Thomas Lyons : Supra note 7, page 18.
17. Arthur Golderg : Equal Justice : The warren Era of the Supreme Court (New York, 1971), p. 6.
18. Walter Murphy, C. Herman Pritchett : Supra 1, page 14.
19. Alpheous Thomas Mason : Judicial Activism Old and New, 55, V.L.R. page 385.
20. Sutherland, J : House Building and Loan association V. Blais dell, 290 U.S. 398, 483 (1934).
21. Brewar, J : U.S. V. Calendra (414 U.S. 338), 1974.
22. Adopted from Corwin Book Review, 56 Harward Law Review, 484, 487 (1942).
23. Ibid.
24. The Federalist No. 51, Madison quoted in A. Mason Free Government in Making, 306 (3rd etd., 1965).
25. Jackson J : Virgina, Board of Education V. Barnette, 319 U.S. 624, 638.
26. Notes on Virginia, : The Writings of Thomas Jefferson, 163 (Memorial Edition, 903).
27. John F. Kennedy, quotee in T. Sorendon Kenndedy, 535 (1965).
28. Mason : Supra note 19, page 412.
29. Wright, J : Hobson V. Hanseen, 269 F. Supp. 401, 1967.

30. A. Cox : The Warren Court : Constitutional Decision as an Institution of Reform, 14 (1968), page 39-40.

31. As Roosevelt did against the 'horse and Buggy' of anti New Deal Court or as Nixon did in his law and order speeches during the 1968 campaign. Or as in India, the concept of committed judiciary and socio-economic programmes can be invoked to supersede judges.

32. Alexander Pekelis : Law and Social Action : Selected Essays. Milton Komirtr ed. (Ithica 1950), page 202.

33. Thomas T. Lynos : Supra note 6, page 22.

34. Brandeis, J : United States V. Moreland, 258 U.S., 433 (1922).

35. Johnson, J : Brown V. Allen, 344 U.S. 443, 540 (1953).

36. Earl Warren : Centurings of Discriminations, the New York Times, October 31, 1970; Speech of September 28, 1968, quoted in Michigan Law Review, LXVII (1966). page 221.

37. Maneka Gandhi V. Union of India, AIR 1978, SC 597.

38. Pathbreaking verdict by justices A.S. Anand and K. Venkateswamy of the Supreme Court of India given on 31.7.97.

39. India Today, March 15, 1996 p.121.

CHAPTER XV

Strengthening of Panchayati Raj—Need for Constitutional Reforms

T.S.N. Sastry

"We cannot realise the full benefit of democratic government unless we begin by the admission that all problems in their incidence require decision at the place, and by the persons by whom the incidence is most deeply felt"

Laksi Harold J.

The Panchayati Raj System is not a new concept in India, and has in existence for thousands of years. With its distinctive institutional character of functioning, it became an integral part of the body politic of Indian Culture. Literally, the term Panchayati Raj (hereafter words referred as PR) means, a body of five or more persons called as *Panchas* either elected or nominated by the people of a village form together to govern the socio-economic, political, administrative geographical, ecological, cultural and legal issues of the people of that village. In short, it is the easily accessible government to the people of the village to cater and administer their day to day needs.

In the ancient and medieval ages it was governed by learned, experienced and honest men of the village. The *Panchas* exercised their powers through various committees, such as, *Gram Sabha* and *Nyaya Panchayats* etc., in fulfiling the aspirations of the people of the rural areas including the enforcement of law and order[1]. From the various studies it can be stated that PR had its pinnacle in the olden days, though there was no direct or systematic State control over the administration of the villages. The life of the rural areas practically remained undisturbed by the political changes in the various periods. In the words of Will Durant, American thinker and historian, "The village community in ancient India (the Panchayat system) is the proto-type of all forms of self-government and democracy that have even been evolved in various parts of the world."[2]

However, with the introduction of land reforms, the centralised system of administration and justice by the British Government led to the disintegration of the PR which was built up through the ages. With the shakeup of the country's socio-economic, political and legal foundations, the institution of PR became a tool in the hands of rich and influential people, instead of serving the people as a social organ. Apart from the reforms introduced by the British from time to time, it is the industrial revolution which had its profound impact on the marginalisation of the village institutions as only mere ornamental institutional set-ups of the Government.[3] Furthermore, with the entry of new class of urbanised society evolved on the edifice of industrial revolution started practically dominating all the aspects of the country (i.e., socio-economic, political, administrative, legal and cultural) and this had mainly affected the system of local government and the needs of the people of the villages were completely neglected. In short, the existence of PR was simply ignored and was made thoroughly ineffective.

Realising the dangers associated with the systematic destruction of PR, Gandhiji advocated the re-introduction of *Gram Swaraj*, or Village Republics in independent India at the time of making the Constitution. He compared *Gram Swaraj* to *Ram Rajya* (i.e., the Kingdom of peace, justice and righteousness). His aim was the Indian independence must begin at the grossroots level than centralization of power in the hands of the State. Gandhiji's main idea behind the theory was to correct the over-westernization and bureaucratisation of the political system of India and to reassert the cherished ethical values of the ancient Indian Society. Therefore, he urged the urbane elite men both in Congress party and in the Constituent Assembly to restructure the Indian Polity on the ideal of *Gram Swaraj* for a perfect democracy based upon individual freedom.[4]

The draft Constitution of India did not contain any reference to village administration and was subjected to severe criticism by a section of members of the Constituent Assembly. However, the followers of Gandhian philosophy had succeeded in mounting pressure on the Assembly to incorporate certain village oriented policies in the final version. As a result the Constitution of India under the Chapter of Directive Principles of State Policy (Article 40) did incorporate village-oriented policy administered by the State.[5]

After the adoption of the Constitution there have been continuing efforts towards democratic decentralization and to restructure the village administration.

POST-INDEPENDENCE PERIOD AND DEMOCRATIC DECENTRALIZATION

Article 40 of the Directive Principles of State Policy has been the most vigorously implemented provision than other provision of the constitution in the last fifty years. Almost all the State Governments in the Union enacted legislations to strengthen the PR. Even the Five-Year Plans of the country emphasized the need to develop the village based administration. Further, the Government of India in the year 1957, appointed the Balwant Ray Metha Committee to study the working of the Community Development Programme and to suggest methods for their effective functioning. The Committee after an exhaustive study tour through out the country, suggest for a suitable restructering of local government to attain the desired goals. The Committee recommended a three-tier system consisting of *Zilla Parishads*, *Panchayat Samithis* and *Panchayats* at the—village level. For the first two it suggested indirect elections, whereas for the panchayats direct election. The committee also opined that the control of the State power should be reduced and adequate resources should be provided to discharge their functions properly.[6] On the basis of the Metha Committee Report, though almost all the States enacted specific legislations, there was no legislation enacted by the Union Government. Due to lack of a Union legislation by the Government of India, there is little uniformity in the PR set-up in all the States. There is a lot of difference with respect to the constitution, functioning and powers of the three tier system in the whole country. These structural differences and the tight grip of State control over the administration of the three-tier system, because of this arrangement could not provide the desired results as aimed by the committee.

The Government of India taking into consideration of the Choatic conditions prevailing in the PR set-up appointed the Ashok Metha Committee[7] in 1977, to study and to suggest suitable mechanism to streamline the concept of democratic decentralization. The committee to overcome the maladies of PR recommended a two-tier system recognising the District as the first point of decentralization. It was opined that the three tier system be replaced by constituting *Zilla Parishads* and *Mandal Panchayats*. It was felt by the committee that *Gram Panchayats* and *Panchayat Samitis* be removed for effective functioning of *gram swaraj*. This Committee too felt that the interference of the State in the administration of PR should be drastically reduced and they should be made independent of themselves in their activities. Although, some states enacted legislation empowering the *Zilla Parishads* with more powers none of them have implemented the report of the committee whole heartedly. As stated already, due to the lack of Central enactment, the variations between the States led to the defeat of the objective of strengthening a real *gram swaraj* or democratic decentralization. The former Prime Minister Mr. Rajeev Gandhi, taking into consideration of the maladies of the PR, called for drastic reforms in strengthening the philosophy of the founders of *gram swaraj*. The call given by the former Prime Minister has once again opened the pandora box on the necessity of strengthening the concept of *gram swaraj*. The Government of India after a wide ranging of debates and discussions has finally amended the constitution and incorporated specific provisions of the constitution of the panchayats under Article 243 of the constitution in the year 1992.[8] The long felt need of constitutional amendment is a welcoming feature for the development of Gram-Swaraj. Though the amendment Act raised the hopes for a sustainable development of PR institutions, with in a short span of time it proved to be a futile exercise. Because, the amendment too has fallen prey to the nexus of political parties and towed the way on the similar lines of the various legislations enacted by the State Governments. The constitutional amendment too has not provided any uniform procedure in systematising the constitution of PR institutions. The amendment Act has neither adhered to the proposals made by the Balawant Ray Mehta or Ashoka Mehta Committees. Instead it towed a comprising formula of both and adopted the proposals of the two. The Act has once again conferred powers on the State governments to enact legislations according to their whimsical fancies. With respect to the composition of Panchayats, it has empowered the States to choose either direct or indirect elections in the constitution of panchayats. It has retained the system of co-optation of the members of the Legislative Assembly, Council of States and Members of the House of the People in the panchayats above the village level. Further, in the constitution of village panchayats there exists an apparent contradiction between the provisions of the amendment Act. For example, on the one hand, Article 243 Clause (c) Sub-Clause (2)[9] specifies that all the seats in the village panchayats shall be filled by direct election. At the same time, on the contrary sub-clause (4)[10] and (5)[11] empowers the State Governments to adopt their own procedures in constituting a village panchayat and its Chairperson by means of either direct or indirect election. With respect to the constitution of panchayats at the intermediary level and at District level it has provided for indirect elections.

In view of the apparent contradictions that exist in the provisions, and the lack of strict governance by the Central Government for the implementation of the provisions, most of the States did not even bother to enact their legislations in accordance with the provisions of the article. Moreover, the provisions of the amendment Act too empowered the States to completely regulate the affairs of the village administration than orienting them as self-sufficient centres of administrative units of the polity.

As a result, the aspirations of the advocates of PR have hardly been realised even after the amendment of the constitution. In view of lack of conscientious efforts either by the Union or by the States, all the steps taken in the last five decades have paved the way for raising tensions and feuds among the rural population instead of nurturing them as the nerve centres of democracy. Ultimately, this has resulted in isolating the rural mass from the activities of PR except for participating in voting once in a while, whenever they are called for. Moreover, it is an unfortunate situation that in several States elections to the Panchayats could not be held due to one reason or the other. If such a trend continuous any longer, it may lead to complete destruction of the very concept of *gram-swaraj*.

The several studies undertaken on the functioning of PR institutions, clearly specify, that instead of transparency to be reflected in their functioning as real units of democracy, they became the scapegoats of the political parties. Further, the coercive tactics adopted by various political parties to woo the voters, and, the continuous experiments with the functioning of their system led the people to hate the village-based administrative units than to participate in them. We can't make further piece-meal experiments with the system any longer. In restructuring them as equal units of democracy, we may have to undertake a detailed examination of the philosophy of *gram-swaraj* and to reconstitute them in accordance with the future needs of the society. As already opined by various sections of the polity and the momentum which is growing infavour of a through over-hauling of the entire system of the governance of the country (i.e., the need for a reformed constitution), it is time to have a re-look at the concept of *gram-swaraj*. Various opinions have already been aired in the restructing of PR. The following suggestions need consideration for the upliftment of village administrative units for the sustainbility of the Indian democracy.

1. To attain all round economic, political, cultural development and social justice in a more integrated manner, there is every need than ever before to renew the constitution and to decentralize the political power up-to the grossroots level. This can be better achieved by incorporating clear cut provisions in the constitution to evolve a uniform four-tier system of governance for the entire country (viz; a stronger Union with better administrative units such as States, Zilla Panchayats and Village or Nagar Panchayats). This will certainly help not only to remove the existing maladies and

confusions about the Panchayati Raj System but tend tc make them to take active part as the real administrative units under a democratic set-up.

2. The Union or the States should possess no power to interfere with their governance. They should be left free to administer themselves. To attain this the village panchayats should be constituted only on the basis of direct election without any provisions for co-optation of Parliamentarians and Legislations. However, in the case of District Panchayats the membership should be fixed at 20 or 25 for viable administration. Accordingly the village or *Nagar Panchayats* should be grouped as 20 or 25 blocks for effective and efficient representation of all the panchayats in the district body. The Chair Person of the District Panchayat and the Village Panchayat should be elected by direct election on the basis of adult franchise, so that the Chair Person can discharge his functions freely without the fear of veto by the members.

3. The panchayats should be elected for a fixed term of five years. To become a member of a panchayat a candidate must secure atleast 52% of the total votes cast, whereas in the case of a Chair Person it should be atleast 55%. By adopting this methodology, the present day maladies of Caste or Community dominance can easily be marginalised to a great extent. In case where no clear cut result emerges, two methods can be adopted. The first is there should be a repolling within a week eliminating the candidates having lost their security deposits without any chance for new entrants into the fray. The second alternative is to follow the system of proportional representation by means of single transferable vote followed at present to the offices of President and Vice President of India. If the second method is adopted, the voters should be well trained in exercising their preference. Infact, by adopting the second method the problem of rigging and bogus votes can be eradicated.

4. To achieve more transperancy and for a feasible administrative efficiency, political parties should be barred to participate in the elections to the local bodies and no

member of a panchayat should be allowed to continue in office more than two terms.

5. As envisaged by the seventy third and seventy fourth[12] amendments of the constitution, the system of reservation to Schedule Castes, Tribes and Women can be continued for a period of ten years. If the new constitution adopts such a formula with in this period without any provision for extension of time-frame it should be the duty of the State to see that these sections should be developed in all aspects with more clear cut welfare measures.

6. For the effective, and smooth functioning of the local bodies it should be prescribed to become a member or chairperson of the panchayat (a) he or she should be a registered voter of that particular village or district and should have spent atleast three years within the geographical area prior to the date of elections to the office of the local bodies. (b) no person below the age of 25 years and above 60 years shall be allowed to contest in the elections. (c) to contest for any office in the panchayat at village or at district level a candidate should have the minimum educational qualification, viz., atleast matriculation (d) at the time of filing of the nomination papers a candidate should be asked to enclose the following documents: (l) he/she belongs to the respective village or district with three years of residence from the taluk or district magistrate. (2) a certificate specifying no criminal charges against him or her from the District Judicial Officer. (3) He/she does not belong to a political party (4) a copy of his/her properties and assets. (5) proof of age alongwith the prescribed educational qualifications and finally physical and mental fitness certificate by a qualified surgeon.

7. *Gram Sabhas* should be constituted at both levels of the local bodies (viz., village or nagar or district panchayat level). Instead of following the existing system of considering all the residents of a village who have attained the age of 21 years as members, it can be rationalised to 30 members either elected by the system of adult franchise or adopting any other suitable method of drawing people having experience

in administration, socio-economic, cultural and legal aspects. In the case of Gram Sabha at the District level the membership should not exceed more than fifteen and they could be elected by the members of the village or nagar panchayats and district panchayats. No member of the *gram sabha* should be allowed to continue in office for more than six years and one-third of the members should retire for every two years. The Chairpersons of the panchayats at both the levels should be the ex-officio members of the *gram sabha*. The Chair Person of the *gram sabha* should be elected amongst the members of it for every three years. It should meet at least four times a year. The *Gram sabha* should be entrusted with powers to draw developmental plans to suggest and guide the members and the Chair Persons of the panchayats, to approve the budget of the panchayats etc. In fact at the village level they should be entrusted to deal with civil and criminal cases of ordinary nature.

8. The District panchayat should be empowered with all the powers of a State Government including the supervisory powers over the *village-panchayats*. All modern and technical equipments be provided to the district bodies. They should be left free to formulate the plans of the economy and more resources be provided at their disposal for a rational allocation of funds tó the village units.

9. A nation level planning should be evolved by the Union government to setup all consumer article oriented industries of small scale sector be established at the district level. As a principle of development, agricultural products, horticultural products, poultry, fisheries, sericulture, medicinal herbs should be set up at the village level.

10. To assist the polity in attaining secular, egalitarian, modernistic and to render cost efficient oriented justice, it is necessary to establish *Nyaya Panchayats* at the District level. To make them as efficient judicial organs, the membership of *Nyaya Panchayats* could be fixed at ten with a provision to co-optation of the District Magistrate, the District and Sessions Judge, and, the Chair Person of the Zilla Panchayat.

The other members of a *Nyaya Panchayat* could be elected by an electoral college consists of the members of all the village or *nagar panchayats* including the *district panchayat*. They should be elected only on the basis of proportional representation by means of single transferable vote. The term of the office of the members of a *Nyaya panchayat* should be for one fixed term of six years or up to the age of 60 years, which ever is earlier. Suitable criteria can be evolved to eligible for the membership of a *Nyaya panchayat*. The *Nyaya panchayats* should be empowered with civil and criminal jurisdiction. In civil cases, they should be given powers to deal with aspects such as property, agricultural successionary and conjugal relations. In criminal cases, they should be given powers to deal with offences relating to property, public health, environmental problems, weights and measure, food adulteration and religious aspects. For the proper implementation of the judgements delivered by the *Nyaya Panchayats*, responsibility be fixed on the village and district panchayats. There should not be any provision of appeal to the regular courts until and unless 2/3 of the total members of the *Nyaya Panchayat* cast their vote in favour of an appeal. This would not only boost the confidence of the rural people in their participation of the work, of the polity but at the same time reduces the pressure and saves lot of time of the judiciary thus allowing it to discharge its functions more effectively and well in time.

11. Community colleges should be established at the district panchayt level to train the members of the village or nagar and district panchayats, *Grama-sabhas* and *Nyaya Panchayats* in areas like social, economic, political administrative, legal, cultural, scientific, technological and community developmental projects. The teachers of the Universities, judicial officers, lawyers, legislators, reputed social workers and administrators can be used as resource persons to train the members. The training should be imparted through comprehensive programmes such as, course work, seminars, lectures, field works by using audio-visual methods. This would certainly help the local bodies to furnish humble, fearless and judicious administration.

12. To make the local bodies economically self sufficient the Union and State Governments should allot more funds to them on the basis of contributions made by the skilled labour of these bodies in industrial and urban areas, apart from their regular funding methods. However at the same time, to sustain as viable economic units of themselves, the local bodies have to conduct community oriented programmes to attract people's participation in laying down roads, construction of drainages, bridges and dams within the district. This type of programmes certainly make them self-sufficient economic centres of the country without depending much upon the other agencies of the polity. For example, the people of Darjeeling hill areas could complete the Palamu micro dam project to supply drinking water and to cover the agricultural fields of thirty to fourty villages with the help and direction of some NGOs in a record time of two months with an expenditure of just two lakh rupees. This example clearly suggests that the local bodies can really become viable socio-economic units of the polity if they try to concentrate in utilising the man power of their geographical areas.

Lastly, to strengthen the concept of *Gram-Swaraj* much needs to be done on par with adopting the above suggestions. This can be best achieved only through a reformed polity with decentralisation of power upto the grass roots level, deregulation of bureaucracy, reduction in paper work and the non-interference of the State in the affairs of the local bodies.

If we have any respect towards the concept of *Gram-Swaraj*. we have to rededicate ourselves with true spirit to achieve the ideal of the father of the nation atleast in this golden jubilee year of our polity. The achievement of real panchayati raj or *Gram-Swaraj* is the only befitting tribute to the father of this great nation for his selfless sacrifices than paying tributes every time either to his statue or his samadhi. If India has to progress let us shed the mentality of depending on the government for everything, their self-sufficiency can be achieved only through the system of panchayati raj.

REFERENCES

1. P. Mathur & Narain, eds., "Panchayati Raj, Planning and Democracy" (New Delhi, 1969); Dayal Rajeshwar: Panchayati Raj in India, (Delhi, 1970); Jathar R.V. : Evolution of Panchayati Raj in India (Dharwar, 1964); Marc Galanter : Law and Society in Modern India, (Oxford, 1989) p. 55.

2. Cited in S.R. Nigarm : Local Government, (New Delhi, 1978) p. 216.

3. Vasant Sathe : Democratic Decentralisation Need for Constitutional Reforms" in Reforming the Constitution, Subhash C. Kashyap (edit) (Delhi, 1992) pp. 150-52.

4. T.S. Devadass : Sarvodaya and the Problem of Political Sovereignty (Madras, 1974) p. 28 et. seq 63, 92, 94 et. el; M.K. Gandhi : Rebuilding our Villages, (Ahmedabad, 1952) Upendra Baxi : The little done, the vast undone : Some reflections on reading Gran Ville Austin's 'The Indian Constitution, J. Ind. L. I. Vol. 9, 1967, p. 343.

5. Gran Ville Austin : The Constitution of India; A Corner Stone of A Nation." (Bombay, 1972) pp. 26-49.

6. Balwant Roy Metha Report, 1957 also see: A.T. Philip and K.H. Shivaji Rao, "Indian Government and Politics" (New Delhi, 1982) pp. 207-17.

7. Ashok Mehta Committee Report, 1979; see A.T. Philip and K.H. Shivaji Rao, ibid at pp. 218-219.

8. This act is called as the Constitution (Seventy-Third) Amendment Act, 1992. This act incorporated a new Provision part IX of the Constitution under Article 243. For details see, V.C. Shukla : Constitution of India. (Lucknow, 9th edn., 1954) pp. 615-22.

9. Article 243 (c) (2) : All the seats in a panchayat shall be filled by persons chosen by direct election from territorial constituencies in the panchayat......

10. Subclause (4) : The Chair person of a panchayat and other members of a panchayat whether or not chosen by direct election from territorial constituencies in the panchayat area shall have the right to vote in the meetings of the panchayats.

11. Subclause (5) the chair person of (a) a panchayat at the village level shall be elected in such manner as the legislature of state way, by law. provide.......

12. For the detailed provisions of the Act, see V.C. Shukla : note 8 at pp 623-30.

CHAPTER XVI

Fifty Years of India's Independence and the Tribal Development in India

T.S. Naidu

INTRODUCTION

The tribals are, by and large, children of nature, their life style being conditioned by their ecosystem. At present there are approximately 200 million tribal people, roughly 4 per cent of the global population. They are found in all regions of the world and number among the poorest of the poor India is the largest concentration of tribal people anywhere in the world except perhaps in Africa. According to 1991 census, the population of the scheduled tribes in the country was 67.76 millions, constituting about 8.08 per cent of the total population, approximately one tribesman for every thirteen Indians. Areas inhabited by tribals constitute a significant part of the backward areas of the country. On the whole it is estimated that the predominant tribal areas comprise of about 15 per cent of the total geographical area of the country.

Tribals form the very segment of the weaker sections are with their traditional skills and resources. They are the most vulnerable sections of the population and they are exploited by the most age-old social and cultural handicaps coupled with environmental factors. The age old exploitation and repression of the tribal have cut them off from the mainstream of socio-economic development of the country as a whole. This was the basic point which promoted our constitution makers to provide guarantee for the protection of the interest of the tribals. Articles 14(4), 46, 244(i) and 339 of the Indian constitution speak of special provisions meant for the administration and control of scheduled areas and tribals therein, for their welfare and protection. Based on these constitutional provisions specific policy enunciations for tribal development have been incorporated in the strategy of economic development in our five year Plans.

In India, different tribal groups are living in various degrees of economic backwardness. They live generally in inhospitable terrain where productivity of the soil is low and their hamlets are found in the interior forest areas along with the hill streams. There are no communication facilitates between the various isolated tribal groups, as well as between the tribal and the world at large. Normally they are below the poverty line, because their average daily income has been estimated about Rs.2. Their lands are dry and there are no irrigation facilities. They do not utilise chemical fertilizers, improved seeds, pesticides etc., in their lands. Tribal area agriculture is, therefore somewhat different from other areas mainly on account of the difference in natural topography. And also the typical topography of undulating and hilly areas has made tribal area agriculture less profitable.

TRIBAL SCENE IN INDIA

A tribe is a group comprising families, alone, or generations, having its own customs, occupying a specific geographic territory, and being independent of, or having little contact with, the dominant national society of the country in which they live. However, the level of tribal economy in our country is quite uneven. On the one extreme, there are tribal communities who are at the food-gathering and hunting stage and, at the other extreme, they have become undistinguishable from the modern agricultural and industrial societies. Similarly, differences have arisen in their educational status. Some of these communities, particularly in the North-East are far ahead of the general educational level in the country but, at the other end, there are communities which are still at a pre-literate stage. They are

Table 1 : Growth of Tribal Population in India, 1961-1991 (in Million)

Sl. No.	Year	Total Population	ST Population	Percentage of ST Growth of to total Population	Index Number of Growth of **Total** Population Base Year 1961 = 100	Index Number of Growth of **ST** Population Base Year 1961 = 100
1.	1961	439.24	29.88	6.80	100.00	100.00
2.	1971	548.16	38.02	6.94	124.80	127.24
3.	1981	665.29	51.63	7.76	151.46	172.79
4.	1991	846.30	67.76	8.08	192.67	226.77

Source:

I. Indian Labour Year Book 1989, Labour Bureau, Ministry of Labour, Government of India, Page.213.

2. Census of India 1991, paper 2 of 1992-Final Population Totals-Brief Analysis of Primary Census Abstracts.

scattered along the length and breadth of the country, from the Himalayas to the Indian Ocean and from the Arabian Sea to the Eastern Frontiers. They have been so specified in 25 states and Union Territories except in Haryana, Jammu and Kashmir, Punjab, Chandigarh, Delhi and Pondicherry. Growth of total population and Scheduled Table (ST) Population in India, 1961-1991 is given in Table 1.

The table 1 shows that the total population have increased from 439.24 million in 1961 to 846.30 million in 1991. The ST population have increased from 29.88 million in 1961 to 67.76 million in 1991. The table explains the steady growth of ST population from the year 1961 to 1991. ST population account for 6.80 per cent of the total population in 1961 increase to 8.08 per cent of the total population in 1991. The index number of total population has increased from 100 in 1961 to 192.67 in 1991. The index number of ST population has increased from 100 in 1961 to 226.77 in 1991. The above data reveals that there has been a sharp increase in the total population over time when compared to ST population.

Table 2 shows the male and female ST population in India in 1971 to 1991. In 1971 census male accounts for 50.45 per cent and female accounts for 49.55 per cent. In 1981 census male accounts for 50.44 per cent and female accounts for 49.56 per cent. In 1991 census male accounts for 50.71 per cent and female accounts for 49.29 per cent. The table shows that in all census there is no difference between male and female per centages.

The state-wise concentration of STs in the country according to 1991 census is given in Table 3. The table shows that about 82.69 per cent of the ST population in the country has concentrated in the states Madhya Pradesh (153,99 lakhs), Maharastra (73.18 lakhs), Orissa (70.32 lakhs), Bihar (66.17 lakhs), Gujarat (61.62 lakhs), Rajasthan (54.75 lakhs), Andhra Pradesh (42.00 lakhs) and West Bengal (38.09 lakhs). Among the States, Madhya Pradesh accounted for the highest number of ST representing 23.27 per cent of the state population followed by Orissa representing 22.21 per cent of the state population. However, there are some states in the North-Eastern part of the country where the percentage of ST to the state total population is very high viz., Mizoram (94.78 per

Table 2 : Male and Female ST Population in India 1971 to 1991 (in Million)

Sl. No.	Year	Total Population	Male Population	Percentage of male to Total Population	Female Population	Percentage of female to Total Population.
1.	1971	38.02	19.18	50.45	18.84	49.55
2.	1981	51.63	26.04	50.44	25.59	49.56
3.	1991	67.76	34.36	50.71	33.40	49.29

Table 3 : State-wise Total Population and ST Population in India as per 1991 Census (in Lakhs)

Sl. No.	*States/ Union Territories*	*Total Population*	*Schedule Tribe Population*	*Percentage of ST to Total Population*	*Percentage to Total ST Population*
1	2	3	4	5	6
1.	Andhra Pradesh	665.08	42.00	6.31	6.20
2.	Arunachal Pradesh	8.65	5.50	63.58	0.81
3.	Assam	224.14	28.74	12.82	4.24
4.	Bihar	.863.74	66.17	7.66	4.24
5.	Goa	11.70	N.E	0.03	-
6.	Gujarat	413.10	61.62	14.92	9.09
7.	Haryana	164.64	-	-	-
8.	Himachal Pradesh	51.71	2.18	4.22	0.32
9.	Jammu & Kashmir	N.A	N.A	-	-
10.	Karnataka	449.77	19.16	4.26	2.83
11.	Kerala	290.99	3.21	1.10	0.47

1	2	3	4	5	6
12.	Madhya Pradesh	661.81	153.99	23.27	22.73
13.	Maharastra	789.37	73.18	9.27	10.80
14.	Manipur	18.37	6.32	34.40	0.93
15.	Meghalaya	17.75	15.18	85.52	2.24
16.	Mizoram	6.90	6.54	94.78	0.96
17.	Nagaland	12.10	10.61	87.69	1.57
18.	Orissa	316.60	70.32	22.21	10.32
19.	Punjab	202.82	-	-	-
20.	Rajasthan	440.06	54.75	12.44	8.08
21.	Sikkim	4.06	0.91	22.41	0.13
22.	Tamil Nadu	558.59	5.74	1.03	0.85
23.	Tripura	27.57	8.53	30.94	1.26
24.	Uttar Pradesh	1391.12	2.88	0.21	0.43
25.	West Bengal	680.78	38.09	5.60	5.62

1	2	3	4	5	6
	Union Territories				
1.	Andaman & Nicobar Islands	2.81	0.27	9.61	0.04
2.	Chandigarh	6.42	-	-	-
3.	Dadra & Nagar Haveli	1.38	1.09	78.99	0.16
4.	Daman & Diu	1.02	0.12	11.77	0.02
5.	Delhi	94.21	-	-	-
6.	Lakshadweep	0.52	0.48	92.31	0.07
7.	Pondicherry	8.08	-	-	-
	Total	8385.84	677.58	8.08	

Source : Census of India 1991, Series 1, Paper-I of 1993., Union Primary Census Abstract for Scheduled Castes, and Scheduled Tribes, Page.13.

Note : 1. Excludes figures of Jammu & Kashmir where 1991 census was not taken.

2. NA-Not Available

3. N.E-Negligible

4. Null Population

Table 4 : Occupational Distribution of ST Population in India,1991

Sl. No.	*Particulars*	*Number*	*Percentage to Total*
1	*2*	*3*	*4*
I	**Main workers**	**2,84,75,765**	**42.02**
1.	Cultivators	1,55,20,576 (54.51)	22.90
2.	Agricultural Labourers	93,08,705 (32.69)	13.74
3.	Livestock, forestry, fishing, hunting and plantations, orchards and allied activities	5,74,642 (2.02)	0.85
4.	Mining and quarrying	2,30,754 (0.81)	0.34
5.	Manufacturing, processing, servicing and repairs in household industry	2,97,098 (1.04)	0.44

1	2	3	4
6.	Manufacturing, processing, servicing and repairs in other than household industry	5,64,956 (1.98)	0.83
7.	Constructions	2,37,456 (0.83)	0.35
8.	Trade and commerce	3,39,301 (1.19)	0.50
9.	Transport, storage and communication	2,43,766 (0.86)	0.36
10.	Other services	11,58,511 (4.07)	1.71
II.	**Marginal workers**	**49,31,573**	**7.28**
III.	**Non-workers**	**3,43,51,042**	**50.70**
	Total Population	**6177,58,380**	**100.00**

Source :Census of India 1991, Series-1, Paper-I of 1993, Union Primary Census Abstract for SC and ST.

Note · Figures in parentheses denotes percentage

cent), Nagaland (87.69 per cent), Meghalaya (85.52 per cent) and Arunachal Pradesh (63.58 per cent) though their total population is not large.

Table 4 presents the occupational distribution of ST population in India, 1991. The table reveals that main workers constitute 42.02 per cent of the total ST population in 1991 census. While the non workers constitute 50.70 per cent, Marginal workers account for 7.28 per cent of the total ST population in 1991 census of the main workers cultivators constitute 54.51 per cent and agricultural labourers 32.69 per cent.

TRIBAL DEVELOPMENT APPROACH IN INDIA

During the initial days, the British administrators thought it expedient generally to leave the tribal alone, because the task of administration in the hill areas was difficult and costly. Secondly, it was considered desirable to keep away the tribals from possible political influence from the world outside. Thirdly, some of the British officers genuinely felt that left to themselves the tribal people would remain a happier lot. The Scheduled District Act of 1874 had kept most of these areas administratively separate. The same situation was allowed to continue under the Government of India Acts of 1919 and 1935. However, after independence this policy was abandoned and a new policy of tribal development and integration was initiated. The constitution of India has made definite provisions for the welfare and uplift of the tribal people throughout the country. A number of commissions and committees were appointed in the recent past to look into the problems of development in the tribal areas in the country. The commissions and committees recommended a number of measures to remove the socio-economic imbalances and also to break down the old psychological barrier which existed in the tribal areas. The Dhebar Commission (1961) recommended an integrated approach based on the minimum essential items like food, drinking water, employment, education, health and village roads. The Task Force on Development of Tribal Areas constituted in 1972 suggested that the ecological, occupational and social parameters of the tribal population should be properly assessed for formulation of a policy and its implementation so that a steady flow of benefits could be assured to the tribal people. The Dube Committee in 1972 tried to define a new strategy for tribal development and suggested that the probiem of tribal development should be defined at the national level and national efforts required for tackling it, worked out. It also suggested an integrated area development approach in consonance with the genius and aspirations of the tribal people.

TRIBAL DEVELOPMENT DURING FIVE YEAR PLAN PERIODS IN INDIA

The problem of development of tribal areas is primarily linked with the backwardness of these areas, poverty of the people and the concept of integration of tribals with rest of the population. For promoting the welfare of the scheduled tribes and for raising the level of administration of scheduled and tribal areas to the state level. 'Article 275 of the constitution provides for grants-in-aid from consolidated fund of India to states for implementation of developmental programmes. In addition the above article lays down as a Directive Principle of State Policy that the State should promote, with special care, the educational and economic interests of weaker sections. On the positive socio-economic front, since the era of planned development in the early fifties, the Government of India have adopted several administrative and financial measures from time to time for implementation of the constitutional responsibility and policy formulations.

Thus, special programmes for Tribal Development have been implemented in our country to benefit tribal population under the backward classes sector from the First Five Year Plan onwards. But at the same time, the First Five Year Plan did not pay any specific and special attention towards the development of tribal areas, because only certain piecemeal attempt such as education schemes, welfare schemes etc., were introduced, these schemes have left no concrete impact on tribal community in the country. During the Second Five Year Plan, recognising the gravity of socio-economic conditions prevailing in the tribal areas, concrete developmental schemes were planned and for the first time, a novel administration system was introduced while creating special multipurpose tribal projects in certain selected tribal areas. On the recommendations of the Varrier Elwin Committee, tribal development block system had been implemented under the Third Five Year Plan. This system was evolved not only to improve the conditions in the tribal areas but also to involve the tribal people in the process of development with the aid of Panchayat raj institution. These schemes and sector Plans which were adopted as the instruments of planned development, resulting in toning up of tribal economy and improvement of social service to a certain extent; but it was found that certain regions and groups in tribal areas still remained very backward, while others recorded a slow-rate of progress.

Against the background of the pronouncement of the two study teams of 1959 and 1969 and the SC and ST commission in 1961, the Fourth Five Year Plan document enumerated that the "problem of scheduled tribes living in compact areas is essentially that of economic development of their areas and of integrating their economy with that of the rest of the country. On the eve of commencement of the Fourth Plan, 489 Tribal Development Blocks had come into existence for economic betterment of the Scheduled Tribes and intensive development of areas with large concentration of tribal population. A number of new programmes were also introduced, besides intensifying programmes which were already, popular. Land colonisation schemes were started and several tribal colonies were established. On the other side, co-operative forming societies had been introduced and a number of concessions were offered to the tribal people by forest, excise, revenue departments etc., in their respective fields. The Fourth Five Year Plan, diagnosing the reasons for the failure of earlier Plans' programmes, as lack of uniform distribution of social services and economic facilities and distribution of natural resources, evolved a new strategy to suit the growing needs and requirements in the tribal areas. Finally, it envisaged a District Level Planning as a correct measure to meet the situation. However, even this District Level Planning could not take concrete shape during the Fourth Plan as actual, planning was not done at the grass root level. By the end of this Plan, limitation of sectorial planning with schematic budgets had brought into sharp focus the gearing backwardness of tribal areas compared to the other areas and the difference between the level of development of tribal region and that of the other.

In view of the weakness of the earlier area-based programme, viz., Tribal Development Blocks and Tribal Development Agencies, a new strategy was evolved in the Fifth

Plan to formulate separate Sub-Plan for areas of tribal concentration. This is intended to achieve an intensity of attention to the tribal areas and devise measures to suit their local ethos. About two-third of the tribal population in the country is estimated to be covered by the Sub-Plans as were in operation in the Fifth Plan. In our country the problem of tribal development was broadly classified into two categories (i) areas of tribal concentration and (ii) dispersed tribals. In respect of the former, it was decided to accept an area development approach with focus on tribal. For dispersed tribals, family-oriented programmes were decided to being taken up. The tribal Sub-Plan includes all the scheduled areas and tehsils/blocks with more than 50 per cent tribal population. For operational purpose the tribal Sub-Plan areas have organised 178 Integrated Tribal Development Project during the above Plan. It is the level at which the entire developmental efforts have been integrated. The strategy of tribal Sub-Plan was implemented in 16 states and 2 Union Territories covering about 65 per cent of the Scheduled Tribes (230 lakh) in the country during the above Plan period.

In the Sixth Five Year Plan, it was noticed that certain pockets of tribal Sub-Plan strategy. It was, therefore, decided during the sixth Plan that pockets of contiguous villages/pockets having a minimum of 10,000 tribal population of which at least 50 per cent are Scheduled Tribes should be covered for intensive integrated development on a Modified Area Development Approach (MADA) under the tribal Sub-Plan. The broad approach of tribal Sub-Plan strategy was continued during the Sixth Plan with greater emphasis on raising of productivity levels in production fields of trial activities with a view to enable a targeted number of families to go above the poverty line, development of adequate infrastructure, and human resource and elimination of all forms of exploitation of tribals. A definite target of assisting 50 per cent of the Scheduled Tribe families to cross the poverty line was adopted during the Sixth Plan for the first time. It can be said that by and large the targets set for the Sixth Plan have been achieved. Against the target of 2.70 million Scheduled Tribe families to be brought above the poverty line, it is estimated by the end of 1984-85, 3.46 million Scheduled Tribe families have been assisted.

Under infrastructure of vital importance for tribal development, some conservation measures have been undertaken in respect of 2 lakh hectors. About 9,000 tribal villages have also been electrified and more than 80,000 villages provided with drinking water supply. The state of Sikkim was added during the Sixth Plan period. An important achievement of the Sixth Plan was to identify 245 MADA pockets of tribal concentration during the Plan period. Additional 20 more primitive tribes were also identified. By the end of the fourth year of the Sixth Five Year Plan, 181 of ITDPS, 245 MADA pockets and 72 primitive tribe projects were in operation in the country. The coverage of Scheduled Tribe population during the Plan rose to about 75 per cent of the total tribal population in the country from about 65 percent of such coverage during the Fifth Plan.

TRIBAL DEVELOPMENT UNDER SUB-PLAN

The Tribal Sub-Plan strategy now in its twelth year of operation continues to be the main instrument for tribal development. In the Seventh Plan, the objective remains to be a judicious mix of area-cum-family development, simultaneously paying attention to the vulnerable section amongst the scheduled Tribes and their dwindling resource base mainly on account of environmental devastation. For the Seventh Plan period about 40 lakh scheduled Tribe families below the poverty line are targeted to be provided economic assistance. In the Seventh Plan, 3 new ITDPs have been added in Sikkim by relaxing the scheduled Tribe population concentration norms, as a special case and by the end of 1987-88, a total of 184 ITDPs are functioning. So for the tribal population covered by ITDP areas in 313.21 lakhs. To improve tribal coverage under the tribal Sub-Plan approach, 285 pockets having a minimum of 10,000 population with 50 per cent or more tribal population have identified, covering a total population of 50.53 lakhs. In addition about 75 Primitive Tribes numbering 13 lakhs have been taken up for development through projected approach. In order to ensure cent per cent coverage of tribals under the Tribal Sub-Plan TSP approach, it has been decided since 1986-87 to include dispersed tribals under the approach while identifying their clusters wherever possible. Forty-seven clusters, each with a total population of 5000 with 50 per cent or more tribal concentration there in, have been identified so far. Among the important contributions of the tribal Sub-Plan strategy over a period of years in our country has been the gradual evaluation of the concept of family-oriented programmes for eradication of poverty in the tribal areas.

Recently the Union Government have decided to set up five sub-groups for an in-depth study of various issues involved in the development of the Scheduled Tribes and Scheduled Tribe areas. The sub-groups have been constituted in pursuance of the decision taken in the meeting of the working group in development and Welfare of the Scheduled Tribes during the Eight Five Year Plan.

The first sub-group will review and analyse the TSP strategy and approach adopted during the Seventh Five Year Plan. It will, suggest approach to be adopted during the Eight Five Year Plan with special reference to identification of special thrust areas for raising the quality of life of Scheduled Tribes.

The Second sub-group will be on protective measures implementation of protective legislation including the Fifth Schedule provisions, and credit and marketing. The third sub-group will review economic development programmes for the Scheduled Tribes and infrastructural and human resources development needs of the Scheduled Tribe areas and suggest financial framework for the Eight Plan.

The fourth sub-group will review the administrative structural in ST areas, the planning process and the monitoring and evaluation arrangements for implementation of TSP schemes/ programmes. All the sub-group while analysing the issues allotted to them shall give special attention to the problems of vulnerable groups especially the tribal women.

In Eighth Plan for the Primitive Tribal groups detailed Plans will be prepared for their economic development, as far as possible, with the family as the Unit. Infrastructure and other developmental needs will be specifically identified so that an integrated Plan is developed. Schemes will be developed which take into account the social and economic organisation of life of these communities, their interests, aptitudes and abilities. During the Plan schemes on water-shed basis, in which sectorial programmes like agriculture, forestry, horticulture, infrastructural and social services will be interwoven in an integrated and viable manner to enable the shifting cultivators to take to settled cultivation.

Originally created for meeting the manpower requirement for exploitation and regeneration of forest resources, the forest villages numbering about 5,000, wherein more than 2 lakh tribal people live, have reminded largely deprived of normal developmental benefits. During the Eight Plan an attempt will be made to reach developmental benefits to forest villages in a manner suited to the situation. Arrangements for review, on a regular basis, of the functioning of developmental schemes in forest villages for their all-round development, keeping in tune with environmental requirements, will be made.

Table 5 shows outlay and expenditure for tribal development programmes in India in various Five year Plans. As compared with the First Five Year Plan the total investment made for tribal development programmes has been increased 50 times in the Fifth Plan, 276 times in the Sixth Plan and further increased to 600 times in the Seventh Plan as a result of operation of new strategy on tribal Sub-Plan to improve the quality of living in the tribal belts.

An over whelming majority of tribal communities in our country have been living in remote and exclusive areas in the thick forests, on hill-slopes and generally in areas with poor natural resources. This natural isolation has deprived them of the fruits of scientific and technological advances on the one side and it has led to their distinctive life-styles, cultures and languages on the other side. Broadly speaking, the tribal villages are small in size, less than half or one-third of their villages in the country. Their life is inextricably linked with collection of minor forest produce, since a large part of their land is covered by forests. Yet another feature of the tribal village is its total dependence on agriculture, including forest labour. They cultivate the land by using traditional methods. As a result the output of their land is very low. Besides, the tribal are being exploited by money lenders-cum-traders, who lend money for agricultural and non-agricultural purposes at an exorbitant rate of interest and purchase the minor forest produce and agricultural produce of the tribals at a very low price. In fact this two way exploitation has led to the development of a pernicious social system called bonded labour. Because of this basic weakness found in the tribal economy, different anti-social elements have started their subversive activities in the tribal areas.

Table 5 : Plan outlay and Expenditure for the Development of the Tribes in India (Rs. in crores)

Sl. No.	*Plan Period*	*Total Plan outlay*	*Tribal Development Programme*	*Percentage*
1	2	3	4	5
1	First Plan* (1951-56)	1,960	19.93	1.00
2	Second Plan* (1956-61)	4,672	42.92	0.90
3	Third Plan* (1961-66)	8,577	50.53	0.60
4	Annual Plans* (1966-69)	6,756	32.32	0.50
5	Fourth Plan** (1969-74)	15,902	75.00	0.50
6	Fifth Plan** (1974-79)	39,322	1,182.00	3.01
7	Sixth Plan* (1980-85)	97,500	5,535.00	5.67
8	Seventh Plan** (1985-90)	1,80,000	12,000.00	6.67
9	Eighth Plan** (1992-97)	4,34,100		

Source: Ministry of Home Affairs, Occasional Paper on Tribal Development, 1986, PP.19-24

Note : *Expenditure **Outlay

Inspite of several measures taken in the above Eighth Five Year Plans from the year 1951, the Government was not able to reach the target of tribal development.

REFERENCES

1. Robert Goodland et al, *The tribal peoples and Economic Development,* The international bank for reconstruction and development, New York, May 1982, P.l.

2. Government of India, *Tribal Development-A statistical Profile.* Backward proper on Tribal development No. 12, Ministry of Home Affairs, New Delhi, 1985, P.V.

3. Alexander Verghese V., *Tribals and Sub-Plans Seminar,* Feb,1983, P.33.

4. Khaund T.P., "New strategy for Tribal Development", *Yojana,* Vol XXVI, August 16-31 1982, PP. 35-39.

5. Government of India, Planning Commission, Draft Sixth Five Year Plan 1978-83, New Delhi: Controller of publication, 1979, PP. 303-304.

6. Government of India, *Seventh Five Year Plan (1985-90),* Planning Commission, New Delhi, Vol II, Oct 1985, P.332.

7. Government of India, *Report of the Working Group on Tribal Development during Seventh Plan (1985-90),* Planning Commission, New Delhi, Dec, 1984, P.3.

CHAPTER XVII

Tasks and Challenges in Preparing Lawyers for the 21st Century

N.R. Madhava Menon

Law performs a variety of functions in modern societies. It sets norms for human behaviour and prescribes standards of conduct with a view to maximise peace and happiness for all. It helps to resolve disputes in generally acceptable ways. Finally, it shapes and directs institutions and structures which enable society to function and progress on desired goals.

CHANGING MISSIONS

Given the varied and dynamic functions of law in organizing human relations, it is not surprising that legal education in Free India could not fully comprehend its mission nor develop the strategies in pursuing its goals effectively. Decades ago, we were discussing the goals of legal education. We still continue to debate the issue as the role of law in development assumes varying shades and degrees of emphasis. Depending on the way we articulate the role of law at a given time, our concept of a lawyer is shaped and the agenda for legal education is formulated. In the beginning, the perspective was around dispute settlement and consequently, the lawyer's education was largely vocational, to be learnt in association with other legal practitioners. Later, University education was felt necessary to give the lawyers a knowledge-base essential to understand the social milieu in which disputes arise and to appreciate the limits and limitations of law in social ordering. The thrust was on problem solving and dispute avoidance rather than on litigation and adjudication. The subjects felt necessary to be studied and the skills required to be developed created the need for a new law school with a different mission than before.

In the latter half of the current century emerged the concept of law-in-society or law-in-development where law came to be looked upon as a policy instrument in governance which, in turn, demanded a vastly different curriculum and teaching methods. Most law schools are continuing the search for appropriate technology to accomplish this dynamic role of law in social engineering and social development.

Values of democracy, human rights and rule of law conditioned by historical and cultural factors influenced the shape of legal education in different countries. Language added another dimension in legal development particularly in India, complicating the situation and making tasks of legal educators still more challenging.

GLOBALISATION AND LEGAL DEVELOPMENTS

Before many developing countries could settle with an acceptable legal education agenda, the political and legal map of the world got changed necessitating another look at the whole exercise. Communism has crumbled and together with it, the process of centralised planning and command economy. The World Trade Organization got established and powerful nations have set the agenda for world economic development. Human Rights as perceived by some Western Countries came to be used as a weapon even in trade relations. Corruption came to dominate all aspects of public life in many developing countries. The process of globalisation is inevitably impacting on human relations threatening cultural integrity of peoples and nations.

The twenty-first century is going to be a totally different world than most of us are familiar with during the last fifty years or more. It is difficult even to comprehend the dimensions of change and the demands of the legal profession in the next millennium. Given the prospects for trade in services, we need to produce a world lawyer comfortable with legal systems other than his own. Given the growth of information and communication technology, we must anticipate the changing styles of advocacy and prepare the future lawyers to be proficient in managing all types of information, not just the Statutes and judicial decisions. For the first time in history, the legal profession is under threat of invasion from other professions unless the profession itself changes its nature and methods of delivery of services. To be able to teach intellectual property laws or natural resources laws or to train students in negotiation and business planning, the law school of the future has to go multi-disciplinary and multi-national in its teaching programmes. This is a challenge which law schools in most Asian countries have not addressed themselves as yet!

BASIC ISSUES TO BE RESOLVED

For quite some time issues agitating the minds of legal educators have been how to facilitate access to the profession to all sections of society, improving the quality of instruction at all levels, imparting skills-education including ethics of the profession and providing continuing education to law persons. Several Committees in different countries have come out with recommendations from time to time. In this connection, I venture to suggest few propositions of common concern to most developing countries :

1. What is the best strategy to strengthen professional legal education while promoting instruction in law as a liberal academic discipline?
2. If law schools are to share the burden of professional training, what is the model appropriate in the circumstances obtaining in different countries? What are the skills, law schools can teach and how?
3. Should a period of training in legal practice be required as a pre-requisite for admission to practice? Who should organize this training and what should be its content and methods?

4. What are the available methods for teaching ethical values in legal education? How does one inculcate the justice mission of the legal system in every law student? What is the role of law schools in educating the students about the lawyer's responsibility to perform public services?

5. How does one evaluate the social relevance of legal education? If curriculum is one measure, how does one go about structuring the core content and the optional agenda? How much of social sciences knowledge a law student should have in order to understand law-in-context or law-in-development?

6. What is the appropriate period of the law course and nature of education one would recommend for entry to the law school?

7. Finally, there is the question as to what type of supervisory and monitoring structure professional legal education should develop within the country and outside, in order to ensure the protection of the maximum interests of students of the community, of the profession and of the system of administration of justice?

There is no doubt that a mechanism which enables the participation of the bar, the bench, the academics and the community will be appropriate to develop future professional legal education. At the regional and global levels similar mechanisms should develop if legal education were to serve the cause of world peace, regional stability and development through law.

A critical re-evaluation of our legal education programme both in terms of substantive content and methodology is required. To be able to do this, we have to have a clear vision of our objects, the challenges we face and the alternatives available to us for advancing the cause of professional legal education. The vocational role of law has come to occupy the central concern in curriculum, planning and development. The socratic and clinical methods of teaching have assumed special place in pedagogy at the law school. There has to be bilateral and multi-lateral co-operation in these matters.

Another welcome development is the increased nobility of law students and teachers integrating a wealth of information and experience to mutual advantage. Systems for regulating entry into the profession are being re-assessed and adjusted with a view to facilitate what I call the emergence of a universal lawyer.

As I look to the challenges ahead and the role of legal education in the new millennium, I find certain dilemmas at the individual and collective levels.

The first dilemma relates to the cataclysmic changes - political, economic, social, technological - which are happening all around at such speed making it difficult for conventional law persons to comprehend, much less to manage it. Society in the 21st century will certainly differ dramatically from what we are familiar with today. The legal order will have many gaps and inadequacies which cannot be solved with conventional wisdom. Even the methods of law require change which will necessitate adoption of skills, varied and innovative. The current debate on curriculum reform and skills training may appear trivial in the context of the brave new world unfolding steadily. Law relating to natural resources, international trade, biotechnology, social and economic rights, rights of minorities, women and children, public interest advocacy etc. are likely to dominate the legal agenda. The techniques of negotiation, mediation and arbitration are likely to overtake adjudication as the dominant method of dispute settlement both in domestic matters and in international issues. Other professions and disciplines will have a critical and sometimes, decisive role in legal policy and in dispute settlement. Are we adequately prepared to respond to these changes?

Another dilemma that I see in the horizon is the continued relevance of private practice at the existing level in the future. The forces which knock at our doors today may have implications to the way legal services are organized, the rewards and privileges provided to it, as well as the ethics and social responsibilities expected of the profession. There is a distinct possibility of emergence of a public sector in the legal profession dictating the agenda in legal work of the future. Legal profession will be forced more often and more intensely to examine the justification for its very existence. A lot of public relations exercises will have to be done as a survival strategy. A new species of public interest lawyer has to be projected who imbibe values of a public servant and who share accountability not just to the profession but to the community organizations and the government. The object of the new role is supporting good governance rather than just service to the client to get what he wants through the legal processes. Public service lawyering will have to evolve different norms, standards and practices.

The law schools will have to foresee this development and prepare themselves for the changes ahead.

CHAPTER XVIII

Problems and Prospects of Higher Education in India

V. Natarajan

I

INTRODUCTION

"In a rapidly changing world of today, one thing is certain, yesterdays educational system will not meet today's need and even so the need of tomorrow"

- Indian Education Commission (1964)

PLUS POINTS

Fifty years in the history of a country is not a vast span but in the life of human beings it may be considered roughly equal to a generation. In these 50 years, people of India have experienced the impact of Higher Education through the effects of Science and Technology: People have witnessed from Radio to Tape recorder, TV, VCR; simple mechanical calculator to electronic Note Books; ordinary bulb to new and varied types of neon and other lighting systems. Considerable changes have taken place in the transport and communication system: the coal driven buses have now become high speed multimedia coaches; ordinary phones to cellulars; telex has replaced fax system. World has shrunken into a tiny ball and attempts are made to colonise Moon and mars. The contribution of research and Higher Education through application of Science & Technology is evident. The 21st century is to see many more miracles. So also in the field of Agriculture, there are innumerable milestones and progress. These are some of the positive developments.

PIT FALLS

Despite our developmental efforts, through education and other efforts, there are negative aspects also. The wolf of poverty is still threatening millions of families. Though there may be transisters, tape recorders or even a TV in some of the huts, there are vast majority of people who could not get even their daily bread including educated youths. The poor becomes poorer. The rich becomes richer. The major or sole culprit for such state of affairs of not reaching the targets planned is all pervasive corruption, emanating from socio-political level. The youths are getting frustrated because of the problems of educated unemployment. Naxalite movements are coming up and frighten the society with terrorism and blood shed. The detrimental effects of higher education in this, cannot be denied because, the English system of higher education introduced to recruit clerks, when expanded into gigantic size, it left behind all the ills of educated unemployed. The root causes are lack of quality, relevance, increased number and mania for white collar jobs.

PROBLEMS AND POLICIES

In "Policies of Higher Education in India", A.S. Desai has vividly brought out with statistical analysis, the major problems of Indian Higher Education and the measures taken to solve those problems by UGC. In view of the financial crunch, these measures become inadequate when considered with the mammoth size of the problems.

It is seen that there has been phenomenal growth in the number of institutions, enrolment of students and teachers. The growth indexes clearly indicate this. But the students teacher ratio is varying between 15.14 and 17.51. It is indeed an achievement in quantity. Naturally when quantity increases with high velocity, the quality would go down unless drastic measures are taken to curb the tendency.

Table 1 : Growth of University System in India 1947 to 1994

Year	*Universities (No.)*	*Colleges (No.)*	*Enrolment (lakhs)*	*Teachers (lakhs)*	*Student Teacher Ratio*
1947	25 (100)	700 (100)	1.05 (100)	N.A	
1960-61	49 (196)	1537 (220)	6.45 (614)	N.A	
1970-71	93 (372)	3604 (515)	10.94 (1042)	1.29	8.48
1980-81	123 (492)	4722 (675)	27.52 (2621)	1.88	14.64
1990-91	177 (708)	7121 (1017)	44.25 (4214)	2.64	16.76
1994	214 (856)	8210 (1173)	50.07 (4768)	2.86	17.51

Note : N.A - Not Available. Growth Index is given in brackets

Source : 1947 & 1994 Policies of Higher Education, AIU, 1985, the rest from UGC theme paper, Vice-Chancellor's Conference 1992

Table 2 : Total number of persons who obtained tertiary level Education 1950-1993 (lakhs)

Fields	*Graduate*	%	*Post-Graduate*	%	*Doctorate*	%	*Total*	%
Arts and Humanities	63.93	38	28.62	58	0.55	37	92.50	43
Commerce	36.47	22	5.11	11	0.08	5	41.66	19
Natural Science	34.52	21	6.67	14	0.64	42	41.83	19
Education	18.66	11	5.98	12	0.04	3	24.68	11
Engineering	7.71	5	0.89	2	0.07	5	8.67	4
Medical	3.77	12	1.00	2	0.01	1	4.78	2
Agriculture	2.38	1	0.65	1	0.11	7	3.14	2
Total:	167.44	100	48.32	100	1.50	100	217.26	100

Source : CURIE of BITS Vol. F(l) April 1994 - 25.26 as in AIU Policies of Higher Education, 1995.

The major problem is that 88 percent of the students are graduates and only 9 percent are PGs. The students involved in Research is only 1 percent. In 1991-92 alone, the number of graduates enrolled in Higher Education was 40.62 lakhs. That means, 40 lakhs of youths join institutions of higher education with aspirations or on compulsion, but have great expectations in life. Even among the 4.38 lakhs of post graduates, only a small percentage joins, with real aspiration for pursuit of higher studies and research, while a major percentage joins PG degree just because they do not find jobs and could not decide what to do.

Of late, there has been increasing stress on importance of Primary education and adult education because, compulsory primary education upto 14 years of age is enshrined in the constitution and adult education is required to make the population literate and to understand the socio-economic developmental programmes. It is not the case with higher education. Though the higher education at graduate level has its own plus points, in our economy, it creates more sociological problems rather than benefits due to adverse socio-economic circumstances.

The students are under a controlled educational environment upto Higher secondary level to certain extent. When they reach college level, the parents and teachers lose their grip over majority of them. Further the teenage is the most immature stage; the sudden freedom creates a vacuum in their minds and the students involve in many psychological problems.

There is frequent unrest in the colleges distorting the very purpose for which college education is planned. Further when they do not get job, they get frustrated and become delinquents. This could be reduced to some extent by giving RELEVANT, quality education by dedicated teachers adopting appropriate ET techniques. The mammoth size of the problem could be visualised when we study the accumulated strength of students over decades.

The Birla Institute of Technology and Science (BITS), Pilani, made a study of the total number of persons who obtained higher education from 1950 to 1993. In fact, these figures, in the following table, show the achievement in providing education to the people of India at different levels and professions. It would also indicate how many of them would be seeking employment in the market and get frustrated.

The Table 2 clearly shows the intensity of the problem due to increasing accumulation of the students of higher education. Over the period 1950-1993, the total number of persons comes to 217.26 lakhs out of which, the number of students of general education comes to 175.99 lakhs or nearly 176 lakhs. The Arts and Humanities students alone constitute 92.50 lakhs. Where are we to find jobs for all of them? Every year 20 to 30 lakhs graduates and post graduates are added to this already agonising strength.

Theoretically the best solution would be what Prof. Adiseshia said: Impose a moratorium for 5 years on the expansion of higher education (Dubhashi, P.R. 1995). Politically such logical considerations never work. In one side, the universities are denied adequate funds, on the other side new universities and colleges are opened. Another paradox is that "on the one hand we do not want such a large number of educated unemployed and on the other we have jobs for which suitable candidates are not available" (A.S. Desai 1995). The UGC has introduced Vocational Courses at graduates level. There are conflicting views on this. Some educationists say that they should be given training in required competencies after graduation. Yet another group says that while they learn they should acquire skills and knowledge through vocational orientation/subjects. This may help to certain extent but all the staggering number of graduates cannot be trained in vocational courses. Then, these vocational courses would themselves become irrelevant.

STRATEGIES

The possible strategies to reduce the problems are: (i) Restrict admission to higher education in a phased manner by increasing cut off points for admission for institutionalised education at the same time providing safeguards for the under privileged sections of society including women. For example, if with the existing facility, only 50% could be admitted, it should be boldly done. In Indian Express dt. 22.7.97, there was a news item with caption "Colleges bid good bye to traditional courses". It is stated that now there is a growing concern at the fact that 70000 students graduate from the 304 colleges in Tamil Nadu every year without any job to speak of at the end of it. Prof. Ponnusamy, the then Vice-Chancellor, Madras University stated that 24 job oriented courses have been given affiliation. Naturally according to the theory of survival of the fittest, demand for traditional course admissions will be reduced. (ii) Provide more wider, cheaper, but qualitative distance education for the people aspiring for general education for education sake or for its intrinsic values, apart from career based courses which will not add to educated unemployed. (iii) Based on a survey of job/man power requirements at local/regional/national levels provide community colleges to provide specific courses according to the needs. (iv) Delink degrees for jobs and aptitude tests for specific jobs should be conducted. There should be no room for subjectivity. All the examinations/Viva-voce should be well defined and objective in nature.

FROM FRYING PAN TO FIRE

The unit cost of higher education is the highest and producing unwanted unemployable graduates not only wastes much required scarce resources but also creates problems of frustration even after spending so much on them, leading to multi-faceted sociological problems which need additional expenditure/funds for rectification.

RELEVANCE

In order to improve the relevance of higher education the following suggestions were made in the conference of Executive Heads, held at Delhi as early as January 1991 (P.R. Dubhashi 1991). Some of them still remain valid:

(a) Introduce career oriented new courses

(b) Undertake applied research and research on local problems to solve them

(c) Involve universities in extension activities so that at least the community around the institution of higher education could improve

(d) Provide consultancy service to Industries and Government. Even in Social Science, it could be done

(e) Set up extra-mural centres of education or community college to provide training in all local needs

(f) Bring out the research outcomes to disseminate the ideas for further development

II

EDUCATIONAL MANAGEMENT

GNANAM COMMITTEE

All these ideals could be achieved if and only when effective modern management models are adopted relentlessly in the universities. The Gnanam Committee (1990) with eminent educationists and management experts has given the *magnum opus* analysing thread-bear almost all management problems of the university system. This was discussed in the CABE meeting and the UGC has also accepted substantial portion of the report (A.S. Desai, 1995).

MAJOR SUGGESTIONS

The most salient suggestions of the Committee are:

(a) Develop participatory management system involving dedicated teachers

(b) More involvement of user groups in curriculum development

(c) Increase accountability of all groups of universities

(d) Decentralise responsibilities and authority

(e) Have long range continuous monitoring and evaluation

(f) Use appropriate model of university management (many alternatives have been given)

(g) Introduce assessment of performance of Universities

(h) Have grievance redressal mechanism

(i) Separate the management of affiliating colleges

AUTONOMOUS COLLEGES

The concept of autonomous colleges was introduced to improve quality of colleges by giving academic freedom to them. In spite of help assured in setting up autonomous colleges, the number did not increase due to various reasons. Only a little more than 100 colleges have become autonomous and it is high time the reasons for not coming forward to take autonomy should be studied and remedial measures introduced so that they could frame their own curriculum to meet the needs of society and evaluate their own students.

BETTER MODERN EDUCATIONAL MANAGEMENT

Y.S. Kiranmayi (1981), while studying Management of Higher Education in India reflected:

It is really unfortunate that though universities are the places where good research has been going on various aspect of management of profit and non-profit organisation, no effort has been made by the administration of university to take advantage of fruits of these research bodies. "Universities preach modern management but do not practice."

The managerial pattern of a university system must necessarily have an in-built flexibility to adopt itself to the changing needs of the country and region it serves and to carry out innovation (Gnanam Committee report). Of late, the concept of TQM is applied for Higher Education.

UNESCO STUDIES

The IIEP, UNESCO has brought out an excellent book based on research on Innovations in University Management (B.C. Sanyal, 1995). It analyses the experiments tried in various developing countries and provides suggestion for improvement in management.

It mainly covers (a) Financial Management (b) Academic staff management (c) Management of research (d) Management of space and (e) Educational delivery system.

In taking stock of the university educational system it states: "A Combination of bureaucratization, unionisation and traditional forms of protection such as tenure and academic freedom have combined to insulate them from the need to adopt.

The academic freedom here refers to pseudo-academic freedom which is used as excuse for not doing the duties and responsibilities.

It also observes "Government intervention is needed because higher education system may, if left to themselves, change too slowly to serve society's broader needs (p.29).

REASONS FOR PROBLEMS

The major reasons for problems in higher education are:

(a) Lack of proper planning, taking into account financial implications. Each and every suggestion involves costs.

(b) Absence of effective internal information system for taking correct managerial decisions.

(c) Absence of financial control system.

(d) Absence of effective mechanism for self evaluation to detect problems by senior staff.

Integrated Management

In order to solve such problems, it suggests: A multiple level integrated management, involving Government, Universities, University executives and Faculty can be quicker to change them than the one which locates decision-making at mainly one level (p.298).

Measures to improve the university management is discussed in detail in this book. The role of Government in formulating suitable and specific policies is stressed. Examples:

U.K: Departments were penalised for low submission rate as percentage of Ph.D. students.

Australia: Published over 50 indicators of performance.

U.K: Published more than 70 indicators of performance.

The role of institutions in proper planning, implementation and evaluation is also explained in detail.

It finally concludes "There must be will to change and the will to adopt to the needs and provision set down in national plans and institution's missions" (p.312).

III

HUMAN RESOURCES MANAGEMENT

So far, some of the general problems have been discussed. Now a few specific problems are analysed.

Human Resources management is the most critical problem throughout the world. Because of political indiscipline, organisations are influenced and there is growing indiscipline everywhere. Dedication and devotion are becoming rare commodities. Since 50 to 60% of the expenditure is on Salaries, Productivity of the university depends on efficient Human Resource Management. There should be measures for controlling work load norms and quality, at the same time providing better emoluments for keeping their status high in society.

PIVOTAL ROLE OF TEACHER

The efficiency and effectiveness of the University mainly depends on the Teachers who form the fulcrum of the entire system. Dr. S. Radhakrishnan said:

"A Good Teacher must know how to arouse the interest of pupil in the field of study for which he is responsible; he must himself be a master in the field and be in touch with the latest developments in this subject, he must himself be a fellow traveller in the exciting pursuit of knowledge".

Teachers' job is such a difficult one and that is why provision for vacation and sabbatical leave, etc. has been given to prepare and equip themselves abreast of time. But, these holidays are sometimes not properly used for academic pursuits.

R.N. Sethunarayanan (1989) while analysing the role and functioning of teachers' organisation in Higher education said, "It should not be forgotten that it is one of the noblest professions. Therefore those who are in charge of teaching must be prepared for some sacrifice. A spirit of devotion is required of all the teachers".

SELF ASSESSMENT EDUCATION

J.N. Kapur (1995) in his article on "Quality of Higher Education" has evolved criteria for measuring quality of learning, quality of teaching, quality of administration, quality of department, etc. A.K. Srivastav and T.B. Singh (1996) have enumerated the criteria for evaluation, teaching, research and extension work in their article on "Performance Appraisal of the Faculty". The UGC has developed a self appraisal report for the self assessment of teachers. The UGC has created the NAAC (National Assessment and Accreditation Council) as an autonomous body to evaluate universities and institutions of higher education. They expect students evaluation of teachers and peer evaluation. Such evaluations become the necessity of mass higher education system for applying systematic management policies. In the initial stage, it will have some adjustment problems but it will remain as the universities are accountable to the Society and Government. If universities are not taking such measures, a day will come when the students and the public would question the quality of education.

THE FOUR WHEELS

Dedication to work is also applicable to students, non-teaching staff and officers. The collaboration and coordination in creating cohesion in the university system by these four units, Faculty, Students, Staff and Officers are essential for the success of the University. These four human resources are like the wheels of a vehicle. The vehicle of University could move well only when the four wheels - the major four human elements in the system cooperate and work. The codes of conduct are like brakes which should be applied when something goes wrong. The Vice-Chancellor has to provide, as the leader of the system, the drive for effective movement. If all the four wheels move in different directions, there will be utter confusion and chaos resulting in educational accident, killing the very spirit of development of society.

IV

FINANCIAL MANAGEMENT INVESTMENT & PRODUCTIVITY

Baron W. Hansford said, "Education is an investment rather than a cost; it is a mortgage payment rather than rent. It is a matter not of how much cost we can afford, but of how much we are willing to invest in the future lives of our children". In consonance with this concept, efforts have been taken to improve the inputs of investment on education.

The total expenditure increased from Rs. 1140 million in 1950-51 to Rs. 87540 millions in 1986-87. The per capita expenditure shot up from Rs. 3.16 to Rs.112.77. As a percentage of the NNP it rose from 1.3 to 3.8 in the same period (A.N. Agarwal, et. al, 1989). The investment on plan funds also increased in absolute figures but decreased in percentage to the total investment on plan schemes from 7.6 in I Plan to 2.6 in the VI Plan (M.M. Sharma, 1992). The percentage of plan allocation to University Education out of total plan funds for education was 9 in I Plan and 25 in IV Plan and 8 in VIII Plan (Department of Education, MHRD, 1994).

NEED FOR FINANCIAL MANAGEMENT

This analysis shows that there is growing concern to invest more on education but due to conflicting demands/priorities, Higher Education is not able to get adequate funds as it used to get in the beginning. Hence, there is urgent need to improve the effectiveness and efficiency of the system. In other words, the system should fulfil its objectives and should improve its output for a particular level of input. This becomes imperative because the unit costs of Higher Education are higher and rates of return are lower. "Today the country is almost spending on education whatever it can afford to spend. If we are not getting all that we get out of this outlay on education, an important explanation lies in whether we are making wise and productive use of what we invest in education" (Amrit Singh & G.D. Sharma, 1981). This would be possible, if and only if, the Higher/University education system adopts/adapts the principles and procedures of modern management of men, machines, materials and money. The university system spends all top level managers from its portals but it is not adopting these principles and procedures. If the individual institutions apply some of the modern management techniques and strategies discussed here, the Higher Education System could improve.

SOURCES AND USES OF FUNDS

First of all, the financial data available in Universities should be converted as Management Information System (MIS) for application of Management Accounting Techniques. An analysis of the sources of income and uses of expenditure would throw very useful information for FM.

A software to analyse the source of income and the expenditure pattern in Universities would be useful in examining the trends of income and expenditure over a period. 80 to 90 per cent of income to the University is from Government and the University's receipt through fees and other sources are falling down. The MHRD should direct UGC/AIU to study the expenditure structure to arrive at unit student expenditure at least once in five years and this should be the basis to formulate national level policy on fee structure. Though any amount of increase in fee may not match with expenditure, it should be periodically increased at least to reduce the increasing burden on Universities, of course, with built-in facility for fellowship/scholarships to deserving poor students.

In the case of new Universities, proper care should be taken to invest money on building, books, equipment on a rational basis so that there is no lopsided development. The principles of Capital Budgeting can be applied here. Further, in the initial stages, the allocation for equipment should be on a lumpsum basis as otherwise, funds for purchase of costly equipment would not be available.

BALANCE SHEET ANALYSIS

Analysis of balance sheet in all possible ways horizontal, vertical, common size statement and ratios would open up new vistas towards better Financial Management (FM). In fact, a method of making Funds Flow Analysis and finding current ratios has been attempted by the author (V. Natarajan 1995) and it is useful in indicating how the working capital could be better managed. This analysis has been made for the first time and it could be refined and improved by further studies.

UNIT DEPARTMENT EXPENDITURE

Another significant area of study is Departmental Expenditure. Per student Departmental Expenditure (PSDE) takes care of the student-teacher ratio and a detailed analysis of PSDE would reveal the departments which require Financial Management Control. Apart from finding the variances from the university mean PSDE, the PSDE for different groups-Humanities, Social Sciences and Sciences-can be determined using standard costing Techniques taking into consideration standard Students Teacher Ratio and standard inputs for ideal academic output. If the PSDE is higher, efforts to bring it down by attracting more students by diversification, etc. can be tried. Developing a software for analysing various indicators relating to Departmental Expenditure will be immensely useful in introducing Financial Management Reforms. It would be possible to make inter-university comparison of unit expenditure of related departments and groups.

RATIO ANALYSIS AND INTER-UNIVERSITY COMPARISON

Modern Management Accounting makes profuse use of Ratio Analysis and Inter-firm comparison. The latin word Ratio stands for reasons and indicates the relation on the proportion of one thing to another and accounting ratios have been developed to diagnose and study the effectiveness of organisations. In Universities such ratios are not used in the FM system and the author has evolved a package of ratios (V. Natarajan 1995) which could be applied on the four parts of accounts and Balance sheet. These ratios package is useful in diagnosing the areas of weaknesses in the University and to suggest remedial measures.

In fact, these ratios could be further refined and improved to include more deeper analyses, if adequate data are available at micro-level. Moreover, the accounts of Universities could be brought under uniform accounting system by a "National Level Committee" so that the accounts can be used for Inter-University comparison, which would reveal a plethora of details for introducing FM reforms in Universities. Another way of making inter-university comparison is through average value of accumulation of assets. Either the values of Assets should be based on market value or it should be deflated for price index so that the comparison could be better. Yet another way is to find the ratios of these average values which could avoid the absolute values.

INVESTMENT STRATEGIES

By quarterly analysis of funds availability, the investment in short term and long term deposits could be planned to increase income from interests.

JUSTICE PUNNAYYA COMMITTEE

With a view to streamline the process of funding institution of higher education, UGC constituted a Committee (1992-93) under the Chairmanship of Justice Dr. K. Punnayya. After making detailed analysis and discussions with various officials and faculty, it gave 71 recommendations in its report. It was on the basis of this report that universities were given freedom to use resources generated by them instead of deducting it from the UGC sanction. The matching grant of 25% was also allowed for the resources generated.

UNIT COSTS

This Committee recommended that the maintenance grant should be based on unit cost from IX Plan. Later Prof. Pylee Committee was constituted and model unit costs for sample universities were worked out. But the concept of unit costs for application for working out grants is a complicated one and so there should be detailed working of unit costs for different departments. Services of qualified Cost accountants connected with higher education could be utilised as consultants. These unit costs now worked out are actual costs. First of all, a standard situation of staff, contingencies, equipment, etc. required for teaching UG/PG/M.Phil/Ph.D courses should be finalised and then unit cost should be worked out for keeping it as a standard yardstick for sanction of grants. Different levels of teachers should form committees and evolve details of standard requirements which are neither prohibitively exorbitant nor too low for providing normal quality education. Without making such elaborate efforts, attempts to introduce unit costs would result in confusion.

Alternatively, another simple method is possible; just as cost of living index, once in a year or a period, the average actual cost for different levels/disciplines could be worked out by computerising the data bases and then the average actual cost may be used as Yardstick. Those Universities which are using more than the average, have to be warned to reduce their expenditure and improve their efficiency by proper control, in a phased manner. Those universities which are using less than the national/regional average may be encouraged with additional grants based on the average so that they could improve their effectiveness and facilities.

V

SPACE MANAGEMENT

OPTIMAL USE

Among the infrastructural facilities space is the most crucial one. In these days of increasing costs of land and building, in order to improve the efficiency of the university system, optimal space utilisation is essential. Wasting space for dumping unnecessary materials without disposing them by adopting proper procedures, would result in increasing unit cost indirectly.

The IIEP, UNESCO has evolved elaborate procedures for better space management. The MHRD/UGC should come out with specific norms for provision of space, for teachers, supporting staff, classes, labs and it should be strictly adhered to.

By computerising time tables of classes, the class rooms and labs could be optimally utilised. It is also stated that there is a tendency among the departments to use only the forenoon slots/periods for teaching and leave the class rooms unused in the afternoon. This creates pseudo-scarcity of class rooms leading to unnecessary conflicts.

OPPORTUNITY COST

The careless use of space, if any, could be rectified if along with the actual departmental expenditure, a nominal rent based on area assigned to the departments is charged before ascertaining unit costs of departments/sections for comparison.

When central facilities like computer centre is used, there is a practice in foreign countries to charge the concerned departments the unit expenditure according to the number of hours used by the staff/student. As otherwise some persons may use it for non-academic wasteful purposes and there will be no control over them.

ALTERNATIVE USE

Alternative uses for labs, common rooms and other facilities can be planned by the HOD's of the departments in a particular building, on mutually agreed terms. In fact there is no need for administration to interfere in space problems, if the teachers/users discuss and solve the issues among themselves in periodic staff meeting at inter-departmental level.

VI

EPILOGUE

GLOBALISATION

Liberalisation and globalisation is the trend in all fields and Indian Higher Education system should also be prepared for this. Australia conducts admission campaign in India. Large number of students from India pursue education in State's, like UK, etc. Hence our education should become qualitative and competitive to retain them here and to attract foreign students.

It is unfortunate that apart from globalisation of positive programmes, negative activities are now-a-days globalised. Everywhere there is political indiscipline which leads to indiscipline in Government departments/Offices and institutions.

It is a vicious circle, each passing on the bug to others. Everyone is pointing out to the defects of the other. People do not look into the pillars in their eyes but only say the other person is having a dust in his eyes. Such trends could be reversed only when every individual introspects and corrects himself for the sake of the institution and country.

BINDING FACTOR

In those days India was able to get freedom because of the sacrifice of the freedom fighters and the integrated patriotism of people. Now, there is no such integrating emotion among the people. Every one is trying to exploit as much as possible and ultimately no scheme, plan or target works: all remain in papers. Public properties like Buses, buildings are burnt. *'Bandh'* for anything and everything, paralyses development.

Japan, which was almost annihilated into dust during world war, could become a tiny but gigantic competitor with developed countries because, the people have integrated patriotism and attachment for their country's uplift. They strike by producing more.

HUMAN WEALTH OR WASTE?

In India we are having precious human resources next to China but, all of them are not used in productive efforts. If a master plan is worked out for effective and productive utilisation of all human resources of India, it could compete with any other country.

ROLE OF EDUCATION & TEACHER

Who could do this miracle? Who could make a beginning to set right chaotic Indian conditions? Here the role of education is significant and that is why Nehru said, "If Universities discharge their duties adequately then it is well with the nation and the people". The next logical step is that, "If Teachers at all levels discharge their duties well, then it is well with the nation and people", because, the teaching profession is unique in character and they form the educated cream of any society or community. If they along with students, determine to introduce positive reforms, the country will prosper well in all fields. From good old days, teachers have been kept in exalted status as guru, therefore, they could command the entire society by their silver tongue and dedicated service.

An advocate has to tell lies for winning his case. A doctor has to move with diseased patients to serve them. An Engineer has to live with machines and materials. There could be dichotomy in their personality. They may preach one thing, advocate one thing and do just opposite to that; it will not affect them or the society but if a teacher teaches one and does differently, it would be keenly observed by students A teacher has to be a model worthy of emulation by students and society because, "the destiny of India is shaped in her classrooms".

TRIPLET FOR PROGRESS

In this year of completion of 50 years of independence, the general thrust of concomitant teaching/learning or mission would be to make the students, community and nation, 'conscientious'. Everybody is conscious of their welfare by any means but "Conscience" is dormant and dumped into dust. Especially the spirit of patriotism in the broader sense of working for society and nation with all related good quality and tolerance for caste, creed, colour and religion, are required at personal level 'to build a strong, integrated, cohesive India, which will not waste its energy in clashes but can contribute for development. From foreigners the educated people are adopting many qualities: dressing, having parties, clubs, etc. but do not follow the quality of punctuality. At the organisational level, discipline should be the watch ward. If the discipline of punctuality is inculcated, all other good qualities would follow.

From the epoch making day of 15th August 1997, Let us take a vow to make India a better Bharath by contributing our best in education.

John W. Garolner said : "An excellent plumber is infinitely more admirable than an incompetent philosopher. The society which scorns excellence in plumbing because it is a humble activity and tolerates shoddiness in philosophy because it is an exalted activity will have neither good plumbing nor good philosophy. Neither its pipes nor its theories will hold water".

REFERENCES

Agarwal, A.N., et.al., *INDIA, Economic Year Book 1989-90,* National Publishing House, New Delhi, 1989.

Amrit Singh and Sharma, G.D., (eds), *University and College Finances,* AIU, New Delhi 1981.

Department of Education, Government of India Educational Statistics *University News* 32/29, New Delhi, 1994.

Desai, A.S., Policies in Higher Education in India, AIU, 1995.

Dubhashi, P.R., Conference of Executive Heads of Commonwealth Universities, *University News*, March 11, 1991.

Gnanam, A. (Chairman) Report: *Towards New Educational Management*, UGC, New Delhi, 1990.

Kapur, J.N., Quality in Higher Education, Measurement and Assurance, *University News*, March 13, 1995.

Kiranmayi, Y.S., *Management of Higher Education* in India, New Delhi, Crown, 1989.

Natarajan, V., *Financial Management Techniques for Universities*, VIKAS, New Delhi, 1995.

Punnayya, Justice Dr. K., *UGC Funding of Institutions of Higher Education*, UGC, 1993.

Sanyal, B.C., Innovations in University Management, IIEP, UNESCO, 1995.

Sethunarayanan, R., The Role and Functioning of Teachers Organisations in Higher Education, *University News*, Vol. XXVII, 1989.

Sharma, M.M. *Financial Management of Universities* in India, Concept Publishing Company, New Delhi, 1992.

Srivastav, A.K. and Singh, T.B., Performance Appraisal of the faculty, *University News*, Nov. 11, 1996.

CHAPTER XIX

Working of the Constitution : Model for a Re-Formed Polity

Subhash K. Kashyap

The fulfilment of the 'tryst with destiny' and achievement of independence on the 14-15 August 1947 midnight was for India the beginning of a long and arduous journey. We had to choose for ourselves a political system that suited our history, ethos, genius and needs. We had to draft and adopt a Constitution for independent India. Above all, we had to build a united and prosperous India and an integrated nation from a highly heterogeneous, widely segmented and fragmented society with many linguistic, regional, religious and other pressures pulling in different directions and a backward, badly battered and exploited colonial economy with abject poverty and vast illiteracy among the people.

We began well. We were fortunate in having a galaxy of patriotic leaders of great calibre, competence and commitment during the early years of the operation of the Constitution. With a view to removing dismal poverty, rampant illiteracy and backwardness, emphasis was laid on planned development. Under successive five year plans, efforts were made to ameliorate the lot of the poor and the downtrodden, build a scientific and technological infrastructure, revolutionise agriculture, diversify manufacture and raise industrial capacity and output. Abolition of Zamindari and other land reforms, liberation of Portuguese and French possessions in India, development of a meaningful foreign policy with cardinal principles of non-alignment and peaceful coexistence with over 100 nations at one time accepting India's philosophy and leadership, conducting of general elections in the largest democracy an earth and peaceful transfer of power more than once from one party to another and surviving many pressures, stresses and strains inflicted on the body politic by malevolent forces, both external and internal, were significant achievements.

Without going into the details, it could be safely asserted that on the political plane, the most remarkable achievements were (i) to bring about and maintain the unity and integrity of the nation and the secular character of the polity, and (ii) to preserve the system of representative parliamentary democracy, ensuring the freedom and dignity of the individual. When we see all around us, these achievements appear still greater since there are very few nations in the world, where really functioning democracy and freedom have survived. We can take legitimate pride in the fact that sonic temporary aberrations notwithstanding, despite very difficult and turbulent times, we were able to work a fully democratic Constitution in such a large populous country with all its variety and diversity for so long and, whatever problems we faced, were sought to be solved within the framework of the existing system without its breaking down, getting abrogated or taken over.

Nevertheless, there is a negative side also. We are passing through very critical times. When we look around, the maladies and ailments that afflict the nation are many. Enough has been written and talked about the constitutional crises after crises faced by us. It is hardly necessary to focus on corruption, castcism, communalism, criminalisation of politics etc. which the present system has generated or strengthened. It is also well-known that during the last decades, it has not succeeded in fulfilling the dreams of the founding fathers in the matter of removing poverty, illiteracy, backwardness or even providing drinking water to all the people.

During the last few years, it has come to be clearly recognised that the present model of our republic has failed to meet the hopes, aspirations and requirements of the people and that a fresh look at our Constitution and political system is called for. The case for some fundamental systemic changes is unassailable. Piecemeal reforms or patchwork solutions will not do. We may have to go in for a new model of polity and a second republic, more in tune with our needs and character.

The latest developments in India affecting the economy of the nation underline the need for greater responsibility and accountability of the political Executive and the administrators to the people through the representative institutions. On the-other hand, the spectacle of several successive hung Parliaments and State Legislatures and minority Governments and frequent General Elections naturally cause grave concern for stability.

While quite understandably the chief concern of the politicians in power is always somehow to retain power and to work for ways to ensure greater stability, in a democracy stability alone is not enough nor is it the highest value. The need for emphasis on ministerial responsibility has become more imperative in the dismal political scenario of today when respect for Ministers and politicians in power has been badly eroded with scams after scams being exposed and with allegations of corruption and crimes of all kinds-forgery, cheating, bribery, conspiracy and the like-being levelled against senior leaders who only till yesterday occupied the highest positions as Cabinet Ministers and as the Prime Minister. Even responsibility to Parliament has ceased to have much meaning in a situation where no party commands a clear majority. The two largest parties in Lok Sabha with the best and the second best mandate from the people are outside the Government and some 13 or 14 small parties stay together to share the fruits of power and form a minority Coalition Government. One of the large parties continues to support it from outside for reasons of its own weaknesses or failings of its leaders. And, for the same reasons keeps now and then threatening withdrawal of support.

The new breed of the so-called representatives of the people have lost their representative credentials and respect and trust of the people. Therefore, we need new mechanisms and devices for ensuring and enforcing responsibility of Ministers and Members of Parliament to the people at large. The hard operative reality of our polity today is that it is no more representative or parliamentary or even a democracy.

While we would not like to dilute the element of responsibility, all are agreed that the country can ill-afford frequent general elections which apart from other implications, cost colossal amounts of money. The choice before us, therefore, is to find ways and means of ensuring greater stability within the parliamentary system. Of the various concrete suggestions that have been made from time to time, the following seem to need consideration:

(i) Country may be divided into 4 or 5 zones and 40 to 50 small States of almost equal size with nearly equal representation in Parliament. Combined with strong zonal councils, this would lead to greater stability, more accountability, stronger Union and better administered and more developed or fast-developing States.

(ii) There is every case for a wholesale review of Union-State relations and decentralization of political power in a four-tier system of governance down to the lowest grassroots levels. With a large number of smaller States and a four-tier system of governance, it may be possible to, involve various groups in governance more closely and this may make the Union stronger and the nation more integrated emotionally and culturally. Distribution of powers should be so designed that only the most essential or minimum necessary powers are assigned to each higher level. For example, whatever can be done by the local grassroots institutions like the Village Panchayats or Municipalities, should be left entirely in their hands. Government at a higher tier should have no power to remove or supersede a duly elected Government at a lower tier. This would ensure greater stability and responsibility at every level.

(iii) Direct elections on the basis of adult franchise should be confined only to Panchayats and local bodies with all the other bodies like State Legislatures, Union Parliament, President etc. being indirectly elected. The Panchayats could elect the Zila Parishad or the like, the Zila Parishads could elect the State Legislatures. The State Legislatures, Zila Parishads and Panchayats could elect the Union Parliament and all four-Panchayats, Zila Parishads, State Legislatures and Union Parliament-could elect the President.

The President of the Republic should be elected for one fixed 5 or 6 year term. In order to be elected President, a candidate must secure more than 50 per cent of the total votes cast and a positive vote from majority of the States and the lower tiers.

The lowest unit at the grassroots should be considered as a multimember constituency. Besides, it could be laid down that in order to be declared a winner, a candidate must secure a minimum of 50 per cent plus votes so that it became necessary for every winning candidate to woo more than his caste, community or narrow group vote bank and seek a wider consensus. The representative credentials of those winning under this system would be above reproach.

(iv) To prevent continued horse-trading and the game of toppling Governments, we could adopt the German practice of a constructive vote of no-confidence in the Council of Ministers. This would make it essential for the House to select a successor simultaneously with the throwing out of the incumbent Prime Minister/Chief Minister.

(v) If no party or pre-election coalition of parties secures an absolute majority of seats in Lok Sabha or in any one of the State Legislative Assemblies and the largest party is not able to provide a stable Government, the President or the Governor, as the case may be, should ask the House to elect its leader. The person so elected may be appointed the Prime Minister/Chief Minister.

(vi) Number of political parties should be restricted by law. Political parties participating in the democratic processes of a nation's governance must themselves be democratic in their internal organisations. They need to be regulated and disciplined by law. Party membership must be open to all citizens without any distinction, party elections must be regular, free and fair. Sources of party funds should be declared and party accounts must be duly audited and open to the public.

(vii) There should be a strict ceiling on the number of ministers- or equivalent posts-both at the Union and State levels.

(viii) Inasmuch as professional politicians have proved to be a menace, membership of Legislature or any other public office should not become a life-long whole-time profession for anyone and no one should be allowed more than two terms. Basic educational and other qualifications should be laid down for contesting election to various offices. Persons with criminal antecedents should not be allowed to contest any election. First conviction should be enough to indicate criminal antecedents.

Every holder of public office should compulsorily make an annual declaration of his assets. No defector or person with criminal antecedents should be allowed to remain a legislator or to occupy any public or party office.

(ix) Gun trotting Personal Security officers on roads and at public functions and guards at residences at public expense have become a special perk and a status symbol in social life. Literally, hundreds of millions are being spent on safeguarding the public men-leaders and representatives of the people-from the people. Public life may have its hazards but then those who feel their lives threatened are free to return to private life instead of becoming a drain on the public exchequer. Public functionaries so secured and removed far away from the people, cannot be expected to remain responsible to the people or responsive to their woes.

(x) Financial costs of parliamentary democracy have been skyrocketing. During the-last four decades they have gone up by more than 100 times. Also, the figures of costs e.g. on Parliament are not realistic inasmuch as much of the expenditure gets reflected under other heads.

A matter often raised is that of the salaries, allowances, amenities, facilities etc., extended to Members. While for some entering Parliament involves financial sacrifice, for many others it provides much sought for rewards and benefits. There are two extreme views on whether Members are heavily pampered and overpaid or they are misunderstood and grossly underpaid. According to one guess, if every member is paid Rs. 100,000 per month-in cash and all perks and direct and indirect financial benefits from the State are withdrawn, the public exchequer would be a gainers.

(xi) Unlike U.K., in India, the Constitution and the laws place no limits on the borrowing powers of the Executive. Even parliamentary approval for any amount of internal or external borrowings as such is not required except that it is part of the budget. This is a significant lacuna and must be plugged. For public borrowing is a charge on the future generations and must be duly controlled. Beyond certain prescribed limits, borrowing proposals should also be subjected to scrutiny by parliamentary committees and a positive vote of the Houses of Parliament.

(xii) The fundamental constitutional directives like the right to a decent living, the right to education and the right to work must be made legally enforceable fundamental rights under the reformed Constitution.

(xiii) It has become a fashion to blame the politicians for all that ails the nation, little is done to educate the citizens in the matter of their own citizenship obligations in a representative, participatory democratic polity. In a democracy, the citizens arc both the rulers and the ruled. The ultimate responsibility is, therefore, theirs.

Lastly, it may need iteration that much needs to be done, a re-formed or new model of polity and national renaissance and regeneration have become categorical imperatives and as the Mother said, the process had to begin with re-forming the Constitution. There is no case or cause for despair. We, as a nation have every reason to have full faith in our future. For, as Sri Aurobindo prophesied, only India could provide the vision that the world needs.

REFERENCES

Subhash C. Kashyap, *Our Constitution - An Introduction to India's Constitution and Constitutional Law*, N.B.T., New Delhi, 1994, Chapter 24, pp. 277-283.

———, 'Reforming Parliamentary Polity' in Ajit M. Banerjee and K.A. Chandrasekaran, *Renewing Governance*, Tata Mc Graw Hill, New Delhi 1996, Chapter 15, pp 277-304.

———, (ed.), *Reforming the Constitution*, UBSPD, New Delhi, 1992, Chapter 1, pp3-33.

———, *Perspective on the Constitution*, UBSPD, New Delhi, 1992, Chapter 3, pp.24-30.

———, *Crime and Corruption to Good Governance*, Uppal, New Delhi, 1997, Chapter 1, pp.1-14.

———, *Basic Constitutional Values*, Ajanta, Delhi, 1994, Chapter I, pp.1-21.

———, Nation and Polity Under Strain, Uppal, New Delhi, 1996, Chapter I, pp.1-20.

CHAPTER XX

A Plea for French Model

B. Krishnamurthy

On achieving independence from the British colonial yoke in 1947, the political leaders of the nascent Indian Union and the constitutional pandits decided to adopt the Westminister model of Parliamentary democratic government, of course slightly modified to serve the Indian needs. Soon, it was felt that this system has failed to deliver goods and there was an attempt to attribute all the ills of the Indian polity to the Parliamentary from of government. That led to a discussion on switch-over to the Presidential form of government modelled on the United States of America or Switzerland.

While leaders like Nehru spoke in favour of the existing Parliamentary model, others like Indira Gandhi, who felt that the present system had not given them enough leverage to govern the country as they felt fit, too time and again advocated structural and functional changes in the Constitutional framework. At this juncture, discussion was initiated as to whether the French system of 'Presidentialism', which is also known as 'mixed system', since it is both Presidential and Parliamentary at the same time, could be regarded as worthwhile for adoption.[1]

However, the Congress government and party soon backtracked on the proposed constitutional changes and Mrs. Gandhi ruled out the changeover from the existing system and made it clear that in her view neither the spirit nor the essential character of the constitution could change. It was pointed out that

Presidential system by itself could not be the panacea for all the ills of the Indian polity.

Even the Swaran Singh Committee which was appointed by the Congress President in April 1976 to suggest changes in the Constitution, declined to recommend any changeover to the Presidenatial system and maintained that the existing system is best suited to preserve the unity and integrity of the country. Still, the Indian politicians, especially of the opposition hue, used to talk about the shiftover to the Presidential system of government and this continues to date without any follow up action of any consequence.[2]

Now, India is celebrating the golden jubilee year of its independence. It is time to look back, to analyse what has happened in the Indian political scenario for the last fifty years and to take stock of the situation. Any impartial observer may accept without any hesitation that in World's largest democracy all is not well. India, which Professor Galbraith had long ago described as a 'functional anarchy', not only continued to be an 'anarchy but also has now become 'non-functional'.[3] This calls for a critical examination to find out what went wrong with the Indian polity and what sort of remedial measures may be taken to set it right.

The most striking feature of the present day Indian polity is its chronic instability. While the Congress Party could offer a semblance of political stability till 1990, other parties, whenever they got an opportunity to rule failed miserably and were unable to complete their full term in office. During V.P. Singh's tenure, the French news papers like *Le Monde* never used to mention the Indian Prime Minister by name and the explanation given was that they were not quite sure of his continuance in office for considerable time and then, why to tax the memory of their readers?

Narasimha Rao was hailed as Chanakya by some quarters for his achievement of entrenching himself in office by hook or by crook for full five years, in spite of the minority nature of his government. However, its scandalous existence has in no way done credit to Indian polity.

The general election of 1996 had thrown up a hung parliament and the BJP government under A.B. Vajpayee could hold on for just thirteen days. The National Front government under Dove Gowda which followed suit, had to rely on the outside support of Congress for its continuance in office. After just ten months, Congress party pulled the rug from under the feet of Gowda. Congress struck once again on the successor United Front government under I.K. Gujral on flimsy ground and imposed an election on the Indian electorate.

Unfortunately for the Indian polity, the general election of March 1998 too has thrown up a hung parliament. Though the BJP and its allies came out as a single largest group, the simple majority still evaded them. The ugly face of coalition politics has come to the fore even by the time Vajpayee and his Council of Ministers assumed office. The coalition partners of the government pull it in different directions and the natural casuality is the political stability.

This instability and the resultant uncertainty has seriously affected the Indian economy as well. From the very beginning, the New Economic Policy and its implementation has been invariably linked with some personalities like Dr. Manmohan Singh and Chidambaram and the prospective of their absence in any Cabinet had shaken the confidence of foreign investors over Indian economy or brought the sensex figures crashing down. As such, the success of the economic reforms in India has been indispensably linked with the governmental stability.

In a democracy elections serve three main purposes: to select representatives of the electorate; to confirm or change governments; and to give legitimacy to government. Unfortunately, the Indian electoral system has failed miserably in all these counts. Religion, community and caste play an unholy role in our elections, thereby reducing our electoral politics to a tribal war among the contenders and their supporters. The political parties choose their candidates on the basis of predominant religion and community in a particular constituency and in turn, the electorate vote for the candidate on the basis of religious and caste affinity rather than on the strength of his/her other qualifications.

Criminalisation of politics manifest more during election times and coupled with money and muscle power has thrown a serious threat to our parliamentary democracy. It is reported that out of the 13,952 candidates who had contested the *Lok Sabha* elections in 1996, 1,500 had a criminal record.[5] Another report of the Home Department mentions that there are cases of "heinous crimes", including rape and murder, pending against 52 sitting MLAs of Uttar Pradesh.[6] The Vohra Committee report on the nexus between crime and politics clearly points out that the government has a lackadaisical approach towards breaking that link, which is "virtually running a parallel government, pushing the state apparatus into irrelevance". From the criminalisation of politics of yester years, the Indian polity has now degenerated into politics of, by and for criminals. If things continue as they are today, the day is not far off, when criminal record may become a prerequisite for entering into and to thrive in the political arena.

The election is supposed to be used as a mechanism to confirm or change the government according to its performance. Unfortunately, the electorate is being influenced by factors like sympathy wave, pre-poll analysis and so on, besides the factors mentioned earlier, and many a times squarely miss the opportunity to pass its verdict on the existing government.

Funding of elections is a very serious issue impregnated with dangerous consequences for the health of democracy. All efforts to have a control over the money spent on the elections by the candidates as well as the parties so far have failed miserably. The political parties engage in various dubious methods to collect funds from big business houses, sugar or liquor barons and other such sources, thus allowing the money bags to have a hold over the polity. Even a honourable politician like Vajpayee has to admit: "No one looks at the colour of money while accepting (political) donations". Their dependence on illegitimate sources of money has irreparably shaken the moral basis of state power and vitiate the popular verdict, which forms the basis of propriety and legitimacy of political authority.[7]

The popular mandate enjoyed by the governments of India so far, whether under the Congress regime or under other parties was always remained questionable. The Congress, during its about four-decades long stint in office, has hardly ever got more than 30 to 35 per cent of popular vote. In spite of that the Congress leaders used to claim, rather shamelessly, that their party alone could afford to give a stable government. The governments under opposition parties too were no exception to this rule, and less said about the last three governments as well as the present one regarding their popular mandate is better.

The popular mandate enjoyed by the Chief Executive of the Government of India, the Prime Minister, too remains unenviable, as he is elected indirectly. The earlier incumbents were at least elected by the electorate of certain constituency but Narasimha Rao, Deve Gowda and Gujral entered parliament rather through back-door, by opting to contest and getting elected to the Rajya Sabha. Especially, Gujral's case was rather precarious, as he was elected to *Rajya Sabha* not from his home state Punjab but from Bihar. This made Laloo Prasad Yadav, the former Chief Minister of Bihar, to comment that Gujral owes his *gaddi* to him, as it was he, who got him elected for the Rajya Sabha and enabled him to become Prime Minister. As such, the questionable popular mandate enjoyed by the Prime Minister has seriously affected the power and prestige of the Chief Executive of the Indian political system as well.

The ideological bankruptcy of the political parties has seriously affected the health of parliamentary democracy in this country. Regional, communal, religious and linguistic diversities and interests have resulted in the multiplication of political parties. Besides this, the personality and ego clashes and rampant self-interests among the leaders have given birth to new factions within them. Resultant multi-party system has reduced the Indian polity into a mockery.

The Congress Party continued to enjoy power for about four long decades encashing on the Gandhi-Nehru legacy and its image as a party which won freedom for India. All these could not save this party from deterioration and degeneration caused by the activities of successive Gandhis and Gandhi-cap clad politicians. Unfortunately for the Indian democracy, there was no alternative to Congress and the alternatives built up by the activities of Jayaprakash Narayan and others, crumbled under the weight of the internal dissensions and personality clashes of the leaders and parties those were thus brought together.

Moreover, opportunistic electoral alliances were formed at state level, in which national parties aligned with regional parties as junior partners. For instance, in Tamil Nadu the Congress party was climbing piggy back on either of the Dravidian parties, the DMK or the AIADMK, according to their availability. In the same way, the BJP and the BSP came up with an strange arrangement in UP according to which the latter party would be in power for the first six months followed by the former subsequently. This anamoly failed miserably when the BSP proved itself to be shrewder and more unscrupulous of the two.

The multiparty system has inevitably lead to multi-cornered contests, which results in polarisation of votes. In such a situation, the successful candidate's representativeness of his constituency becomes rather questionable. This has also caused fractured mandate for political parties in the general elections of 1996 and 1998, which has made coalition governments at the central level unavoidable.

In vast plural societies like the one in India, coalition governments are not only inevitable but also desirable. However, to be successful, coalition should be based on positive ideologies and programmes and not on negative tendencies. Moreover, legislator's respect for people's mandate is absolutely essential for the survival and stability of an honest coalition.[8] Without that no coalition, either pre-poll or post-poll could lost long. Neither the Vajpayee government in which the Coalition partners take part proves better than the United Front-Congress exercise of 1996-97, in which the latter offered outside support. The main thrust of both the Common Minimum Programme and the National Agenda seems to be sticking to power as long as possible and these experiments in no way augurs well for future coalition governments at central level.

Parliamentary democracy, by its very nature, brings both the legislative and executive wings of the government into close contacts. Under this system, the Chief Executive, the Premier and his Cabinet, could be in power, as long as they retain the confidence of the legislature and this entails the Premier to do everything at his disposal, to maintain his majority. Defection and lack of party discipline prove to be big problems, and saving his *gaddi* from the pulls and pressures of legislators seems to be the main preoccupation of the Chief Executive rather than governing the nation for the welfare of the people.

On the other hand, with a brute majority, the Chief-Executive could bulldoze the legislature. In such a situation he could replace the institutionalised politics by personal politics which would result in the erosion of institutions, especially the Parliament and would lead to the growing importance of individuals and their agents, who blatantly violate just about every rule in the book. What Vajpayee said about Indira Gandhi is perhaps applicable to all her successors, more so to Rao, who could do it, inspite of the minority character of his regime: "Nehru used to avoid Parliament only when it was unavoidable. Indira Gandhi used to attend it only when it was unavoidable".[9]

Moreover, the Executive deny the members of Parliament their right to information and often refused to part with the details. Doctored or partial reports of the Committees and Commissions were placed before the House. For instance, the Vohra Committee report which ran into "hundreds of pages", as admitted earlier by Minister for Parliamentary Affairs V.C. Shukla, when placed before the House contained just twelve pages, with a cryptic gap in the numbering sequence-para 3.7 is followed by para 6.1.[10] The Congress, both as a ruling party and as a dominant power extending support to the UF government from outside prevented any meaningful debate on the Joint Parliamentary Report on the Bofors scandal or on the Interim Report of the Jain Commission on the Rajiv Gandhi Assassination case.

The decline of the Parliament under Indira Gandhi and her successors was complete with the members of Parliament themselves would "rather make money on the side than debate the important issues of the day", as Madhu Limaye, veteran Parliamentarian puts it.[11] The rate of attendance and the quality of discussion are rather poor. Most of them are driven by Party whip-rather than by their sense of duty to the nation or commitment to the electorate.

Again, the Parliamentary system insists on that members of Cabinet must be the member of either House of Parliament and in case a non-member is inducted in, he or she must get elected to the Parliament, within six months of their assumption of office. This actually stands in the way of appointing technocrats or experts in the field concerned into the Cabinet. In the given situation, in which good and efficient people have no chance of getting elected to the *Lok Sabha*, it is very difficult to get right person for right job.

To overcome this discrepency, politicians have often taken recourse to get themselves elected through *Rajya Sabha*. However, the members of *Rajya Sabha* are required to be "ordinary resident" of the state from which they have filed their papers. This law is violated by political leaders of all kinds of parties. The list of these carpet baggers includes even otherwise respectable names of Gujral and Dr. Manmohan Singh, who have filed false residence papers in Bihar and Assam, respectively.[12]

To be precise, the "Parliamentary Democracy' in India is infested by severe maladies, which have reduced the body-politic, much weak, unstable and less effective. Its guiding principles—parliamentary supremacy and the representative government—are floated with impunity by self-seeking politicians of the day. Much flawed leadership, indifferent bureaucracy and directionless masses have thrown serious challenges to the very existence of the Indian political set-up.

After detailing the problems faced by the Indian Polity, it is imperative to analyse and pin-point what needs to be done to stem the rot and to set it back on rails:

(a) to ensure political stability;

(b) to plug the loopholes in the present electoral system by appropriate reforms and to make it more effective;

(c) to arrange for state funding of elections which will considerably reduce the nefarious influence of tainted money on that key political process;

(d) pan-national election for the Chief Executive so as to create a strong executive with legitimate popular mandate and an ensured term of office;

(e) to curtail the evil effects of multi-party system;

(f) to create an environment in which all the organs of government work in unison, with respect to each other and not at cross purposes; and

(g) to introduce the idea of parliamentary incompatibility which delinks the membership of Cabinet from that of Parliament. This will ensure the appointment of technocrats and experts in the Cabinet on the one hand and will prevent people with money and muscle power from entering into politics on the other, since they will not have incentive to waste their resources for elective public office.

After studying the problem and pin-pointing what is to be done, let us now try to find out, how this is to be done? Any meaningful lesson could be drawn from other political systems, especially from the Presidential Systems of Executive?

In the process of answering these questions, the present paper aims to advocate the 'Presidentialism' of France as an alternative to the existing system of government in India. However, this study is limited in its scope and treatment and only a few striking features of the political system under the Fifth Republic of France are examined here. Again, the paper suggests the French system not in toto, but, in parts, which, it is believed, would help in plugging certain loopholes in the existing Indian system.

France is known as the 'laboratory of political systems and since 1789, eleven systems have been tried, out of which five, including the present one, were 'Republican'. The Republican form of government was tried again and again, since it was found, in the words of Adolphe Thiers, first provisional President of the Third Republic, "a Republic divides us (the French) least".

The Third and Fourth Republics suffered much from the unstable governments. Only six out of the fourteen Presidents under the Third Republic could complete full seven years term. Cabinets were recklessly overturned by the Parliament at an average rate of once every eight months.[13] This miserable situation continued under the Fourth Republic and for instance, Pierre Mendes France's government, which could retriéve France from the colonial squabbles of Indian sub-continent and Indo-China lasted only seven months and seven days.

As such, the first priority of the constitutional makers of the Fifth Republic of France was to find out a mechanism which would offer a stable government for France in the future. In this the present constitution has remarkable success. For the last forty years, France under the Fifth Republic enjoys the bliss of a 'stable' government. Franois Mittercand, who became the first Socialist President under the Fifth Republic in 1981 could complete two consecutive terms of seven years each, no mean achievement. In France, continuity of government is given by the President, who is both the Head of the State and the Government.[14]

The 'plebiscitarian' element of the Fifth Republic that strikes the attention of any observer is direct election to the Chief Executive of France. Originally, the President was elected indirectly by an electoral college consisting of members of Parliament, departmental and municipal councillors and supplementary delegates from larger municipal councils. To enhance the prestige of the Chief Executive, Charles de Gaulle introduced direct election to the President in 1962. This ensures the Head of the State and the Government enjoy country-wide mandate and unassailable legitimacy.

The French electoral system is based on the principle of 'simple majority' also known as the 'first-past-the-post system'. Under this system in both the Presidential as well as Parliamentary election the winning candidate has to get absolute majority of votes i.e. more than all the votes got by his opponents together. This ensures the representativeness of the winning candidate unquestionable. None getting absolute majority in the first ballot, run-off elect is conducted a week later and in this only those candidates a who receive 12.5 per cent of the total first-ballot votes may stay in the race.

One striking feature of the run-off elect or the second ballot is the 'withdrawl agreements' among fraternal parties. To ensure a decisive victory of a candidate in the parliamentary or presidential elections, candidates belonging to the fraternal parties used to withdraw from the race, thereby building up two distinct groupings, in spite of the multi-party system prevailing in France. Such two-bloc or two-coalition party configurations have been taken place among the French Communist, Socialist and some left-wing radicals to the left (the Union of the Left) on the one hand and among the Gaullists and the Union of French Democracy and other Centrist groups to the right on the other. This arrangement has reduced the evil effects of multi-party system to a considerable extent. Moreover, any political party which receives less than 5 per cent of the votes will not be represented in the National Assembly and the votes cast in its favour will not be taken into account under the 'exclusion clause'. This step is intended to discriminate against smaller parties and to discourage them.

Another interesting feature of the French electoral system is the provision for *suppléant* or 'shadow Deputy', whose name appears on the ballot along with the candidate. As such, a substitute to the Deputy gets elected at the same time as members of the National Assembly. In case, a member of Parliament is inducted into the Cabinet, his substitute assumes his place in the legislature.

Article 23 of the Constitution of the Fifth Republic of France deals with 'Parliamentary incompatibility', which means that the members of the Cabinet should not be members of the Parliament. In case, a member of Parliament is inducted into the Cabinet, he is expected to resign his parliamentary membership, which, as mentioned earlier, will be passed on to his substitute. This clause enables the French President to seek for efficient hands and technocrats beyond the bounds of the legislative body and to secure right person for right job.

Occasional by-elections too is taken care of by the French system through the provision for substitutes. On the death of sitting members of parliament, vacancies are filled up by these substitutes and if no substitute is available then only by — elections are held. Again, if a former-minister who has passed on his seat to a, substitute wished to return to the National Assembly, by — election held. Moreover, no candidate is allowed to contest in more than one constituency, which is permitted and so always causes by — elections in India.

.The French system has also certain interesting features regarding electoral expenses and state funding of elections. The candidates are expected to deposit 100,000 francs, which is reimbursable only if the candidate receives 5 per cent or more of the votes in either ballot. He is entitled to have certain amount of free publicity or rather the cost of it is reimbursed to those who obtain 5 per cent of votes cast. This publicity materials include posters on official hoardings and printing and postage of election addresses and cards. The main purpose of this arrangement is to provide equality among candidates. Moreover, parties with candidates put up in at least 75 constituencies have the right to a certain amount of radio and television time. Besides this, unofficial postures, letters and launching of short period newspapers too are in practice.

The French law also prohibits the publication of opinion poll results relating to the election for a period of one week prior to polling day, as it is prone to influence voters unduly. Thus, the system takes care to not allow the opinion polls to vitiate the public opinion for or against any political party or individual.

The French system has also found a solution to the problem of absenteeism widely prevalent among the parliamentarians. The member could now delegate his vote only for five reasons and no member may cast a proxy vote for more than one of his colleagues at a time. The member is required not only to vote in person but also regularly. Parliamentary salaries have been increased but the total is divided into two parts: a basic salary and an 'attendance bonus' (*indemnité de fonction*), which is offered as per the member's attendance. Moreover, concerned member is also penalised for non-attendance and the Assembly's Standing Orders provide that absence for three consecutive Commission sittings without valid explanation entails the member's resignation from the Commission and the loss of a third of the attendance bonus, until the opening of the following session. Absence without valid explanation for more than a third of the votes by ballot in any month entails the loss of a third of the monthly attendance bonus and two-thirds of it is forfeited in case of absence for more than half the votes.

Yet another significant feature of the French constitution is the institution known as Constitutional Council, decisions of which shall be binding on the executive and parliament and on all administrative and judicial authorities. This Council is the highest body to pass judgement on the constitutional validity of laws and rules of procedure. It also supervises the election of the President and of members of the Parliament.

The French system has also proved its resilience when a situation, unforeseen by the authors of the Constitution of the Fifth Republic, occurred in 1986. In the parliamentary election of that year Gaullists under Jacques Chirac were victorious and secured majority. However, Mitterrand, who became President in 1981 continued to be in power, since his term of office would be over only by early 1988. This brought out a peculiar situation known as cohabitation in which President was from one party and the Premier and his Cabinet colleagues were from another party. Same thing happened once again in 1993 and then in 1995, which continues till date. The French system has absorbed this oddity quite admirably.

The above discussion clearly brings out the strong points of the French system under the Fifth Republic and how much we can draw from it, to make our polity much effective and enterprising. Prof. Gupteshwar, after comparing and contrasting both the Presidential system of the US and the Presidentialism of France, concludes: "We want a strong President, directly elected by the people of India, as in France today, and not just through a cumbersome electoral, collegiate process as in the USA which, in practical terms, is regarded as the mouthpiece of party plenums."[21]. For India, at present, stable government is the need of the hour. As such, what else could have been a better model to follow, than the time-tested French system under the Fifth Republic?

Yet another factor that goes in favour of adopting the French system is that a parallel system is already existing in India and so, switching over process will be smooth and easy. As in the case of India, France too has a 'bicaphalous' executive consisting of the President as well as Premier and his Cabinet. What is now needed is to make the President both Head of the State as well as the Government, as in the case of France.

Again, as India, France too has a multi-party system and not a bi-party system as in the case of the US or the UK. However, the French system has admirably overcome the evils of the multi-party politics and has provided the possibility of two coalition party configurations.

It may be argued against the adoption of French system on the ground that organising direct election to the Chief Executive or conducting nation-wide referendum in a country of India's magnitude is a gigantic task and will cost enormously. Still, it is worth spending as the Chief Executive of any democratic country must have a country-wide mandate and he must represent the entire country. He must be above narrow party politics. To avoid double expenditure, we may fix the term of both the President and the Parliament at five years and can have simultaneous elections. Again, referendums to be held only on issues of great significance and in the forty years experience of Fifth Republic, referenda were held just seven times only. And in a democratic Republic, is it not desirable to consult the entire population on issues, which are going to have country-wide repercussions?

Moreover, some critics point out that Charles de Gaulle has developed the Presidentship of France as quasi-monarchical. Some even feared that de Gaulle would eventually turn out to be a dictator. But, he proved them wrong and has left-behind a great tradition. In 1968, when France had not responded favourably to his reform package, de Gaulle coolly resigned his post and withdrew himself into political oblivion. As is the case, not only the French political system but also the fine traditions developed by de Gaulle, are worth emulating by any head of a democracy.

To be precise, it may be maintained that it is not the political system, but only the men, who operate it and for whom it is operated, contribute to the successes and achievements of the polity of any country. The statement of Joseph de Maistre made in 1811 that "every country has the government it deserves" holds good even now. After all, the key to a successful and effective Indian polity lies not in the political system that we are going to adopt but in the precise way that we are going to adopt and to build up on it.

REFERENCES

1. K. Gupteswar, "Wanted : President, Indian Style" in *The Academy Law Review,* Vol. XII, No. 2, 1998, pp. 85-107. I have drawn a lot from this article for the present paper, for which I am quite indebted to Prof. Gupteswar.

2. At the 1997 Golwalkar Memorial Lecture, A.B. Vajpayee advocated switch-over to Presidential system and to adopt the French model, which he felt would ensure stability. After coming to power, BJP continued to advocate the Presidential system and Union Home Minister recently maintained that the Cabinet system is not a part of the basic structure, and so, a constitutional amendment is quite permissible. However, this stand is stoutly opposed by the Congress and the Left Parties.

3. Rajni Kothari, "Towards System Transformation - An Agenda" in *Politics India,* January 1998 p. 13.

4. Rajinder Puri, Political System and Agenda for New India" in *Politics India,* January 1998, p. 18.

5. The Hindu, (Chennai), May 3, 1998.

6. *India Today,* August 31, 1995, pp. 117-119.

7. *India Today,* March 31, 1996, pp. 29-42.

8. Jayaprakash Narayan, "Federalism and Coalition Governments - The Indian Experience" in *Politics India,* January 1998, p. 37.

9. *India Today,* July 15, p. 75.

10. As No. 6, p. 118.

11. As No. 9, p. 75.

12. *India Today,* July 31, 1993, p. 45.

13. William Safran, *The French Polity,* Second Edition, Longman, New York, 1985, p. 6.

14. Dorothy Pickles who has written on both the Fourth and the Fifth Republic of France clearly mentions that the Constitution of 1958 is a "plan for winning the last war and is an overreaction to experiences of ineffective governments".

15. Under the Fifth Republic, the President enjoys a comparatively long tenure of seven years, popularly known as *septenet,* while the term of Parliament and consequently the Premier and his

Cabinet, even if they complete full term in office is just five years. Hence, it is the President who gives continuity to the government.

16. Peter Morris, *French Politics Today,* Manchester University Press, Manchester, 1994, p. 80.
17. Dorothy Pickles, *The Fifth French Republic,* First Indian edition, B.I. Publishers, New Delhi, 1978, pp. 56-57.
18. Paul Godt; (ed.), *Policy-Making in France From de Gaulle to Mitterand*, Pinter Publishers, London, 1989, p. 14.
19. Jack Hayward, *The One and Indivisible French Republic,* New York, 1973, p. 99. Safran (No. 13, p. 136) maintains that "a cabinet like that of President Eisenhower, which consisted of "nine millionaires and a plumber," would be unthinkable in France ...... Fifth Republic cabinets have contained a significant proportion of graduates of the elite schools. For example, ten of the fifteen ministers in the Chirac government were graduates of the *grandes écoles*. In the first Mauroy government, nine ministers wer professional civil servents and of these, six were graduates of the National School of Administration (ENA), but fifteen were university professors or public school teachers....."
20. Pickles, No. 17, pp. 91-92.
21. Gupteswar, No. 1, p. 106.

Index

C

D

E

T

U

V

W

Y

Z